Creativity
and cultural diversity

About the editor

Dr Marilyn Fryer is Founder/Director of The Creativity Centre Ltd and co-founder of The Creativity Centre Educational Trust. She is a chartered psychologist, experienced academic and qualified teacher specialising in creativity research and consultancy. Formerly Reader in Psychology at Leeds Metropolitan University, she has nearly 20 years experience of creativity research and of developing and delivering accredited creativity courses at HE and professional levels.

Marilyn has published and presented internationally, mainly in the United States, Asia and Europe. She has received various awards in the UK and overseas for creativity research and development and has acted as consultant on creativity and innovation to major public and private sector organisations, including government bodies.

Creativity
and cultural diversity

edited by
Marilyn Fryer

The Creativity Centre Educational Trust

Published in Great Britain by
The Creativity Centre Educational Trust
1 Whitehall Quay
Leeds LS1 4HR

British Library Cataloguing-in-Publication Data
A catalogue record for this book is available from the British Library

ISBN 0-9548116-0-7

Printed and bound in Great Britain by
The Shipley Print Company
Shipley, West Yorkshire

Cover design by
Julia Fryer

Contents

Acknowledgements

The involvement of everyone who contributed so willingly to this book is greatly appreciated. This includes Barry Fryer who helped edit and format the text. It was the vision and tenacity of Caroline Fryer which made the international conference, *Creativity and Cultural Diversity,* a reality. That event was the catalyst for this book.

The production of the book was partly funded by Arts Council England (Yorkshire) and the European Social Fund under the Equal Community Initiative Programme. The contents do not necessarily reflect the opinion or position of the European Commission and/or the Department for Work and Pensions. We are very grateful for their support.

EUROPEAN UNION
European Social Fund

Marilyn Fryer

Creativity & cultural diversity

Introduction

It is relatively easy to travel the world and to see, *en route*, very different examples of creativity, but it is far less easy to uncover how creativity is perceived, valued or practised in different countries and cultures. Yet it is vital that we try, otherwise we are restricted to the most readily available information about creativity which usually reflects the views and practices of the most dominant cultural groups. Whilst such information is undoubtedly valuable, ignoring less accessible information can mean that equally valuable knowledge and skills become lost. Then there is a real danger that only one or a few approaches to creativity will dominate education and training provision. Yet creativity thrives on a multi-perspective approach.

At present, not all creative education and training reflects its client groups. In the UK, for example, the school curriculum does not fully reflect the creative achievements of all the cultural groups it serves. So many young people lack role models and learning materials with which they can readily identify. Disaffection can result. How creativity is currently defined and developed in UK education and training tends to reflect a mainly white, Western approach, rather than our diverse society. This not only puts people from minority ethnic groups at a disadvantage, it is everyone's loss.

This book does not attempt to deny the relevance of dominant views on creativity. To do so would be misguided. Instead a key aim is to help redress any imbalance. But it is just a beginning.

In fact, this book is just one outcome of The Creativity Centre's creativity and cultural diversity strategy. The book was conceived in conjunction with our 2002 international conference on *Creativity and Cultural Diversity* described on page 183. Another outcome is our *Science Alliance* schools project (see Appendix).

As will be seen from the following chapters, the authors have drawn on very different cultural sources to support their arguments. Some established but difficult-to-access work will be new to many readers, whilst here and there seasoned creativity researchers may well find an idea or argument that reminds them of earlier work.

In one sense, this book represents a snapshot in time. The picture is not simple, since we have all been influenced by many cultures over the centuries. Trying to identify the contributions of different cultures to creativity is not at all straightforward. In fact, it's rather like 'trying to catch a particularly elusive fish, by hopefully casting different kinds of bait at different depths, without knowing what goes on beneath the surface!' (Oppenheim, 1966, p. 49). As you read the following chapters, you won't always find clear cultural differences in views about creativity. Look instead for the 'elusive fish'. Fortunately, this is not a

1

random catch of authors, so hopefully you will find rather more fish than you might ordinarily expect!

Overview

The chapters which follow were written by authors from Africa, Asia, Australia, the USA and Europe. There are chapters by some of the *Creativity & Cultural Diversity* conference presenters, as well as invited contributions from other colleagues - from China and Singapore, for example. The views that the authors present and the evidence they cite are entirely their own. Theirs is the responsibility and the credit. Their biographical descriptions included below are designed to set their work in context, rather than provide a full account of their considerable achievements.

African perspectives on creativity and innovation - Elizabeth Rasekoala, D.Univ.

In her chapter, Liz argues that African perspectives on creativity have for too long been denied, undervalued and marginalised. She cites examples of early creative achievements in Africa and explores the driving force behind them. She discusses the effect of Western colonialism, highlights differences between African and Western value systems, and makes a powerful plea for the future.

Liz Rasekoala is a chemical engineer with 18 years' work experience both in her native country, Nigeria, and the UK where she now lives. Liz is founder of the UK-based African-Caribbean Network for Science & Technology. She also initiated and developed the Ishango Science Clubs (for which she received an Innovation Award from the Commonwealth Association of Science, Mathematics and Technology Educators) and the RESPECT Campaign. In 2000, she was conferred an Honorary Doctorate by Sheffield Hallam University in recognition of her outstanding contribution to the enhancement of equality issues in maths, science and technology education in the UK and overseas.

Creativity as a social phenomenon - Arthur Cropley, PhD

That creativity does not occur in a vacuum, but in a social context, has long been stressed by Morris Stein. In this chapter, Arthur discusses the *role* of the social context in creativity and the way in which the focus of attention has shifted away from aesthetic or artistic creativity towards the social ends creativity serves. But, as Arthur points out, this raises a key question for us all.

This chapter includes a useful discussion of the nature of creativity (see also Rogers, 1954 and Kneller, 1965, in Fryer, 1996). Of particular interest are Arthur's views on creativity in Australia, especially the match/mismatch between what employers want and what the education system provides. Here there is a certain resonance with the work of Sen and Sharma (see their chapter).

Professor Arthur Cropley is an Australian who has spent much of his working life in Canada, Germany and elsewhere. In 1978, he became Professor of Psychology at the University of Hamburg. From 1992 to 1995 he was Professor at LaTrobe University, Bendigo (Victoria) before returning to Hamburg. He became Professor Emeritus in 1999 and is presently living in Australia, where he is Adjunct Professor of Engineering at the University of South Australia. He has published and presented internationally and is author of 19 books on creativity, lifelong learning and the adaptation of immigrants. From 1989-96 he was editor of the *European Journal for High Ability*. He received the 1997 Creativity Award of the World Council for Gifted and Talented Children.

'I shall be many': the garland making perspective on creativity and cultural diversity – M. K. Raina, PhD

The title chosen by M.K. could not be more apt, not least because this chapter is itself a garland of multiple perspectives on creativity and cultural diversity. M.K. criticises the 'narrow ethnocentric boundaries' of most creativity research and calls for much more cross cultural research. He is especially concerned about the dominance of any one cultural perspective. He argues that instead we should adopt a 'garland making' perspective which allows a diversity of approaches to flourish. The field of psychology also has its multiple perspectives and methodologies and it is appropriate that M.K. should argue for their wider use in creativity research.

In the course of his discussion, he contrasts Western and Oriental approaches to creativity and sheds light on the origins of some very different perspectives and traditions. This includes highlighting the links between the creation myths and the creativity traditions of various cultures.

His insights into the Indian cultural tradition and the effect on present day thinking are particularly valuable. These also inform the discussion of Rekha Sharma Sen's findings. Indeed, M.K.'s chapter offers so many valuable insights into cultural influences on creativity, the state of creativity research and the way in which it needs to develop in the future.

M.K. Raina's distinguished career includes the post of Professor and Head of the Department of Educational Psychology and Foundations of Education, in the National Council of Educational Research and Training, New Delhi, India; as well as Dean of Research and Chairman of the Educational Research and Innovations Committee of the Council. He is currently Professor Emeritus of the Indian Council for Social Science Research, Jawaharial Nehru University, New Delhi. M.K. has produced many publications and presentations and received many awards. He was nominated for the Torrance Creativity Award of the National Association of Gifted Children in the USA. In 1996, he was awarded the First World Council Creativity Award of the World Council for Gifted and Talented Children. The World Council described him as 'an outstanding model of creative thinking, as well as the promoter of the importance of creativity'. In 1997, he delivered a keynote address to the World Council in Seattle, Washington, entitled 'Recognizing Indigenous Creativity'.

Creativity: the antidote to the argument culture - Vincent Nolan

Vincent decries the argument culture which is embedded in Western institutions. He suggests a more productive alternative, drawing on his expertise in *Synectics* to propose a useful model for conflict resolution – one which is much needed in today's world.

Vincent Nolan started his own business in 1971 as a licensee of the American innovation consulting company, Synectics Inc. In 1984, he merged his business with Synectics Inc. to form the International Synectics Corporation and continued as Chairman of its European subsidiary, Synectics Ltd, until retiring from that in 1991. Prior to setting up his own business, he was Head of Management Services and Assistant Director, New Business Development, for Rank Xerox Ltd. Vincent continues to work as a part-time consultant in the field of innovation and change. He has written various books and articles on innovation and change and is Editor of *Creative Education*, published by the Synectics Education Initiative in 2000.

How to shape the innovative culture in your organisation - Jon-Chao Hong, PhD, Ming-Yueh Hwang and Chan-Li Lin

In discussing how to shape the innovative culture of organisations, Jon-Chao Hong and his colleagues draw on the wisdom of both East and West, whilst directing our attention to cultural differences between the two. Interestingly, they argue that the difference between gifted and mediocre people often lies in their ability to detect and solve problems. But what makes one group succeed over another? This is a key question they address.

These authors are based at the National Taiwan Normal University where Dr Jon-Chao Hong delivers the Program of Innovative Management. His interests include creativity training for enterprise managers and students. His publications include work in the area of knowledge management, thinking systems and problem solving. Dr Ming-Yueh Hwang is the chairperson of Social Education. Her particular interest is in innovation management in social education institutes. Her publications are focused on innovation strategy in museum management and resource-based learning in museum work. Chan-Li Lin is a doctoral student at the Department of Industrial Education. His special interests include innovation management and creativity training.

Metaphor and Creativity - Martin Shovel & Martha Leyton

We know from cognitive psychology that even when we see physical objects we are interpreting what is before our eyes to make sense of what we see. In other words, just about all seeing involves interpretation or 'seeing as' and we draw on our experience to do this (see for instance Matlin, 2004). In social perception even more interpretation is involved.

What Martha and Martin have done is to remind us that, in making sense of situations in this way, we often unwittingly use metaphor. In particular, they alert us to the role of metaphor in the everyday language we use to frame our perceptions. Much of the time we are unaware of this, but once aware, we can take steps to change the metaphors we use and thus get a fresh view of the situations in which we find ourselves. The authors then discuss what influences our choice of metaphors.

Martha Leyton is an experienced teacher and facilitator who studied English at the University of Sussex. She has taught in further education for several years, worked with business clients to develop their communication skills and run access courses for students wishing to enter higher education. She now works freelance. This includes writing and editing education/training related publications. In 2001 she set up *CreativityWorks* with Martin.

Martin Shovel is a leading freelance cartoon illustrator, writer, experienced teacher and workshop leader. After gaining a philosophy degree from the University of Sussex, Martin taught English to foreign students. His work includes an innovative cartoon-based approach to language teaching, as well as the production of a best-selling language teaching book.

Challenges for creativity in Singapore and Japan: Confucius' influence and professionalism - Yuichiro Kubo

In what ways are Japan and Singapore the same or different? In this chapter, Yuichiro points out which values are shared by these two countries and where any differences lie. He then discusses their effect. Yuichiro identifies the challenges for the development of creativity in Japan and Singapore. His conclusions are based both on his knowledge of modern life and the teachings of Confucius and the Neo-Confucians.

As a Japanese lecturer living and working in Singapore, Yuichiro Kubo is in a good position to compare Japanese and Singaporean cultural differences. He is based in the Language Centre of the Department of Interdisciplinary and General Studies at Temasek Polytechnic.

Creative Southeast Asians - Alice Lee

In charting examples of highly creative Malaysian people, Alice Lee cites Dr Ng Aik Kwang who reminds us that 'East is not East and West is not West - the picture is more complicated than that'. In charting these biographies, Alice reveals patterns of experience and personality characteristics typical of highly creative people.

Alice Lee is a graduate of the University of Singapore and holds an MA from the University of London. In 1982 the award of a UNESCO scholarship enabled her to go to Ohio University, Athens. Alice is currently writing her second book. Her first, *Creative Personalities in Malaysia*, was co-authored with Professor Leonard Yong.

Synergy of East and West for greater creativity - Zulfi Hussain

Zulfi argues that greater creativity may be achieved through synergy between Eastern and Western approaches. He highlights the East's tremendous creative contribution and he discusses the role played by religion in this.

He also points out that creativity education and development rarely address how individuals envisage creativity. This is in keeping with my own research findings. Prior to my Project 1000 investigation with UK teachers (Fryer, 1989; 1996) there had been a dearth of research in this area. However, my findings revealed very clear differences in perceptions of creativity between groups and this was directly linked to their preferred teaching styles.

Zulfi Hussain came to the UK from Pakistan as a boy and experienced a clash of cultures at first hand. He is a chartered engineer, an experienced manager and runs his own business, *Global Synergy Solutions Ltd*. Zulfi is Chair of the Asian Business Development Network (ABDN) and holds a number of other key posts such as Member of the Government's National Minority Ethnic Advisory Group.

Women's creative development - Kathy Goff, EdD

Kathy argues that too little is known about creativity in everyday life and about the creativity of women, for which she suggests some reasons. One is that women are disadvantaged when men are the judges of creativity, since they tend to prefer work like their own. This has some resonance with the results of Project 1000 (Fryer, 1989; 1991) which revealed that male and female teachers had quite different criteria for judging the creativity of their students' work. Kathy highlights the importance of living creatively, as well as suggesting ways in which women's creativity may be supported.

Kathy Goff earned her doctorate in adult education at the University of Georgia, USA under the direction of Dr E Paul Torrance. She is a certified gerontologist, researcher and department head. In 1991 she co-founded *McGoff Creative Enterprises*. Kathy has delivered many presentations, workshops and publications on the creativity of adults, with particular emphasis on women and elders. In 2002, she was a keynote presenter at the E Paul Torrance Lecture Series.

The role of gender in creativity - Joanna Kwasniewska

When Joanna explored the role of gender in creativity among engineering and arts students, she made an interesting discovery. She discusses the theoretical and practical implications of this discovery and usefully sets these in the context of earlier research.

Joanna obtained her Masters in Psychology, on which her chapter is based, from the Warsaw School of Advanced Social Psychology, where she teaches. It was her experience as a painter and photographer which stimulated her interest in the psychological aspects of creativity. Her PhD is concerned with modelling in creativity. Joanna conducts workshops in creative problem solving for business participants and others.

Education reform and fostering creativity in Japan - Kenichi Yumino, PhD

Kenichi Yumino assesses the contribution of the West to post World War II Japan and points out differences between Japanese and Western societies. He puts forward his views on what Japan now needs to address and he discusses the role of creative education in this process.

Dr Kenichi Yumino is Professor at Shizuoka University in the Faculty of Education and he is Principal of the Attached School for Special Education. He has published and presented internationally in the area of creativity and has made a major contribution to Japanese creative education.

Early influences on Creativity in Great Britain - Lynda Foster, PhD

Over 25 years ago, Lynda Foster left the USA to make her home in the UK. When she arrived, she was surprised by the differences she found in conceptions of creativity between the USA and the UK. Lynda discusses these and contrasts her experience of creativity education in the UK then with what is

6

happening today. She also reports findings from her study of early influences on 24 creative people in the UK.

Dr Lynda Foster obtained her Masters and Doctoral Degrees in the United States, studying with Dr E Paul Torrance at the University of Georgia. She has worked with the Georgia Public Schools' gifted and talented programmes and with the American School in London - to set up a similar programme. Lynda is a primary school governor, conducts creativity workshops for teachers, parents and children, and is a valued Trustee of The Creativity Centre Educational Trust.

Creative thinking in the early years of education - Anna Craft

Anna explores interest in creativity in education in the UK from a historical perspective and highlights the difference between everyday and paradigm-shifting creativity (cf. Fabun, 1969 and Ausubel, 1978). She cites a definition of creativity adopted by the UK's National Advisory Committee on Creative and Cultural Education (DfEE, 1999) which is quite similar to Stein's definition (Stein, 1984), apart from not mentioning the social context of creativity.

Anna's argument that creativity may be thought of as on a continuum accords with the 'democratic' view of creativity propounded by psychologists such as Guilford (1950) and Weisberg (1986) and with Ghiselin's 'higher' and 'lower' creativity (Ghiselin, 1963), as discussed in Fryer (1989).

Anna Craft is a Senior Lecturer in the Open University's Faculty of Education and Languages and is working on the Masters Programme and courses contributing to the Foundation Degree. She has published widely and is currently a (mainly remote) visiting scholar at Project Zero at Harvard University. In 2001, she co-initiated the Open Creativity Centre with Bob Jeffrey.

Teachers' conception of creativity and its nurture in children: an Indian perspective - Rekha Shama Sen & Neerja Sharma, PhD.

This chapter explores how Indian teachers perceive creativity and how they think it can be nurtured. Since these are the questions which occupied me in the UK in the mid to late 1980s, it is particularly interesting to find out what these authors have discovered in India.

Rekha and Dr Sharma argue for an ethnographic approach to the study of creativity and discuss the fundamental differences between Eastern and Western perceptions of creativity. They also usefully draw attention to the duality in the Indian psyche which makes people individualist and collectivist at the same time. In addition, they recognise the role of creativity in bringing about cultural change as well as the impact of cultural change on creativity.

Rekha Shama Sen is a lecturer (Selection Grade) at the Indira Gandhi National Open University in New Delhi, India where she designs and develops programmes of study in Child Development and Disability. This chapter is based on her doctoral research. She has published and presented in the areas of creativity, early childhood care and education, disability and distance education. Her paper entitled 'Defining access and equity in the context of the differently abled' was nominated for the best paper award at the conference of the Asian Association of Open Universities.

Dr Neerja Sharma, Reader, teaches Child Development at the Lady Irwin College, University of Delhi. Having obtained her Masters and Doctoral degrees from the same university, she has worked in the areas of childhood disability, adolescence and early childhood. In 1988 she led the establishment of the Enabling Centre (an innovative primary education program for children with disability as a laboratory for university students) as an example of linkage between higher and basic education. In 1998, she was a visiting research fellow at the Special Education Centre, University of Newcastle, Australia. She has undertaken academic assignments throughout the world.

As well as publishing research papers and book chapters, Dr. Sharma has authored *Understanding Adolescence, Identity of the Adolescent Girl* and *Evaluating Children in Primary Education*. She was an expert on a World Bank study on primary education in diverse poverty situations in India (2003). She is currently involved in writing a chapter (as co-author) on research in Human Development for a publication of the Indian Council of Social Science Research. She is Director of PhD Studies for Rekha.

Using Creative Methods to teach English in China - Ma Xiaolei (Diana) and Wang Yan (Lily)

Diana and Lily describe how they have devised their own creative method of teaching English in China in order to engage their students in enjoyable and deep learning. They adopt a holistic approach which takes account of the many different functions language serves, student attitudes, motivation and preferred ways of learning. Learning a language, they argue, involves much more than learning the grammar and meaning of words. It involves appreciating the beauty of the language, the people, and their literature, culture and traditions.

These enthusiastic teachers describe their syllabus and their well-thought out teaching methods which, despite the pressure on teachers, can be used to help students become creative and independent learners.

Ma Xiaolei is based in the Department of Foreign Languages in Beijing Normal University and Wang Yan works at Beijing No. 8 High School. They both hold first degrees in English Literature and Masters Degrees in TEFL. They have each produced a number of publications and have both been involved in the Teachers' Action Research in the Formative Assessment of Foreign Language Teaching. In 1997 Wang Yan achieved first prize in the National English Teacher Competition in China. In 2000, Ma Xiaolei authored 'Familial Education: the Foundation of School Education'.

QCA's creativity project - Margaret Talboys

Margaret summarises a three year project, *Creativity: Find it, promote it*, conducted by the Qualifications and Curriculum Authority (QCA). The QCA maintains and develops the National Curriculum in England and associated assessment, tests and examinations; and accredits and monitors qualifications in colleges and at work. The Creativity Centre was pleased to contribute to this project.

Margaret is a Principal Officer with the Qualifications and Curriculum Authority. She has taught all phases of education in the UK and overseas. Her roles have included generalist and specialist teaching, advisory work and headship. Since 1990 she has been involved in the formulation, monitoring, review and development of the National Curriculum for England and its assessment and the National Qualifications Framework. She has particular responsibility for Art and Design in the curriculum. Margaret is Director of the QCA project, *Creativity: Find it, promote it*, a description of which may be found on www.ncaction.org.uk/creativity/index.htm.

References

Ausubel, D.P. (1978) The nature and measurement of creativity. *Psychologia: an International Journal of Psychology in the Orient*. 21, 4, 179-91.

DfEE (1999) *All Our Futures: Creativity, Culture and Education* (Report from the National Advisory Committee on Creative and Cultural Education). Sudbury: Department for Education and Employment.

Fabun, D. (1969) *You and Creativity*. New York: Macmillan.

Fryer, M. (1996) *Creative Teaching and Learning*. London: Sage/Paul Chapman Publishing.

Fryer, M. & Collings, J. A. (1991) Teachers' views about creativity. *British Journal of Educational Psychology*. 6, 207-19.

Fryer, M. (1989) Teachers' Views on Creativity. PhD thesis, Leeds Metropolitan University.

Ghiselin, B. (1963) Ultimate criteria for two levels of creativity. In Taylor, C.W. & Barron, F. [Eds.] (1963) *Scientific Creativity: its Recognition and Development*. New York: Wiley.

Guilford, J.P. (1950) Creativity. *American Psychologist*. 5. 444-54.

Kneller, G.F. (1965) *The Art and Science of Creativity*. New York: Holt, Rinehart & Winston.

Matlin. M.W. (2004) *Cognition*. New York: Wiley.

Oppenheim, A. N. (1966) *Questionnaire Design and Attitude Measurement*. London: Heinemann.

Rogers, C.R. (1954) Towards a theory of creativity. In P. E. Vernon [Ed.] (1970) *Creativity*. Harmondsworth: Penguin.

Stein, M.I. (1984) *Making the Point*. Amagansett, NY: The Mews Press.

Weisberg, R.W. (1993) *Creativity: Beyond the Myth of Genius*. New York: Freeman.

Elizabeth Rasekoala

African perspectives on creativity and innovation

As we begin the 21st century, creativity and innovation seem to be new buzzwords in the lexicon of advancement. The potential contribution of creativity and innovation to advancing sustainable economic growth and enhancing social inclusion, is immense. However, perspectives on creativity and innovation have increasingly become dominated by a narrow, overwhelmingly 'Eurocentric' focus, disempowering and excluding the majority of the world's populace from its benefits, discourse and agenda. For too many of the world's poor, people of colour and women, their creativity and innovation enterprise seems to be contextualised in a realm that they do not recognise in their daily lives.

For the people of the African continent, their perspectives on creativity and innovation, for so long denied, undervalued and marginalised, are a crucial starting point in understanding the demise of advancement on the continent. Africans are still trying to come to terms with the trauma of the arrested development of their societies, through the often brutal interface with so-called Western civilisation, which interrupted their development path along cultural, spiritual and value systems that were uniquely theirs, having been handed down through generations. These value systems were the driving force for their creativity and innovation, in science, technology, numeracy etc., which have been interrupted by the dominance of Eurocentric values.

There are numerous examples of the creativity and innovation of Africans, underpinned by their cultural and spiritual value systems, such as the Benin bronzes, the Gold Mines of Great Zimbabwe, the Ishango Bone, the Yoruba Number System and the Dogun of Mali and their study of the stars. The driving force behind these scientific and technological developments was the cultural and spiritual need to pay homage to spirits and natural phenomena that were deemed to be the powerful forces behind creation and the sustainability of the Earth, such as the Sun, the Moon, the Stars, Thunder, Rain, etc. The impact of the Christian missionary zeal in converting many Africans to Christianity rendered these cultural and spiritual systems as primitive and forms of paganism, which were to be eradicated. Unfortunately, the profound impact of this indoctrination was to interrupt the creative flow and development of many Africans.

Key elements of the creativity of Africans, and the values which underpin them, can be seen in aspects of their lives, which from the Western viewpoint, appear to be contradictory. For example, in Western society, which is very much driven by individualism, people unrelated by family or blood ties have pretty much the same names. However, in African societies, where the needs of the community prevail above those of the individual, every person has a different name, and surnames are only shared by people who are linked by

11

blood ties or marriage. This might seem contradictory unless one understands that within the communal ethos of African societies, every individual is deemed to be of supreme value. Thus, family elders devote a considerable amount of creative thought and energy to choosing a name when a child is born. This process involves an intuitive study of the child, and involves wisdom and judgement on the part of the family elders, so that the name given to the child is one that makes a profound statement, relating to that child as an individual. In this same ethos, the legal sense in Western societies of a child being illegitimate because he or she is born outside wedlock, is one that does not exist in African societies. Every child, regardless of the circumstances of its birth, is a valued member of society.

Another seemingly contradictory aspect of African societies is that of punctuality or time keeping, or lack thereof. In Western societies, punctuality is very much a valued trait, based on a sense of good manners and self-discipline. However, in African societies, the concept of time is very much seen as an individual's gift to give to another. As a gift, it cannot be demanded.

In the global drive for the development of creativity and innovation, there is a profound need for an African Renaissance, so that African societies and countries can develop the confidence that they have lost, through the Eurocentric emasculation of the cultural and spiritual values which have underpinned their creativity and innovation. Thus, Africa can assert its rightful place and contribute to global developments.

Arthur Cropley

Creativity as a social phenomenon

Recent discussions look at creativity from a social rather than aesthetic point of view. They emphasise its importance in innovation, growth, personal welfare and the like, and judge it according to criteria such as usefulness, ethicality and social acclaim. Thus, the focus is on 'functional' rather than 'aesthetic' creativity. Society is ambivalent about creativity and experiences two opposing forces: conserving forces that slow down or resist change and innovating forces that favour it. Not all conservation is reactionary or undesirable, and not all innovation is beneficial. Furthermore, creativity can be achieved through evolutionary as well as revolutionary change. Thus, what is needed in society is a balance between the two forces.

The dawning of the age of creativity

According to the Nomura Institute, the development of human society has involved four 'ages'. We have passed through the age of agriculture, the age of industry and the age of information, and are now said to be entering *the age of creativity*. Indeed, although scholarly interest in creativity stretches back to antiquity - to take a single example, Plato's *Ion* - there has been a surge of interest in recent years, perhaps even the dawning of an age of creativity. Although earlier discussions focused mainly on art, literature, music, dance and similar areas, what I call 'aesthetic' or 'artistic' creativity, the situation changed drastically about 50 years ago. The turning point was the successful launching in 1957 by the then Soviet Union of the first artificial earth satellite, Sputnik 1. In the USA and most North American-Western European societies this event led to a wave of self-criticism that centred mainly on the argument that the Western world's *engineers* had failed *because they were not creative enough*. In the USA, the subsequent *National Defense Education Act* adopted a concept of creativity going beyond the aesthetic and accepted it as an important practical factor in the prosperity, even survival of society, thus launching the age of social creativity.

Adopting a human capital approach, writers in the intervening years (e.g. Walberg and Stariha, 1992) have given considerable attention to creativity in applied and theoretical sciences ('scientific/intellectual' creativity), as well as in management and manufacturing on the one hand, and administration and even the military, on the other ('survival/prosperity' creativity).

The general argument is easy to summarise. In the face of rapid societal change that is, among other things, political (eg. terrorism, achieving fairness in international relations), economic (demands for the elimination of inequalities between rich and poor nations), industrial (eg. offshore manufacturing, globalisation), social (eg. adaptation of immigrants, integration of minorities), demographic (eg. breakdown of the family, ageing of the population), environmental (eg. global warming, gene modified crops), and biotechnological (eg. communications, health), societies will stagnate, even perish, unless their leaders in all fields become more creative. Thus, creativity is no longer seen as purely the domain of aesthetes and intellectuals dealing with questions of truth and beauty, often in an intensely private way (as important as these issues may be), but as a pathway to the society's prosperity and as a means for making the nation strong and safe.

Creativity and the social context

The essence of any kind of creativity is *production of novelty*. This was defined by the psychologist Bruner (1962) as the process of achieving 'surprise' in the beholder by deviating from how things have been done until now. It is the contrast effect that yields the surprise. In other words, creativity does not occur in a vacuum, but in a social context. Indeed, what is regarded as creative in one era or society can be uncreative in another. Brahms was unable to obtain the important musical post he sought in his native Hamburg, because his music was initially judged to be too conservative. He had to go to Vienna to find acceptance. Einstein's PhD dissertation was rejected by the *technischer Hochschule* in Zurich. The French mathematician Galois, founder of the theory of groups, was killed in a duel in 1832 at the age of 20. He worked frantically on his notes almost until the moment of his death, which he correctly anticipated because he knew that the duel was grossly unfair. Because of his desperate obsession, it was thought by his contemporaries that he must have been working on something of great importance, and his writings were examined closely. However, the ideas he left were judged to be of no particular value. Several years passed before the society's fund of mathematical knowledge advanced sufficiently for the creativity of his work to be recognised.

In a sense, then, it is not the product or the process itself that determines whether something is creative, but (a) the particular setting (the impact of the novelty on the existing 'state of the art') and (b) the reaction of the people in that setting (their willingness and ability to recognise creativity). This view was supported by Csikszentmihalyi (1996), who argued that creativity is no more than a positive category of judgment in the minds of observers, a term they use to praise products that they find exceptionally good. When a number of observers - especially experts - agree that a product is creative, then it is. This is one of the 'paradoxes' of creativity (Cropley, 1997): Social recognition or *acclaim* is necessary. Thus, creativity not only serves social ends such as economic development (see above), but is also defined in terms of social criteria.

Surprise can be produced through mere unregulated self-expression (eg. daubing paint on paper, writing text in any way that pleases the writer, or picking out notes at random on the piano) or by means of simple production of variability (doing things differently from the usual regardless of accuracy, meaning, sense, significance or interestingness). However, as Heinelt (1974) argued, such unfettered production of simple variability may well cause surprise, but is not genuine creativity. He added 'quasicreativity' to Cattell and Butcher's (1968) concept of 'pseudocreativity'. The latter produces novelty only via lack of discipline, rejection of what already exists and simply letting oneself go - blind nonconformity.

Quasicreativity, on the other hand, certainly has many of the elements of genuine creativity - such as a high level of fantasy - but the connection with reality is tenuous. An example would be the 'creativity' of daydreams. Pseudocreativity and quasicreativity differ from 'genuine creativity' because the latter requires a further element over and above mere novelty. A product or response must be *relevant* to some issue that the society regards as worth looking at and must offer some kind of *effective* response to the issue, even if the relevance and effectiveness only become apparent after the fact. Victor Kayam rejected the opportunity to acquire the rights to *Velcro* because he could see no use for it. Until somebody else did, in terms of the present social definition of creativity, *Velcro* remained uncreative.

A further crucial property of creativity as a social phenomenon arises from the fact that the concept has highly positive connotations. It is difficult, for instance, to think of novel forms of terrorism as creative, even though they might, in a purely formal sense, satisfy the criterion of introducing useful (to the goals of the terrorists) novelty. Furthermore, in a second paradox of creativity, revolutionary new ideas and products that are well-intentioned, and may even achieve significant social good, often open the way for serious negative consequences for society, regardless of the intent of the people producing them. The highly acclaimed discoveries of people like Jenner and Pasteur, to take one example, laid the foundations for germ warfare! Thus, creativity has a 'dark side' (McLaren, 1993). Nowadays we are experiencing a climate of 'general intoxication' with creativity (*ibid.*), so that this problem has become particularly acute and the need for social responsibility is increasingly being stressed (see, for instance, discussions of cloning human beings). As King (1992) argued, the term 'innovation' should only be applied to change introduced with the deliberate intention of *benefiting* the system into which it is introduced. Thus, the *ethical* element takes on particular importance (Grudin, 1990).

Society's rejection of some novelty

Not all deviations from the commonplace are equally acceptable to a society. Pseudo- and quasicreativity are usually treated as harmless dreaming, letting off steam, etc., even if they are regarded as having no social value. However, some behaviour that deviates from the social norms goes beyond what the society will tolerate and awakens anger, resentment or rejection. Those who introduce such intolerable novelty are sometimes regarded as deranged or crazy. Indeed, one of the oldest ideas about creativity is that it is linked to madness (eg. Lombroso, 1891). In the former Soviet Union, for instance, regime critics who attempted to introduce novel (for the Soviet Union) ideas about government and economics were regularly declared to be psychiatrically ill. Cropley (2001) summarised evidence showing that there really are similarities between the thinking of creative and psychotic individuals, and that both differ in a similar way from people who introduce no novelty. However, there are also important differences between the insane and the creative. In the present paper these differences will not be looked at in a psychological way as in Cropley (2001), but from the viewpoint of usefulness, ethicality and the like (i.e. from a social point of view - see Table 1).

In some cases, deviation from the usual is treated not as crazy but as criminal. Of course many of the behaviours that lie outside a society's norms and are labelled criminal, really are unacceptable in anyone's terms. Obvious examples would be murder or beating up and robbing elderly people. However, other proscribed behaviours are really guilty only of deviating too much from what the society will tolerate at the present time. Perhaps the best known 'classical' example is the sentencing of Galileo in 1633 for supporting the now commonplace Copernican position that the earth orbits the sun. The degree of novelty was too much for the society to tolerate. The society's reaction to levels of novelty that exceed the limits, i.e., that introduce intolerable levels of surprise, are closely connected with the age, occupation or social role of the person involved. An artist is allowed to be more outrageous than an engineer or a brain surgeon, for instance.

Creative products

According to economic theory, returns on investments in rich countries should have been lower during the second half of the 20th century than during the first, because the stock of capital was rising faster than the workforce. However, the fact is that they were considerably higher. The decisive factor that defeated the law of diminishing returns is now seen to be the *addition to the system of new knowledge and technology*, i.e. innovation. Innovation involves the practical insertion of novelty into a functioning system, i.e. what might be called 'applied' creativity. It currently accounts for more than half of economic growth in more technologically developed societies (*Economist Technology Quarterly*, 2002, p.13). As Higgins (1994) put it, the task of this applied kind of creativity is to generate new and valuable ideas, products and processes, 'devices or systems that *perform tasks or solve problems*' (Horenstein, 2002, p.2). Burghardt (1995) referred to this not as applied but as *functional* creativity, contrasting it with *aesthetic* creativity that, in his view, has no functional purpose, only aesthetic purpose. It is this functional creativity on which the present paper focuses.

An essential element of functional creativity is the devices or systems that perform tasks or solve problems, in other words, the *products*. Although earlier discussions of creativity gave considerable emphasis to tangible products (eg. Gordon, 1961; Roe, 1952; Rossman, 1931), this aspect has not received as much attention as might be expected in recent years, perhaps because modern research has been dominated by psychologists and educators. I have argued, as have other writers such as Albert (1990), that it is too difficult to define creative products in a practical, objective way, because the concept is so subjective; and have recommended focusing on creative *processes* and characteristics of the creative *person*, thus treating creativity as a sociological or psychological phenomenon. Although I do not want to reify creativity, repeating the mistake made by treating 'intelligence' as though it were a real and tangible entity rather than simply an explanatory construct used to make sense of observable behaviour, the creativity of products is not as diffuse a concept as it might at first appear.

Cropley and Cropley (in press) defined four key properties of creative products. Somewhat modified for present purposes, these are:

- *novelty* (the product introduces something that is new in a particular setting)
- *usefulness* (it does what it is supposed to do in that context)
- *beauty* (the product is understandable, complete, well finished and internally harmonious)
- *seminality* (it opens up possibilities in contexts other than the one into which it is being introduced).

Extending Taylor's (1975) idea of 'levels' of creativity, Cropley and Cropley argued that the criteria just listed form a *hierarchy*. Although in theoretical discussions novelty is the main characteristic of creativity, in practical settings the first criterion in the hierarchy is usefulness. For instance, if a bridge falls down instead of carrying traffic across a river, no amount of novelty or beauty can justify its cost. However, although usefulness is a necessary criterion for functional creativity, it is not sufficient on its own. A product that is simply useful is not creative but 'routine'. Of course, routine products can be extremely helpful, but because they lack novelty they are not creative.

The second necessary criterion is novelty. In the case of aesthetic creativity, novelty may be sufficient on its own (i.e. aesthetic creativity may not demand usefulness), but in the case of functional creativity it is insufficient without usefulness. When a product's usefulness is *supplemented* by novelty it achieves the lowest level of functional creativity and can be labelled 'original' (useful and novel). The further addition of beauty yields an 'elegant' functional product (useful, novel and beautiful), and usefulness, novelty and beauty supplemented by seminality yield 'innovative' creativity. 'Original', 'elegant' and 'innovative' products can all lay claim to 'functional' creativity, although at successively higher levels.

Functionally creative products that solve concrete and practical problems in economics, business, manufacturing, science, engineering and the like can be contrasted with the 'merely' aesthetic products of some forms of art, music, literature, etc, in which the primary focus is on novelty and/or beauty rather than on practical usefulness, with the result that usefulness in a specific, concrete, physical situation is missing. Of course, it can be argued that such products display their own form of usefulness, since they solve aesthetic problems such as how to communicate an artist's sense of wonder. However, this form is different from the usefulness that is seen in functional creativity. Without decrying aesthetic creativity, the present paper defines usefulness in a functional way.

Kinds of novelty

A framework has now been established for distinguishing among the four forms of introduction of novelty into a social setting (functional creativity, aesthetic creativity, madness and criminality). This is based on the six criteria discussed above: novelty, usefulness, beauty, seminality, ethicality and social acclaim. Table 1 shows how this can be done. Here, a plus sign means that a criterion is satisfied, a minus sign that it is not, and a question mark either that the role of the particular criterion for this form of novelty production is unclear or the property in question is possible but not necessary. Thus, for instance, criminal novelty is obviously novel and useful (to the criminal), and therefore receives plus signs in these areas. However, it is clearly unethical and does not receive social acclaim, since it is illegal (at least officially), and therefore receives minus signs on these two dimensions. It is unclear whether novel criminal behaviour can be beautiful, since it is conceivable some people could regard it in this way, and it is possible but not necessary that it be seminal (i.e. that it open up new perspectives for novel kinds of criminal behaviour in other settings). So, criminal novelty receives a question mark for both beauty and seminality.

Society's ambivalence about introducing novelty

Despite its value to society, the introduction of novelty is not always greeted with unreserved approval. To take the example of education, in a recent survey in Australia (Government of Australia, 1999) employers complained that three-quarters of new university graduates show 'skill deficiencies' in creativity, problem-solving and independent and critical thinking, and are therefore unemployable. Despite the apparent desire for creativity, Cooper, Altman and Garner (2002) concluded that the system discourages it. Cropley and Cropley (2000) summarised a number of earlier studies that concluded that universities in the USA do not favour the emergence of creativity in engineers, and Fasko (2000-2001) reported that more recent evidence supports this view. At the school level the situation may well be much the same.

	Deranged	Criminal	Aesthetically creative	Effectively creative
Usefulness	-	+	?	+
Novelty	+	+	+	+
Beauty	-	?	+	?
Seminality	-	?	?	?
Ethicality	?	-	+	+
Social acclaim	-	-	+	+

Table 1: Forms of novelty production

Despite the fact that Feldhusen and Treffinger (1975) showed more than 25 years ago that most teachers have a positive attitude to creativity, in their classrooms properties and behaviours actually associated with it are frequently frowned upon. The evidence is that teachers discourage traits such as boldness, desire for novelty or originality, or even actively dislike such characteristics (for a summary, see Cropley, 2001). Thus, although there are calls for creativity there may be limited effort to foster its emergence, or even dislike of people who display it.

Thus, societies simultaneously admire creativity and dislike it. There seem to be two apparently competing forces at work, a force favouring introduction of novelty and a force opposing it. These contrasting forces are shown in Table 2.

The mechanisms of conservation

People acquire knowledge of the *status quo* of a society via learning, in the usual course of events, largely during childhood. The learning process is often referred to as 'socialisation'. They learn specific behaviours in concrete situations such as how to obtain and consume food or move about in safety, how to treat other people in face-to-face contacts, or how to obtain information. They also acquire special cultural skills such as a language and techniques for dealing with stress, anxiety and the like, as well as social roles and a self-image, a concept of the 'good' person and ways of distinguishing 'us' from 'them'. These are acquired through interactions with the various instruments of socialisation: family, schooling, peers, role models, media, etc, by means of reward and punishment, imitation and rule learning.

Learned behaviours and rules are reinforced by having an affective or evaluational component. Thus, children learn not only that 'we' do something in a particular way, but that those who do it differently are stupid, ignorant, wilfully wrong or evil. When I was a child I was taught to cut food with the fork in my left hand and the knife in my right, retaining the fork in my left hand when using it to place food in my mouth and always using it with the tines pointing downwards—even when eating peas. It was explained to me that those who eat differently are uncouth and lacking social finesse. When I first encountered the North American way of transferring the fork to the right hand after cutting

19

the food and spooning it up with the fork held 'upside down' I was amazed at how many uncouth people there were in Canada! As Fromm (1980)

Force	Effect	Change mode	Benefits
Conserving	Change: • is relatively slow • builds on what already exists • may appear to be blocked.	'Evolutionary'	Despite change: • the world remains orderly and understandable • existing knowledge and skills remain useful • people's feeling of security is not threatened • experts' self-image of competence is preserved • power structures and the like remain intact.
SLOGAN: 'If it ain't broke, don't fix it!'			
Renewing	Change: • is rapid (paradigm shift) • sweeps away what already exists.	'Revolutionary'	As a result of change: • novelty is obvious • progress is often rapid • problems are often solved quickly • people are encouraged to introduce novelty • existing structures are threatened.
SLOGAN: 'Altius, citius, fortius!'			

Table 2: Opposing forces of change in a society

put it, societies have 'filters', and these inhibit divergent behaviour or even thinking. Societies conduct 'surveillance' (Amabile, Goldfarb and Brackfield, 1990) to detect and deter people who deviate.

Social discouragement of divergent behaviour need not involve direct attitudes to creativity or active suppression of it. For instance, social norms involving 'correct' ways of behaving or the social image of what a 'normal' person is like can inhibit creativity, even when they seem to have nothing to do with it, and the negative influence may not be readily observable. For instance, Lindauer (1993) showed that although famous male and female artists both experience their peak years between 30 and 50, it is common for men to continue to be productive in their 60s or even later, whereas this is unusual in women. This suggests a social effect - in this case possibly sex role expectations - on creative activity. Dudek and Hall (1991) showed that architects who resist social pressure to retire and hand over to the young are creatively productive for many years more than those who retire early.

Some people may have a vested interest in maintaining the *status quo*. For instance, scientists who have invested a lifetime's work in a particular paradigm are likely to resist dramatic novelty, among other things by withholding acknowledgement from those who deviate. As a result, introducing novelty can require a special form of courage (Motamedi, 1982). To return to Galileo, giving influential support to the heliocentric view of the solar system posed a great threat to existing cosmological theory, as well as imperilling the souls of a large number of people. It is not surprising that it was labelled criminal. When Ignaz Semmelweiss dramatically reduced the incidence of death from puerperal fever in Vienna in the 1840s by getting staff in the lying-in hospital to wash their hands before touching pregnant women, far from showing gratitude, his colleagues labelled him a crackpot.

The need for both forces

Some writers interpret society's resistance to the introduction of novelty in dramatic terms. According to Sternberg and Lubart (1995), societies are gripped by a 'climate of conformity' or, as Burkhardt (1985) put it even more forcefully, by '*Gleichheitswahn*' (a psychosis of sameness). To such writers, being creative means 'living your life your own way' (Moustakis, 1977) or displaying 'contrarianism' (Sternberg and Lubart, 1995), i.e. fighting against the psychosis of sameness and defying the climate of conformity. To some of these writers the conserving force in society is opposed to the innovating one and is therefore pernicious, even evil. Certainly, as King (1992) emphasised, creativity often or even usually involves an *intention* to bring about change and thus a deliberate challenge to the *status quo*. As a result, it brings change in a way that differs from the effects of natural evolution with the passage of time - it is *revolutionary* rather than simply *evolutionary*.

However, in my view not every act of contrarianism (undisciplined, disruptive or ignorant behaviour, or defiance, aggression or nonconformity) should be acclaimed in the name of creativity, and not every demand for knowledge, accuracy, speed, practised skill and the like should be condemned as arising from a conformity psychosis. The former are not always unequivocally good, nor the latter always bad. The society makes a substantial effort to train its members in its ways because this brings them the benefit of being able to function effectively in a socially structured environment. Indeed, acquisition of the social rules has an important survival value. To take a simple example, if city children do not know how to cross the road safely in high traffic areas, many of them will die. Most people would probably prefer the brain surgeon operating on them or the jet captain landing their jumbo to deviate only a little (if at all) from the tried and trusted, i.e. *evolving* rather than making revolutionary changes. The society too has a strong interest in maintaining the achievements of the past and preserving the best of the national culture (i.e. changing by evolution rather than revolution). This is painfully obvious in, for instance, the Baltic States, whose national traditions, languages, even identity as separate peoples have been gravely threatened by excessively rapid and widespread change in the course of attempted Sovietisation. First nations in North America, New Zealand and Australia may well applaud the benefits of, say, modern medicine, but regret the changes that have almost destroyed their individual cultures.

Equating introduction of novelty exclusively with revolutionary change implies that the forces of conservation block all innovation. However, conservation is not the same as total absence of change. Sternberg (1999) argued that novelty can be introduced in one of seven ways:

1. *conceptual replication* (novelty is produced by transferring what already exists more or less unchanged to a new field);
2. *redefinition* (the known is seen in a new way);
3. *forward incrementation* (novelty is produced by taking the known further in an existing direction);
4. *advance forward incrementation* (the novelty not only extends the known in an existing direction but goes beyond what is currently tolerable);
5. *redirection* (it extends the known in a *new* direction);
6. *reconstruction and redirection* (it breathes new life into an approach previously abandoned);
7. *re-initiation* (it begins at a radically different point from the current one and takes off in a new direction).

The first six of these involve building on what already exists rather than introducing something entirely new. At least the first three seem to me to involve 'evolutionary' rather than 'revolutionary' change (see Table 2). Miller (2000) too emphasised that the commonest form of production of novelty involves building on the already known.

Blind, wholesale novelty may fail to satisfy social criteria such as usefulness, even if it introduces novelty. There are also other factors that can hinder a society's acceptance of change. Even if the novelty is useful, possibly beautiful and seminal, revolutionary change may introduce it at a *pace* that is beyond what a society can tolerate. The area of change may be too central to the psyche of the society in question or too sensitive to permit an overnight paradigm shift. Powerful vested interests may wish to maintain the *status quo*. Thus, there may well be situations where an evolutionary process leads to successful introduction of socially acceptable, relevant and effective novelty, where revolutionary novelty would not. Thus, from the point of view of creativity and culture, introduction of novelty requires both conserving and innovating - revolution to be sure, but also evolution.

References

Albert, R. S. (1990) Identity, experiences, and career choice among the exceptionally gifted and talented. In M. A. Runco (Ed.) *Theories of Creativity*, pp.13-34. Newbury Park, CA: Sage.

Amabile, T. M., Goldfarb, P. and Brackfield, S. C. (1990) Social influences on creativity: Evaluation, coaction, surveillance. *Creativity Research Journal, 3*, pp.6-21.

Bruner, J. S. (1962) The conditions of creativity. In H. Gruber, G. Terrell and M. Wertheimer (Eds.) *Contemporary Approaches to Cognition*, pp.1-30. New York: Athenaeum.

Burghardt, M. D. (1995) *Introduction to the Engineering Profession* (2nd ed.) New York: Addison Wesley.

Burkhardt, H. (1985) *Gleichheitswahn Parteienwahn* [Sameness psychosis]. Tübingen: Hohenrain.

Cattell, R. B. and Butcher, H. J. (1968) *The Prediction of Achievement and Creativity*. New York: Bobbs-Merrill.

Cooper, C., Altman, W. and Garner, A. (2002) *Inventing for Business Success*. NY: Texere.

Cropley, A. J. (1997) Creativity: A bundle of paradoxes. *Gifted and Talented International, 12*, pp.8-14.

Cropley, A. J. (2001) *Creativity in Education and Learning*. London: Kogan Page.

Cropley, D. H. and Cropley, A. J. (2000) Fostering creativity in engineering undergraduates. *High Ability Studies, 11*, pp.207-219.

Cropley, D. H. and Cropley, A. J. (in press) Engineering creativity: A systems concept of functional creativity. In J. C. Kaufman and J. Baer (Eds.) *Faces of the Muse: How people think, work and act creatively in diverse domains*. Hillsdale, NJ: Lawrence Erlbaum.

Csikszentmihalyi, M. (1996) *Creativity: Flow and the Psychology of Discovery and Invention*. New York: Harper Collins.

Dudeck, S. Z. and Hall, W. B. (1991) Personality consistency: Eminent architects 25 years later. *Creativity Research Journal, 4*, pp.213-31.

Economist Technology Quarterly (Sept. 21, 2002, pp.13-14) Thanksgiving for innovation.

Fasko, D. (2000-2001). Education and creativity. *Creativity Research Journal, 13*, pp.317-328.

Feldhusen, J. F. and Treffinger, D. J. (1975) Teachers' attitudes and practices in teaching creativity and problem solving to economically disadvantaged and minority children. *Psychological Reports, 37*, pp.1161-2.

Fromm, E. (1980) *Greatness and Limitations of Freud's Thought*. NY: New American Library.

Gordon, W. J. (1961) *Synectics*. New York: Harper.

Government of Australia. (1999) *Higher Education Funding Report, 1999*. Canberra: Government Printer.

Grudin, R. (1990) *The Grace of Great Things: Creativity and Innovation*. New York: Ticknor and Fields.

Heinelt, G. (1974) *Kreative Lehrer/Kreative Schüler* [Creative teachers/creative students]. Freiburg: Herder.

Higgins, J. M. (1994) *101 Creative Problem Solving Techniques—The handbook of new ideas for business*. Winter Park, FL: New Management Publishing Company.

Horenstein, M. N. (2002) *Design Concepts for Engineers* (2nd ed.) Upper Saddle River, NJ: Prentice Hall Inc.

King, N. (1992) Modelling the innovation process: An empirical comparison of approaches. *Journal of Occupational and Organizational Psychology, 65,* pp.89-100.

Lindauer, M. S. (1993) The span of creativity among long-lived historical artists. *Creativity Research Journal, 6,* pp.221-40.

Lombroso, C. (1891) *The Man of Genius*. London: Scott.

McLaren, R. B. (1993) The dark side of creativity. *Creativity Research Journal, 6,* pp.137-44.

Miller, A. I. (2000) *Insights of Genius*. Cambridge, MA: MIT Press.

Motamedi, K. (1982) Extending the concept of creativity. *Journal of Creative Behavior, 16,* pp.75-88.

Moustakis, C. E. (1977) *Creative Life*. New York: Van Nostrand.

Roe, A. (1952) *The Making of a Scientist*. New York: Dodd Mead.

Rossman, J. (1931) *The Psychology of the Inventor: A study of the patentee*. Washington, DC: Inventors' Publishing Co.

Sternberg, R. J. (1999) A propulsion model of types of creative contribution. *Review of General Psychology, 3* (2), pp.83-100.

Sternberg, R. J. and Lubart, T. I. (1995) *Defying the Crowd: Cultivating creativity in a culture of conformity*. New York: Free Press.

Taylor, I. A. (1975) An emerging view of creative actions. In I. A. Taylor and J. W. Getzels (Eds.) *Perspectives in Creativity*, pp.297-325. Chicago: Aldine.

Walberg, H. J. and Stariha, W. E. (1992) Productive human capital: Learning, creativity and eminence. *Creativity Research Journal, 5,* pp.323-40.

M. K. Raina

'I shall be many': the garland making perspective on creativity and cultural diversity

The Hindu God of Creativity, Lord Vishvakarma, who is believed to manifest himself in the activities of the universe in a multiplicity of forms and forces has said, 'I shall be many'. In order to consider God's words and creatively respond to his emphasis on manyness in matters which are universal (Guilford, 1980, Passow, 1987) and basic to Man, one cannot afford to be led by false presuppositions which leave their mark deep in the minds of men, dividing nation and nation, knowledge and knowledge, man and nature (Tagore, 1988). To transcend the limitations of limited thinking and overcome the suspicion of whatever is beyond the barriers we have built, we must cultivate the greatness of soul which identifies itself with the soul of all people and not merely with that of one's own. The fifth century philosopher of language in India, Bhartrhari said: 'The intellect acquires critical acumen by familiarity with different traditions. How much does one really understand by merely following one's own reasoning?' Gaining insightful understanding of creativity and searching for Lord Vishvakarma within the amazing diversity and cultural pluralism that characterises our contemporary societies, necessitates adopting Bhartrhari's resilient perspective (*dristi*) which provides us with unbounded opportunities to understand the creativeness of variety, creativeness of the human will and the pleomorphic and eternal varieties of creativity, Vishvakarma is indicating.

The question of creativity and diversity is no ordinary question and it might be argued that the question of how many answers there are to any great human question is itself a great human question to which I believe there is only one answer, that being that there are many answers. It is unfortunate but true that our concept and understanding of creativity may not have claims to universal legitimacy since our skewed discussions of the phenomenon are largely based on studies of societies which are homogeneous and uniform (Raina, 1993, 1999). Interestingly, most creativity research has not resulted in the enlargement of our vision of creativity beyond the ethnocentric confines (Gruber, 1988, personal communication). Though we have some inquiries which can count as attempts to break the bounds of a single ethnocentric point of view (Simonton, 1989, personal communication), most of the creativity research has been pursued within narrow ethnocentric boundaries, following the framework of Western ontology of the mind. In fact, not many researchers have seriously studied how various civilizations and philosophies have defined and approached creativity. Only a few have remained seriously committed to transcending the limitations of any one culture and being enlightened and inspired by views and concepts other than the Western ones. One notices an inevitable lack of understanding and appreciating 'a global vision of the potential for creative achievement' (Meador, 1999, p.325). The greatest amount of attention has been given to creativity studies in 'developed, achieving societies' and most of the research has been nation-oriented rather than international, resulting in the neglect of cross-cultural research. In 1959 Mead, as a result of her studies, pointed to 'the light that cross-cultural studies can throw on the problems of creativity' besides providing, to some extent, foundations for theory development. Creativity research will have to become more cross-cultural (less time-bound and less place-bound) if it is to answer such questions as 'What are the pervasive philosophies of life in different periods that influence the magnitude and character of the creative work that will be undertaken? What kinds of values contribute to what types of individuals in what places during what historic periods' (Getzels, 1975).

We have to acknowledge the cultural specificity of theories, making it problematic and questionable if theories of one culture are applied uncritically to the empirical reality of another culture. For instance, there are the Indian habits of mind and there are the Western habits of mind nurtured over time by specificity of community's experiences and these may differ crucially. It is these habits of mind that are imbricated deeply in the respective conceptual frameworks. The multiperspectivalism that fosters creativity also invites people to recognise that every conception of truth exists within a cultural context that frames it and gives it meaning (Bjornson and Waldman, 1989). With this as the backdrop, I will attempt to indicate how different philosophical orientations have influenced the way different cultures have approached and conceptualised creativity, and how the character of creativity has been influenced by the diversity of cultural myths. Issues like creativity and cultural differences, creative discontinuity and the way cultures have perceived creative individuals will also be examined. In addition, I want to address how the nurturing practices in different cultures are tied to their philosophical orientations. I also attempt to outline the approach that to me seems vital for understanding cultural diversity and creativity.

It is universally accepted that culture works as the natural stimulus to creativity in praxis and theory, exploring the possible and the improbable worlds. The two are father and daughter of each other as the Rigvedic myth puts it (Pandeya, 1981). Gokak (1992) suggests that the most congenial state of being comes into existence when the creative consciousness apprehends its environment fully, knows its cosmicity and becomes one with it. We, the people interested in creativity, consider variety as an expression of human creativity and we have to equally respect diversity and richness of environments, as they influence the understanding of creativity across cultures. In the absence of this framework, our concepts and findings will have limited generalisabilty and validity, distinctly noted by MacKinnon (1987) in the form of questions: 'But what about creativity in the more primitive and undeveloped countries? Would the definition of creativity generally accepted by European and American psychologists be valid for those other societies and cultures?' To this, I may add those societies which have remained exploited and where the colonialism of the mind is more subtle and pervasive. Or even the question of creativity in those cultures which are characterised by pluralism and find such pluralism congenial to their psyche. And what about creativity where there is greater chaos, increased suffering and unimaginable destruction, where unity has not been reached and yet there is not full separation? What shape will creativity take in those societies which are static, crystalline, harmonious primitive societies where one finds '[the] complete form of mature human being often of a homogeneity and simple integrity which we at times might envy' (Erikson, 1963). Such analyses will perhaps not remain exclusive to a particular country, but will relate to a great part of humanity.

To accomplish this task meaningfully, we will have to adopt the garland making worldview as against the charcoal burning worldview. Mahabharata admonishes the ruler to:

'Be like a garland maker, O king; not like a charcoal burner.'
--Mahabharata, XII.72.20

This famous statement from the Mahabharata contrasts two divergent worldviews. It asks the king to preserve and protect diversity, in a coherent way. The metaphor used is that of a garland, in which flowers of many colours and forms are strung together for a pleasing effect. The contrast is given against charcoal, which is the result of burning all kinds of wood and reducing diversity to homogeneous dead matter. The garland maker celebrates diversity, whereas the charcoal burner is reductionist and destroys diversity. The former respects multiple visions, pluralism and diversity of thought, whereas the latter strives for a homogenised and fossilised state, in which dogma and irrational prejudice run supreme. I think we, as creativity researchers, have to realise the charm and the challenge in adopting the garland making perspective. Torrance (1979, p.ix) experienced the rewards in adopting such a framework and he explained how his concept of creativity was influenced after his visit to Japan: 'We like their concept of "satori" which is a little like the American concept "aha". But in other ways it is very different and seems to capture the essence of something I have been struggling to achieve, along with my students, for some years.... I have been in Japan for about two weeks and already Japanese concepts of creativity have begun to influence our thinking'.

The garland making worldview in the context of creativity research stresses moving from exclusivism and intolerance, to inclusiveness and tolerance, in studying different cultures, minds and mental universe. This presupposes an unhesitating commitment to build uninhibitedly based on insights from both East and the West and an open-mindedness to consider creativity as an infinite and endlessly diverse phenomenon which provides meaning and purpose to many in life and a sense of human purpose in relation to cosmos. This perspective decries universalising a particular culture and inferiorizing or ridiculing others' discoveries in various domains as only myths. It advocates giving honour where honour is due. This is the concept which I have dared to articulate In the form of a phenomenon which I called the Torrance Phenomenon (Raina, 1996; for interesting comments on this, see Magyari-Beck, 1996).

The question of the minds and the societies

Each culture, as Gardner (1989) has shown, evolves over history its own view of human nature, growth, potential and limitations, and there may be as many views and realisations of human potential as there are discrete societies in the world. In approaching a subject as complex as human potential, it is vital to explore the larger spiritual, religious and cultural forces and symbols which have shaped a society; and engage ourselves with the mind of a nation in its richness, its variety, its profundity, its depths and its heights in the broad area of philosophy, and with the powerful moulding force which the philosophies have exerted on the many-sided cultures of the people throughout the ages. Hu Shih, the great Chinese intellectual and philosopher, has been quoted as saying that every people has a unique character in terms of which that particular people must be understood, and this essential character or mind of a given people consists essentially of the deepest philosophical convictions. The philosophies, the religions and the basic cultural patterns have been so deeply engrained in the minds that we must understand these in their fullest significance, in themselves and, in many cases, for the world at large. To quote an example, 'dance' - movement in space and time, especially in the Indian context, cannot be viewed in isolation from the most significant framework of the philosophical thought and the psychical concerns of the Indian people (Vatsyayan, 1983). However, it is important to appreciate that there are some nations made up of more varieties of religion, more philosophies and greater complexities of cultural practices than others. As in the case of India, honeycombed by myriad diversities, with a graduation of opposites that are simultaneously pronounced and subtle, there is no one past but many pasts, infinite variety of philosophical concepts, methods and attitudes that make up the Indian philosophical tradition. It would, therefore, be distortion to speak of single personalities, single vision and one past. Any attempts at simplification will amount to falsification.

Understanding is a very complicated matter. We cannot understand another people if we look through biased eyes, with the conviction of superiority or with the assumption that what is different from our own must therefore be worthless. The Mexican Nobel Laureate Octavio Paz (1995, p.90) has made a profound observation that 'much as I find barbarous the belief that one race is superior to another, treating all cultures as the same strikes me as a modern superstition'. (An example of how such an attitude can impede correct understanding of creativity in other cultures is recorded by Torrance (1988): 'The United States has never shown much inclination to learn from the Japanese. Our stereotype of the Japanese is one of imitators, copyists, and adaptors. The facts available today should cause us to reassess the Japanese as a source of insight and know-how about creativity'). What is required is genuine understanding which must be comprehensive, and comprehensive understanding must include knowledge of all fundamental aspects of the mind of the people in question. It is the spirit of humility, open-mindedness, cordiality to alien ideas and determination that will help in understanding cultures, creativity and diversity. Bateson (1994) is absolutely right when she says: 'What would it be like to have not only color vision but culture vision, the ability to see the multiple worlds of others?'

Conceptualising creativity: the richness of diversity

Being a global issue, the idea of creativeness has been considered as deeply rooted and central in both the Occident and the Orient. I think, Albert and Runco (1999, p.17) are right in mentioning that 'long before the Christian view of creativity had begun to emerge, there were efforts to grasp the meaning for humanity of what we now recognise as creativity'. However, I believe that creative thought in the Oriental traditions cannot be treated as a single undifferentiated entity, as one notices endless complexity and diversity in the way these traditions have dealt with issues of existence and wholeness. One realises immense difficulty in dealing with these issues, particularly when in certain cultures one notices not only a fusion of flavours, but a fusion of times as well, a succession of epochs, a superimposition of peoples, religions, institutions and languages; not only a plurality of doctrines, gods, rites, cosmologies, and sects, but also conglomeration and juxtaposition (Paz, 1995, p.86). One can only imagine what a challenge it would be to make a sensitive study of creativity in such cultures, without jumping to conclusions. Only a garland making perspective will possibly yield results.

Creativity being infinite involves many creative processes, with many layers, many levels of involvement and intent. Some important differences have been noticed in underlying goals, which reflect a more basic cultural difference generally recognised between East and West. Anantha Murthy (in Sharma, 1996, p.28) has elaborated the differentiation thus:

> The great thing about the West is their living culture, what they have built, what they have achieved. Their cultural progression has been unchristian, but their entire mental make-up has been influenced by Christianity. So there is a constant friction between their religion and their everyday existence. This tension has produced some of the best literature in the West. The kind of intensity you find in Tolstoy is possible because he believes in a religious truth which runs counter to the logical progression of his civilization. Similarly with Dostoevsky's *The Brothers Karamazov*. The Indian philosophical system is altogether different; it is all-inclusive. *Prakritai Namah Vikratai Namah. Namah* to *Prakriti*, and to *Vikrati* as well. So our creativity has to be very different. Our entire philosophical system does not have any scope for an intensity born out of friction. Our intensity is that of *Bhakti*.

Every civilization is a vision of time. As Paz (1995, p.184) believes 'institutions, works of art, technologies, philosophies, all that we make or dream is a weave of time. An idea or a sense of passage, time is not mere succession; for all cultures it is a process that has a direction, or points toward an end. Time has a meaning. Or, more precisely: time is the meaning of existence, even if we believe that existence has no meaning. The opposing attitudes of Hindus and Christians toward the human condition – *karma* and Original Sin, *moksha* and redemption – are also apparent in their visions of time'. I believe that these visions of time underlie differences in approaching issues relating to creativity. Analyses of the Western theory of creativity, which is supposed to be more product-centred with its cognitive problem-solving orientation (Lubart, 1999), from the point of view of Indian philosophical tradition which emphasises process-centered creativity, with its ultimate goal being personal enlightenment, has brought into focus the varying intellectual traditions from which stem notions of creativeness. Whereas Eastern cognition is believed to be interested in consciousness itself, Western cognition is interested in the objects of consciousness. The emphasis on science in the West associates creativity with inventiveness, and in the religious traditions like India, with spiritualization. The paradigm artist in Indian thought, for example, is the potter as against the carpenter in Western (Greek) thought. The Indian aphorism, '*Yat pinde tatso brahmande*' – 'In microcosm lies the macrocosm' – is manifested in the fact that the potter is also called Prajapati, the progenitor. His equipment and action are symbolic of the cosmic forces of creation. The carpenter cuts segments and rearranges his material reality (the wood) and is therefore a 'maker'. The potter's material reality (the clay) is like water in the ocean not measurable or segmentable and the potter therefore does not 'make' – he merely makes manifest a form that inheres in the material and is present to him in his mind. The potter is not the 'master' but a *sadhaka*, a devotee, a Yogi who yokes his mind to the object and gives form to the substance. Further, analysis indicates that the Hindu mind views the creative process as a means of suggesting or recreating a vision, however fleeting, of divine truth and regards art as a means of experiencing a state of bliss akin to the absolute state of *ananda* or *jivanmukti* (release in life). The image of dancing Siva, Nataraja, is the supreme symbol of all aspects of life as much as dance itself, which represents the synthesis of all aspects of creative activity. True creativity in human consciousness is the cosmic 'dance of Shiva', as envisioned by Capra (1977, p.242): '… a great rhythmic process of creations and destruction, of death and rebirth, and Shiva's dance symbolised this eternal life-death rhythm which goes on in endless cycles'. This made someone sing: In creation I see Your glory; In dissolution I see Your glory.

The Oriental concept of creativity stresses themes of development and progress towards the realisation of the universe. The *Chandogya Upanishad* describes the ascent of knowledge, identifying Brahman step by step with different realities. There is a whole order of human values (not to speak of the ever-recurring cosmic terms) which serve as stepping-stones in the ascent and are discarded only by the recognition of something greater transcending them. Brahman does not fall from the sky as some incomprehensible revelation; it is discovered by going through the whole range of human realms of freedom. Brahman is neither this nor that; it is only the unlimited (in Panikkar, 1977, p.674). The Chinese view of cosmic creation has been described as an ongoing process, developing and unfolding. In contrast, Judaic and Greek views of cosmic creation involve an abrupt production of the universe by an uncreated being who brings order to the formless void. As noted by Lubart (1990), the modern Western concept of creativity stems from this origin; therefore, the perceived spontaneity of creativity and the locus of creativity in the individual logically belong together.

Among the creative forces of the universe, the Indian texts often emphasise sexual desire (*kama*). One reads in the Atharva Veda: 'Desire arose in the beginning, which was the first seed of thought' (19.52). Kama is a god because desire, in its purest and most active form, is sacred energy: it moves humanity and all of nature. It is generally recognised both in the Brahmanic and Buddhist speculative thought that the seat of creation, and hence of art, lay in *kama* and in *vasana* which contributed towards experiencing pleasure and happiness. Such a desire, urge or impulse is generated obviously by the inter-action of the subject (the perceiving and cognising human being) and the object (the material itself, the visible world of men and things and the invisible world of ideas, visions, thoughts and images). According to Indian tradition *Kamayati*, the artist's conscious creative desire to seek articulation and establish communion with his fellow-beings by projecting himself to them, or at any rate with his other self, to enable him to perceive and see himself in his created object, is central to the creative process (Ray, 1974). The distinct Eastern view is reflected in the description of the creative artists found in Maduro's (1976) anthropological field study of traditional painters of India.

The character of creativity: the diversity of cultural myths

To some it may seem disingenuous and somewhat primitive, yet one notices increasingly many endorsing the belief that theories of creativity derive from cultures' creation myths (Sinclair, 1971; Raina, 1999; Dharwadker, 1999), providing a prototype for framing implicit conceptions of human creativity (von Franz, 1995). 'The cosmogony', wrote Eliade (1963, p.32) 'is the explanatory model for every creative situation: whatever man does is in some way a repetition of the pre-eminent 'deed', the archetypal gesture of the Creator God, the Creation of the World'. Mason (1988, p.697) has pointed out two sharply differentiated beliefs throughout Western history about the character of creativity. 'One of these beliefs - Judaeo-Christian and neo-Platonic - has occupied such a dominant position that the very existence of the other has been obscured and ignored. Yet the evidence for the second belief is no less extensive or vivid. Moreover, this second belief seems to bear a closer relation to the character of creativity displayed by people regarded as 'creative', as well as to what we have learnt about creativity in this century from psychologists. Attitudes to creativity in the modern period have generally been based on the first tradition, but the activities of creative people have borne out the validity of the second tradition'.

Various cultures and traditions have brought into focus varying images, myths, metaphors and notions of creativeness and the processes underlying it. According to the Indian tradition, Lord Vishvakarma is the Primordial Creator and Supreme Patron of Arts, Crafts and Creativity. A symbol of Total Centered Consciousness, he is at once the Great Architect of the Universe and Spirit of the Creative Process. He is also known as Vishvakarmaya: Creative Power of the Whole Universe. Vishvakarma the 'All Creating' appears as an independent Hindu deity as early as the last book of the Rig Veda. Mahabharata (l. 2592) speaks of him as the Lord of arts, master of a thousand handicrafts, carpenter of the gods and the builder of their palaces divine, fashioner of every jewel, first of craftsmen, by whose art men live, and whom, a great and deathless god, they continually worship. Every artist or poet therefore has a share in the divine artistic power and intuition (pratibha), and is himself a human representative of the Divine Architect. In fact, Maduro's study of modern Nathdwara painters indicates that the painters perceive themselves that way. One also comes across conceptions suggesting the idea of God (Siva) as the Original Artist (Baumer, 1985). The creative process is described as the continuity of Brahma, Vishnu and Mahaeswara working in tandem creating, maintaining and destroying to re-create. The trident which is a symbol of the Hindu trinity represents creation and preservation, but also dissolution. 'The cycle of creation and destruction is the fundamental law of nature; hence creation is not represented as merely positive and dissolution as merely negative. They are the two opposite ends of the cosmic ladder, with preservation as the center of balance' (Mookerjee, 1987, p.6). Creation is not a making but 'a pouring forth', which is the root meaning for the Sanskrit word for creation, srsti. Such a myth expresses a worldview that insists on continuities, on transformations.

According to the Indian tradition, the most basic motivation in creation is the desire on the part of the Supreme Being to extend Himself for the sake of lila or 'play' or enjoyment. Creation could, therefore, be understood as Self-extension. Richer than the English word play, it means divine play, the play of creation, destruction and re-creation, the folding and unfolding of the cosmos. It has been the central term in the Hindu elaboration of the idea that God in his creating and governing of the world is moved not by need of necessity but by a free and joyous creativity that is integral to his own nature. Asked why God creates, Hindus liken the divine to a child at play. Tagore (in Raina, 1997) recalled the Indian theory of creation as play (lila) and claimed that he was beating the creator at his own game and creating forms that missed their chance in actual existence because God did not provide a place for them. Charmed by this concept, Nachmanovitch (1990) was prompted to write a full book on the topic of play (lila) and creativity.

The Chinese view of cosmic creation has been described as 'an ongoing progress – a developing, an unfolding' (Sinclair, 1971, p.83). In contrast, Judaic and Greek views of cosmic creation involve 'an abrupt production of the universe – by an uncreated being who brings order to the formless void' (Sinclair, 1971, p.84). Further support to the creation myth–creativity belief is offered by Ben-Amos (1986, p.80): 'In some African cultures – the artist at work is viewed as enacting or recreating the origin myth'. The Dogon weaver, who draws threads from the spindles of a loom, is symbolically identified with Nommo, a primordial being, who wove together four elements to make the universe. It may be rewarding to discover any truths hidden within the rich symbols in different cultures and see if these are confirmed by modern science. In summary, concludes Lubart (1990, p.43), the hypothesis that modern views of creativity stem from cultural creation myths seems plausible and deserves further research. However, unfortunately not many in the field of creativity take such myths, metaphors, parables, legends, stories, political rhetoric and poetic afflatus, tales, narratives both verbal and written, images, similes or philosophical speculations which transmit concepts, and are also goal- and context-sensitive, abundantly used in various texts, very seriously and generously. One would be greatly mistaken in judging them as naïve or euphemisms for primitivism, even though some, from other cultures, may find themselves at a loss in comprehending the terms, concepts and allusions which characterise other cultures.

Creativity and cultural differences

Though the universality of creativity is amazing, it is no less amazing to see how creativity across cultures, at various periods of development, in line with their worldview, has taken various shapes and forms. Cross-cultural research on creativity has shown that creative expression differs in kind, rather than magnitude, in different cultures (Saarilahti, Cramond and Sieppi, 1999). Very early in his research, Torrance (1996) wondered how cultures differed in their attitude regarding being different or exceptional in any important way. The promise and excitement in these multi-cultural studies is evident in indicating how cultures differ and what significance this difference has for our understanding of creativity. Analyses have shown that in different societies, particularly the traditional or indigenous sociocultural systems, original ideas, processes and products can be accepted and promoted more easily when they are placed within the framework of the values of the sociocultural system. Thus, ideas that emphasise more skills of verbal expression and more collective spirit, like modification and improvement, will be encouraged more than radical or uncommon ideas. Thus, in some indigenous cultures, creativity can take the form of modification and adaptation – the trend that has been observed by investigators in some other similar sociocultural context. Nathdwara painters in India, in most cases were not concerned with creating completely new images, but hoped to demonstrate their ability to recreate and reinvigorate inner images in a divergent and unusual way. Analyses of research have indicated that the kind of creativity Indian society nurtures is closely related to the cultural definitions of the high and the low, the legitimate and the non-legitimate, and the pure and the impure.

Multi-cultural studies of creativity (Torrance, 2002) have yielded many insights regarding culture and creativity, indicating that in some cultures a rather severe discontinuity is noticed in creative functioning and development in children at about ages 9 and 10 (fourth and fifth grades). In some, development is relatively continuous. In others, there is little growth during the elementary school years. In most, however, there are discontinuities. There are a number of indications that these discontinuities occur within a culture whenever children in that culture are confronted with new stresses and demands. Results have indicated that where British and American influences have been strongest, the discontinuities are clearest; where the native culture and language predominates, the continuities are clearest. In India, children in Sikh and other native cultural schools showed continuity in development, whereas the fourth-grade slump was apparent in mission schools and private schools, which reflect strong British influences. In the first three grades, children in the latter schools functioned at higher levels than those in native culture schools but showed little or no growth. Discontinuity in the US-dominant culture is attributed to the process of ego development, rearing and peer expectations. However, such a phenomenon may not exist in a continuous culture like India where the process of ego development takes place according to a model that differs sharply from the normative model of Western psychology, and continuity in the Indian case reflects a continuity of emotional and social environment (Raina, 1989).

Different cultures tend to foster their own distinctive intellectual styles and exhibit different attitudes about uniqueness and divergence, aspects that are crucial in creativity in any culture which, in turn, presumably influences the form that creative expression will take. In Indian literature, the dominant form is an aural-visual verse narrative and the highest excellence has been achieved in the epics. In English literature the highest excellence has been achieved in drama, and in Russian literature in the novel. Theories may investigate such cultural specificities if they are to ask relevant questions about compositions. Drawing on anthropological materials from different primitive cultures, Mead studied the relationship between the forms provided by a culture and the creativity of the individuals within the culture, on which statements of regularities may be based.

One should, therefore, be cautious in approaching creativity, particularly in those cultures that are traditional and multicultural, because vast differences can exist in the ways in which creativity is manifested and perceived, which further establishes the relevance of a garland making framework to studying creativity. Even within a particular society, varying cultural definitions of divergence and social sanctions may be available to the divergent in that society. For example, in a society where the traditional concepts of the high and the low intersect status and class differences, that which is divergence in one sector or stratum need not be so in another. Thus, although the Brahminic concepts of creativity and divergence are dominant in India, they are not the only ones current in the society (Nandy & Kakar, 1980).

The cultural levers: the rewarding and punishing forms

The emergence of creative persons (as we know them) may presuppose a certain view of the individual on the part of the culture and of the individuals themselves. To arrive at such an understanding, not only laypeople but many other important sources in different cultures could be analysed to arrive at implicit theories of creativity in various cultures. These could be derived from various indigenous texts and practices rather than from a European psychology perspective, the application of which would be disastrous since what gets construed remains dominated by imagination rather than reason and reality. In some cultures, one may even find elaborate details about psychological and physical characteristics of the great person, called *Mahapurusa* (Kramrisch, 1990) in India, such as Buddha. Reflecting on such individuals, *Chandogya Upanishad* (in Panikkar, 1977; p.683) speaks of the fullness – that which is fullness is immortal, but that which is limited is mortal – that leads to greatness in a man. Some of these qualities influenced Valmiki's perception, portraying these in a richly textured portraiture of Rama, the timeless beau ideal of the Indian imagination. It is significant to note how often Valmiki emphasised the absence of speech blemishes in Rama. He is portrayed as 'intelligent, soft spoken, willing to speak first, he is felicitous in his choice of words' (*buddhiman, madhurabhsahi, purvabhashi, priyamvada*). Felicitous speech (*priyamvada*) was, to the pristine Hindu mind, the first of the major excellences. Besides felicitous speech, truthfulness (*satyavachana*), restraint (*dama*), compassion (*daya*), all subsumed under the golden rubric, *dharma* (virtue) and are considered as excellences. According to Vedanta, the purity and harmony of thought, speech and action forms the basis for expression of artistic and scientific creativity (Raina & Srivastava, 2000). In fact, artistic creativity in India aims at the realisation of placidity even in action. As Krsna mentioned in *Bhagwad Gita*: 'He who sees inaction in action, and action in inaction is intelligent in men, he is a Yogi and a doer of all action.... Whose undertakings are all devoid of plan and desire for results, and whose actions are burnt by the fire of knowledge, him the sages call wise'. From various texts from different cultures, I am sure, one will discover rich portraiture of a creative person as perceived by different cultures.

I think while analysing the cultural roots of creativity, it is imperative to realise that one understands the nature of the culture as well as the creative individual in that culture; otherwise inferences drawn lose relevance and meaning, sometimes reflecting shallowness. For example, in certain cultures creativity may presume a certain marginality and, in the matter of culture, a certain dialectic between the classical and the folk (Nandy, 1995). Inferences about creative individuals can become questionable and at times dangerous in a situation where creative individuals do not self-consciously fit in with that model of creativity which the present generation of cultural experts find comfortable or of those who have a very limited or peripheral understanding of creativity. An example of this is the question of the plurality of the selves, partly traditional and partly Western, with which many creative persons live, a trait if not understood in the right perspective may lead to inane and deformed interpretations of creativity and creative work. One may even notice in the case of Indians, a significant bicultural component within their personality; what was once learnt as a technique of survival has now become a character trait, a part of the society's cultural repertoire. Reflecting on this, Nandy (1990, 1993, p.42) while analysing Satyajit Ray, a distinguished film director, who lived with a plurality of selves – a part of him was as deeply Indian as a part of him was Western – noted: 'It is my belief - or, if you like, my prejudice - that a less defensive use of this bicultural component can be a major source of Indian creativity even in the foreseeable future'. Sustaining plurality, Ray participated in defining the spatial and temporal dimensions of his culture; he stretched its boundaries to make his understanding of Indian culture a lasting part of the culture. Whether his culture shaped him adequately or not, he shaped his culture by altering its contours.

It would also be interesting to study the development of creative individuals in various societies to suggest possible sources of creativity and innovation. Simonton's studies (1989, personal communication) have indicated that at least specific principles of creative genius have been transhistorically invariant. However, it still needs to be explored why, contrary to the common Western assumption that creativity needs freedom, Russian scientists seemed to do best when political conditions were worst. Six Nobel Prizes were awarded to Soviet physicists for work done in the 1930s and 1940s, a period of tyranny and terror. By applying Gruber's methodology (Gruber, 1989, Raina, 1997) to a subject from a non-Western culture (see Gruber, 2000), I developed a great confidence in the potential of this approach in studying creatives from diverse cultures. I am hopeful something useful will emerge as a result of such coordinated studies.

The impact of a given culture cannot remain as constant, noted Ludwig (1992). Many other factors need to be taken into account. A holohistorical (cross-historical) study of the causes of creative florescence in particular periods of time in certain countries has shown that the more politically fragmented a civilization, the higher its creativity level. Studies are also available that indicate creativity tends to thrive more during civil disturbance and ideological diversity than during times of political cohesiveness, tranquility and uniformity; the more traditional, monolithic, stable, and homogeneous the culture, the less tolerance for innovation and change. In creativity research in multicultural nations and composite cultures, it will be interesting to explore whether the interface between two or more cultures has the potential for emergence of creativity.

Through cross-cultural and transhistorical surveys, Simonton's 1975 and 1980 studies identified many factors that explain the emergence of creativity in various periods in history. A certain degree of affluence in a society and physical proximity to one or more larger cultural centres are other conditions that have often been linked to creativity. To the extent that a culture embodies or maintains these political, economic and geographical conditions, that culture should be more conducive to creativity. However, we also know that when attempts have been made to homogenise the appearance of heterogeneity and assault made in the name of 'progress' and when creative urges have been released unharnessed, unchannelled, they have boomeranged and turned counter-productive. In other words, whenever creativity as individual or collective expression is sought to be controlled from without and not from within, it has erupted as 'violence', 'intolerance' and its worst and most destructive forms as all that we recognise by the word 'fundamentalism' (Vatsyayan, 1991). Whether some cultures possess these conditions more than others over the course of history, and how these cultures support these traits, are topics that deserve further research (Lubart, 1990).

Cultural diversity & alternative modes of nurturance

Some idea of creativity is present in the thinking of all cultures; and creativity, as a basic experience of people, is universal (Krippner and Arons, 1973). Accordingly, various cultures have provided many intuitive windows for understanding and nurturing creativity. In fact, 'non-Western modes of mental processing increase the arsenal of initiatives available and open several windows for a large number of inventions' (Goonatilake, 1987). It is interesting to notice that after his visit to China, Gardner (1989) realised clearly that the story of creativity is much more complex than he had imagined, or, as he became fond of putting it in a Chinese idiom, there is a 'long march to creativity'.

Reassessing various cultures 'as a source of insight and know-how about creativity' (Torrance, 1980) becomes critical as it can develop in us a new sensitivity, as it did in case of Torrance while visiting Japan: 'Through our exposure to Japanese culture, we developed a great respect for our own intuitive ways of knowing' and he further recorded that though he had realised the significance of practice and persistence of creative thinking before coming to Japan, 'Its true importance, however, did not dawn upon me until my Japanese experience. During the first week in Tokyo, this insight had been clamoring for recognition. The real flash of insight – the 'aha', the 'satori' – descended upon me during a fantastic tempura meal at the feet of one of the greatest tempura chefs'. Further, Torrance (1982) wrote: 'We might learn such lessons as developing a national climate for creativity... provision for rewards for creative achievements, respect for intuitive ways of knowing and solving problems, training in persistence and self-directed learning, ability to use freedom from within "the rules"'.

To those who advocate the use of creative problem solving techniques, it may be revealing that the 'grand parent of all creativity stimulating techniques' (Stein, 1991), Alex F. Osborn (1963) sought support, though not commonly acknowledged, for his procedures, from the techniques of 'Hindu teachers who made use of *Pariprashna* while working with religious groups' (p.151). (Osborn unfortunately incorrectly spelled it as: 'Prai-Barshana' in his book). *Pariprashna* or *Atiprasna*, questions that transcend comprehension by man's normal consciousness and emerge from the depths of human consciousness were used by the teachers of the Upanishads who never deviated from the strict rules of logic; but with logical clarity they have shown how logic is limited in its scope. While they have pointed to the realms beyond the mind, they have not even once derided the role of logic and reason. To utilise reason in order to show inadequacy of reason is a difficult undertaking, but the teachers of the Upanishads have displayed a remarkable mastery over this technique of transcending the mind with the help of mind (Mehta, 1970; p.3). In fact, the *Upanishads* are not concerned with the conclusion of thought; they are concerned with the process of thinking. The scientific approach of Vedanta is nowhere seen more clearly than in the *Prasna Upanishad* where the teacher and students are engaged in a truly scientific inquiry into the nature of things.

Having performed his work, the teacher would permit his students the flight of the alone to the Alone.

There is no doubt that the activity of questioning is central to the thinking process, and to ask a new question is to open a new horizon for thought. However, the form and pattern of questioning is deeply coloured by the tradition from which it arises, but once an answer is given, it creates its own space for evocation which is infinite, touching the horizons of other traditions. Thus the *Upanishadic* maxim *tat tvam asi* could be conceived only in a tradition, where the question 'who am I' had such crucial significance, but once the answer was proposed 'I am that', it created its own space of amplitude, causing a resonance in European cultures, unfamiliar to such a mode of questioning, but became instantly receptive to answers once it was articulated (Verma, 1993). However, it is my conviction that the packaged 'corporate' marketable techniques will become futile in addressing questions that are arranged by each tradition in a certain pattern, where they create their own space from which the right answers are elicited not from the 'other', but from the depth of the tradition itself. Packaged procedures may be good at eliciting novel responses in a particular tradition, for no less significant questions like 'What are the various uses of a brick', but may not yield much when it comes to answering questions like Gargi asked from Yajnavalkya: 'That, O Yajnavalkya, which is beyond the heaven, which is below the earth, which is between heaven and earth, which is called past, present, and future – in what is it interwoven? In what is its warp and woof?' Such questions can find answers in traditions where neither rationality nor its opposite, but something else, call it wisdom, which includes but supersedes rationality, is central.

Underlying such processes is the need for what Sitakant Mahapatra (1999) calls, extension of borders, made possible through *samvaad* and *vagvaad*, ongoing processes of deep dialogue that involve sharing and trust building. In this context, the 'groundbreaking treatise' (Krippner, 2001) by Sisk and Torrance (2001), which suggests various procedures drawn from a variety of sources in different cultures, is quite revealing. However, it is important to acknowledge that, ultimately, the devising of strategies for conceptual creativity is itself an exercise in creativity. And, hence, these strategies can neither be fixed in number nor be used in such a way as to ensure the result deterministically. The exercise of strategy is as much a creative act as its discovery, for ultimately it is an invocation of the same mystery and power that lies at the root of the universe and ourselves (Krishna, 1988).

Thinking about creativity in certain cultures does not focus attention solely on problems of the creative individual, as we commonly do in our discussions of the creative process, but goes beyond it and shows equal concern for issues that relate to what has been called *contricipation* (Stein, 1990), a process actively followed by a person who in India is called as *sahrdaya*, a time honoured concept. No longer a unit, *sahrdaya* is a part of creative continuity that has the imagination and culture to be able to enjoy aesthetically and provide joy and enthusiasm to the creator. Those people who possess aesthetic sensibility or are in a state of aesthetic receptivity are said to be 'gifted with, or possessed of,' heart' or 'having same heart (as the poet)' (*sahrdaya*). Thus he or she is a crucial component in nurturing creativity according to Indian cultural tradition. One has to realise that other diverse cultures may equally be emphasising such elements in the description of the creative process.

Some religious traditions which have emphasised the process of achieving transforming experiences, awakening and liberating of consciousness, have evolved a timeless mentoring paradigm to build up inner resources of the seeker to move from darkness to light, from untruth to truth and from death to immortality. Mentoring as it has occurred and evolved over a period of time in different cultures is deeply embedded in the history of a culture. The person may be called *guru*, sponsor, patron, tutor, sensei or something else, depending on the culture and time in history. One notices a strong tradition of mentoring in various cultures and societies like the Arab culture, Romanian culture, in the United States, in India, in Spain, and Japan. Torrance's project on transcultural research on mentoring has provided many insights into the richness and complexity of mentoring relationships.

While considering the issue of nurturance, it is important that we think of mobilisation of the intellectual power generated within each community by taking a retrospective look at cultural roots. 'Certain native creative abilities – which social scientists refer to as "endogenous creativity" may help provide appropriate development alternatives' (Raina, 1997). Nurturance of endogenous creativity will result in national particularity, mobilisation of the intellect in the task of regeneration, self-recognition of national traditions of identity; alternative creation of such a reformulated national identity, reestablishment of firm and healthy roots with specific past in each nation which is undergoing a lagged process of development. However, no one will deny the need for creative extension and assimilation of one's own tradition by a creative assimilation and adaptation of the modern intellectual traditions.

Search for a 'new synthesis'

That all human cultures, even the most rudimentary, in accordance with their own logos, have developed a variety of models of mental processing and of how the mind works and creates, makes us recognise the legitimacy of relative realities and pluralistic worldviews and decentres our metatheoretic orientation. Our perspectives become richer when we become sensitive to the unlimitedness of environments and also of minds and models in various societies which made Harry Passow (1987) make a passionate plea to explore further the differences in Eastern and Western approaches in order to nurture creativity effectively. In spite of his personal commitment to the Eastern 'way', David Bohm does not advocate the wholesale adoption of Eastern modes of thought and action, but rather the search for a 'new synthesis', as he calls it, one which has regard 'to the great wisdom from the whole of the past, both in the East and in the West' (p.24). Bohm (1981, p.19-20) goes on to speak:

Why, then, do we not drop our fragmentary Western approach and adopt these Eastern notions which include not only a self-world view that denies division and fragmentation but also techniques of meditation that lead the whole process of mental operation non-verbally to that sort of quiet state of orderly and smooth flow needed to end fragmentation both in the actual process of thought and in its content?

It is therefore imperative that different cultures and subcultures be studied to gain insight into creative functioning and to better understand the character of scientific and psychological inquiry itself. Only in this way will there be any genuine interchange among cultures, any increase in understanding that takes full account of the other form within the individual's cultural framework, which can be brought into sharper focus by comparing it with the representational worlds of individuals belonging to other cultures. We will begin to approach authoritative answers only after we have carried out careful ethnographic studies in different settings and understood the assumptions and values that permeate these settings. Much can be learned from the ethnographies of cultural anthropologists. The risk of imposing an alien ontology and an alien epistemology will not be productive; instead indigenous ways of looking at creativity in specific sociocultural perspectives in terms of culturally provided categories may be justified. Active alternatives like hermeneutic and phenomenological approaches have potential within creativity research that has scarcely been explored.

In the psychological study of creativity, as an alternative to what has been called the methodological battle cry of prediction and control, which serves as the criterion for evaluating our practices, we might see the legitimacy of psychology as variously dedicated, for example, to articulating multiple perspectives, fostering appreciation of others, and not as a way to shun people who are different. We must understand the person beneath categorisation, building relations among people, furthering people's sense of well-being, or generating a self-reflective consciousness, noted Misra and Gergen (1993). 'A monolithic framework does not create a critical mind', remarked the religious philosopher David Hartman (in Friedman, 2002). Hartman elaborated: 'Where there is only one self-evident truth, nothing ever gets challenged and no sparks of creativity ever get generated. The strength of America has always been its ability to challenge its own truth by presenting alternative possibilities. That forces you to justify your own ideas, and that competition of ideas is what creates excellence'. The fact that anyone undertaking cross-cultural research should have a sense of balance and empathy acquires added significance in studies on cross-cultural differences in creativity. Acquiring empathic sensitivity to other cultures requires immersing oneself in that culture's worldview in order to observe in oneself the effect of such an immersion. This garland making perspective will help celebrate the manyness which is reflected in *Atharvaveda* (16.3.6) which says, *Samudro Asmi Vidharmana* 'the Unbounded Ocean am I', hinting at infiniteness of creativity that exists in humans across all cultures. And for an appropriate methodology to understand this infiniteness, I am fond of quoting Confucius who said that the approaches to sagehood are as many as there are sages.

References

Albert, R. S. & Runco, M. A. (1999). A history of research on creativity. In R. J. Sternberg (Ed.), *Handbook of Creativity.* New York: Cambridge University Press.

Bateson, M. C. (1994). *Peripheral Visions: Learning along the Way.* New York: Harper Collins.

Ben-Amos, P. (1986). Artistic creativity in Benin Kingdom. *African Arts, 19* (3), 60-63.

Bjornson, R., & Waldman, M. (1989). Introduction. In R. Bjornson & M. Waldman (Eds.), *Rethinking Patterns of Knowledge.* Columbus. Ohio: The Ohio State University.

Bohm, D. (1981). *Wholeness and the Implicate Order.* London: Routledge and Kegan Paul.

Capra, F. (1977). *The Tao of Physics.* NY: Bantam.

Dharwadker, V. (1999). *The Collected Essays of A. K. Ramanujan.* New Delhi: Oxford University Press.

Eliade, M. (1963). *Myth and Reality.* New York: Harper Torchbooks.

Erikson, E. H. (1963). *Childhood and Society.* New York: W.W. Norton.

Friedman, T. L. (August 29. 2002). Learning about all religions is a strength of this nation. *Columbus Dispatch* (Forum Section).

Galtung, J. (1981). Structure, culture and intellectual style: an essay comparing Saxonic, Teutonic, Gallic and Nipponic approaches. *Social Science Information, 20,* 817-856.

Gardner, H. (1989). *To Open Minds.* New York: Basic Books.

Getzels, J. W. (1975). Creativity: prospects and issues. In I. A. Taylor & J. W. Getzels (Eds.) *Perspectives in Creativity.* Chicago, IL: Aldine.

Goonatilake, S. (1987). Inventions and the developing countries. *Impact of Science on Society, 147,* 223-231.

Gruber, H. (1988). Personal communication. Newark, NJ: Rutgers University.

Gruber, H. E. (1989). The evolving systems approach to creative work. In D. B. Wallace & H. E. Gruber (Eds.) *Creative People at Work.* New York: Oxford University Press.

Gruber, H. E. (2000). Foreword. In M. K. Raina, *The Creativity Passion: E. Paul Torrance's Voyages of Discovering Creativity.* Stamford, Connecticut: Ablex.

Guilford, J. P. (1980). Foreword. In M. K. Raina (Ed.) *Creativity Research: International Perspective.* New Delhi: National Council of Educational Research and Training.

Kramrisch, S. (1990). Marks of the great being: Mahapurusa-laksana. In R. Chatterjee (Ed.) *The Golden Book of Tagore.* Calcutta, India: Rammohun Library & Free Reading Room.

Krippner, S. (2001). Foreword. In D. A. Sisk & E. P. Torrance, *Spiritual Intelligence: Developing Higher Consciousness*. Buffalo, NY: Creative Education Foundation.

Krippner, S., & Arons, M. (1973). Creativity east, creativity west. *Fields within Fields*, 4, 25-31.

Krishna, Daya. (1988). Thinking vs. thought: strategies for conceptual creativity. *Journal of Indian Council of Philosophical Research*, 5, 47-57.

Lubart, T. I. (1990). Creativity and cross-cultural variation. *International Journal of Psychology*, 25, 39-59.

Lubart, T. I. (1999). Creativity across cultures. In R. J. Sternberg (Ed.) *Handbook of Creativity*. New York: Cambridge University Press.

Ludwig, A. M. (1992). Culture and creativity. *American Journal of Psychotherapy*, 46, 454-469.

Mackinnon, D.W. (1987). Some critical issues for future research in creativity. In S.G. Isaksen (Ed.) *Frontiers of Creativity Research: Beyond the Basics*. Buffalo, NY: Bearly Limited.

Maduro, R. (1976). Artistic creativity in a Brahmin painter community. *Research Monographs*, 14, 222. Berkeley, CA: Center for South and Southeast Asia Studies, University of California.

Magyari-Beck, I. (1996). The Torrance phenomenon. *Creativity Research Journal*, 9, 411-414.

Mason, J. H. (1988). The character of creativity: two traditions. *History of European Ideas*, 9, 697-715.

Mead, M. (1959). Creativity in cross-cultural perspective. In H. Anderson (Ed.) *Creativity and its Cultivation*. New York: Harper.

Meador, K. (1999). Creativity around the globe. *Childhood Education*, 78, 324-325.

Mehta, R. (1970). *The Call of the Upanishads*. Bombay: Bharatiya Vidya Bhawan.

Misra, G. & Gergen, K. J. (1993). Beyond scientific colonialism: a reply to Poortinga and Triandis. *International Journal of Psychology*, 28, 251-254.

Mookerjee, P. (1987). *Pathway Icons: The Wayside Art of India*. London: Thames and Hudson.

Nachmanovitch, S. (1990). *Free Play: Improvisation in Life and Art*. Los Angeles: Jeremy P. Tarcher.

Nandy, A. (1990). Satyajit Ray's secret guide to exquisite murders: creativity, social criticism, and the partitioning of the self. *East West Film Journal*, 4, 14-37.

Nandy, A. (1993). How 'Indian' is Ray? *Cinemaya*, 20, 40-45.

Nandy, A. (1995). An anti-secularist manifesto. *India International Centre Quarterly*, 22, 30-63.

Nandy, A., & Kakar, S. (1980). Culture and personality. In U. Pareek (Ed.) *Survey of Research in Psychology*. Bombay, India: Popular Prakashan.

Osborn, A. F. (1963). *Applied Imagination*. New York: Charles Scribner.

Pandeya, A. N. (1981). Endogenous intellectual creativity: Reflections on some Etic and Emic Paradigms. In A. Abdel Malek (Ed.) *Intellectual Creativity in Endogenous Cultures*. Tokyo: The United Nations University.

Panikkar, R. (1977). *The Vedic Experience*. Berkeley: University of California Press.

Passow, A. H. (1987, August). *Presidential Address: Expanding Awareness of Creative Potential: an international perspective*. Paper presented at the 7th World Conference on Gifted and Talented Children, Utah State University, Salt Lake City. UT.

Paz, Octavio. (1995). *In Light of India*. (trans. E. Weinberger). New York: Harcourt, Brace & Company.

Raina, M. K. (1980). Introduction. In M. K. Raina (Ed.) *Creativity Research: International Perspective*. New Delhi: National Council of Educational Research and Training.

Raina, M. K. (1984). *Education of the Left and the Right: Implications of Hemispheric Specialization*. New Jersey: Humanities Press.

Raina, M. K. (1989). *Social and Cultural Change and Changes in Creative Functioning*. New Delhi: National Council of Educational Research and Training.

Raina, M. K. (1993). Ethnocentric confines in creativity research. In S. G. Isaksen, M. C. Murdock, L. Firestein & D. J. Treffinger (Eds.), *Understanding and Recognizing Creativity: the Emergence of a Discipline*. Norwood, NJ: Ablex.

Raina, M. K. (1996). *Guru-shisya Relationship: The Possibility of a Creative Resilient Framework*. Athens, GA: Torrance Center for Creative Studies.

Raina, M. K. (1996). *Talent Search in the Third World: The Phenomenon of Calculated Ambiguity*. New Delhi: Vikas.

Raina, M. K. (1996). The Torrance phenomenon: extended creative search for Lord Vishvakarma. *Creativity and Innovation Management*, 5, 151-168.

Raina, M. K. (1997). 'Most dear to all the muses' - Mapping Tagorean networks of enterprise: a study in creative complexity. *Creativity Research Journal, 10*, 153-173.

Raina, M. K. (1997). Recognizing indigenous creativity. In J. A. Leroux (Ed.) *Connecting the Gifted Community Worldwide*. Seattle, Washington: The World Council for Gifted and Talented.

Raina, M. K. (1999). The divine creativity: the mythical paradigm and Lord Vishvakarma. In Stein, M. I. (Ed.) *Creativity's Global Correspondents—1999*. New York: Winslow Press.

Raina, M. K. (1999). Cross-cultural differences. In M. A. Runco & S. R. Pritzker (Eds.), *Encyclopedia of Creativity*. New York: Academic Press.

Raina, M. K. & Srivastava, A. K. (2000). India's search for excellence: a clash of ancient, colonial and contemporary influences. *Roeper Review, 22*, 102-108.

Ray, N. (1974). *An Approach to Indian Art*. Chandigarh: Punjab University Press.

Saarilahti, M., Cramond, B. & Sieppi, H. (1999). Is creativity nurtured in Finnish classrooms? *Childhood Education, 78*, 326-331.

Sharma, M. (1996). U. R. Anantha Murthy. In *Wordsmiths*. New Delhi: Rupa.

Simonton, D. K. (1975). Age and literary creativity: a cross-cultural and transhistorical survey. *Journal of Cross-cultural Psychology*, 6, 259-277.

Simonton, D. K. (1980). Thematic fame, melodic originality, and musical zeitgeist: a biographical and transhistorical content analysis. *Journal of Personality and Social Psychology, 38,* 972-983.

Sinclair, E. C. (1971). Towards a typology of cultural attitudes concerning creativity. *Western Canadian Journal of Anthropology, 2,* 82-89.

Sisk, D. A. & Torrance, E. P. (2001). *Spiritual Intelligence: Developing Higher Consciousness.* Buffalo, NY: Creative Education Foundation.

Stein, M. I. (1990). Anabolic and catabolic factors in the creative process. *Creativity Research Journal, 3,* 134-145.

Stein, M. I. (1991). On the sociohistorical context of creativity programs. *Creativity Research Journal, 4,* 294-300.

Tagore, R. (1988). *Sadhana.* Madras: Macmillan India Limited.

Torrance, E. P. (1979). *The Search for Satori and Creativity.* Buffalo, NY: Creative Education Foundation.

Torrance, E. P. (1980). Lessons about giftedness and creativity from a nation of 115 million over-achievers. *Gifted Child Quarterly, 24,* 10-14.

Torrance, E. P. (1982). Education for 'Quality Circles' in Japanese schools. *Journal of Research and Development in Education, 15,* 11-15.

Torrance, E. P. (1988). Reflections on emerging insights on the educational psychology of creativity. In J. Houtz (Ed.) *The Educational Psychology of Creativity.* Creskill, NJ: Hampton Press.

Torrance, E. P. (1996). Foreword: The Torrance phenomenon: extended creative search for Lord Vishvakarma. *Creativity and Innovation Management, 5,* 149-150.

Torrance, E. P. (2002). Future needs for creativity research, training, and programs. In A. G. Aleinikov (Ed.) *The Future of Creativity.* Bensenville, Illinois: Scholastic Testing Service.

Vatsyayan, K. (1968). *Classical Indian dance in Literature and the Arts.* New Delhi: Sangeet Natak Academi.

Vatsyayan, K. (1991). The role of art in social transformation. *India International Centre Quarterly, 18,* 155-172.

Von Franz, M-L. (1995). *Creation Myths* (rev. ed.). Boston: Shambala.

Acknowledgements

My grateful thanks are due to U. R. Ananthamurthy; Todd I. Lubart; Vidya Niwas Misra; Dean Keith Simonton; E. Paul Torrance; Kapila Vatsyayan; Partha Raina who reviewed the manuscript, in full or in parts, at various stages. For all their generous help, I am immensely grateful, particularly for clarifying my own concepts and in helping me understand the role of cultural differences. Ashis Nandy's thoughtful work has always helped me to develop my arguments and I am pleased to acknowledge his deep insights. Of course, they should not in any way be held accountable for any imperfections that remain or for any of my conclusions.

Vincent Nolan

Creativity: the antidote to the Argument Culture

We tend to talk about 'Creativity' as though it is a single, indivisible entity, admittedly with many diverse applications in the arts, science, business, education and so on - the whole of life, in fact.

I would like to 'unbundle' creativity a little and distinguish three quite separate, though related, facets: Creative Thinking, Creative Behaviour and Creative Action:

- *Creative Thinking* is the familiar process of generating new ideas, new concepts, goals and wishes, new perceptions of problems, by brainstorming, synectics, lateral thinking, 'out of the box' thinking, etc. Whatever label you choose, the output is new *thoughts*, which in themselves do not change anything in the real world until they are implemented in some way.
- *Creative Behaviour*[1] is the set of behaviours that have been developed to facilitate the creative process - initially the 'suspend judgement' rule which is the foundation of brainstorming (and subsequent creative techniques, including Synectics) plus all the additional behavioural methods which have been added over the last 70 years.
- *Creative Action* is doing new things, ranging from things the individual has never done before, like a first parachute jump, to things that are new to the world, like the Wright Bros. taking to the air in a heavier-than-air machine. Creative Action is experiment and innovation (the Department for Trade and Industry in the UK restricts 'innovation' to the *successful* implementation of new ideas, but experimental action is an essential precursor to innovation).

Of the three, I have come to regard *Creative Behaviour* as the corner stone of creativity, because it underpins both the others - you will not generate truly new ideas without an environment that permits speculation and emotional risk-taking. And equally, experimentation requires a supportive environment that encourages steps along the learning curve. 'No such thing as a failed experiment, only experiments with unexpected outcomes' (a widely repeated saying attributed to Buckminster Fuller); we have to treat experiments in a way that reflects that meaning of the word.

However, what excites me is that *Creative Behaviour* has much to offer outside the specifically creative field   you have only to re-label it *Constructive Behaviour* to highlight its potential for everyday situations of all kinds. In the creative process, the behaviours are made explicit and specific and their productive potential becomes manifest - which is why training in creative techniques is such a good route to learning how to behave constructively.

'It is truly astonishing', writes Edward de Bono[2] 'that Western culture has never developed an idiom of "constructive" thinking. We have the absurdity of "argument" as our basic idiom. We worship the absurdity of "debate"'. Strong words, but undeniably true. Deborah Tannen[3], in her book *The Argument Culture*, assembles a mass of evidence, particularly from politics, the media and the law, that entirely supports de Bono's position. My own experience, mostly in business, does the same (unfortunately, de Bono makes his point in such a polemical way, he evokes exactly the adversarial response he is criticising!).

Not only is it astonishing, it is wasteful and destructive. Debate and argument are essentially adversarial activities and, regardless of the outcome in terms of the subject of the debate, the relationship between the protagonists will probably have been damaged. One party may think they have 'won' the debate, but they are likely to have paid a high price: the loss of the respect/affection of the other. The loser, in my experience, will nearly always set up a return bout, on their own ground, which they are sure to win. It may not be another debate; it may be as unilateral as a withdrawal of co-operation or reduction in commitment to shared activities (when I encounter debating at work, I have an image of factory chimneys belching smoke into the atmosphere - wasting energy and polluting the environment!).

Our political institutions (such as Parliament and Congress), our legal system and our education system are all inherently adversarial. The media aids and abets the argument culture because argument is deemed to be entertaining. The prevailing assumption is that 'debate' is a good thing and the habit of debating is widely encouraged in school debating societies and university unions (a training ground for future politicians). Small wonder that managers, especially graduates, unthinkingly turn to debate to resolve issues - 'we must debate the issue', they say, automatically and with relish. The habit is ingrained from their education and they are not aware that constructive alternatives exist.

Of course, debate has its place. I see it as a form of intellectual sport, analogous to boxing or the martial arts in the physical world. As with sport, it can valuably develop intellectual muscles and skills (perhaps there is a Tai Chi of debate?). That is probably why it is so highly and excessively prized in our education system. Like any sport, it can be an enjoyable activity for those who are good at it and want to participate in it. It is appropriate for the pub, dinner party or debating society; at the highest level of skill, it can be entertaining for an audience to watch (like sport).

However, the participants need to be *consenting* adults - nobody should be forced to debate any more than they should be forced to box. Many people dislike the activity. The participants also need to be reasonably well-matched and to operate within an agreed set of rules (as in boxing or fencing). These preconditions are rarely met in the everyday working of organisations, so debate can have only a very limited role as a working tool.

I am *not* suggesting that differences of view should be ignored or swept under the carpet. On the contrary, I see them as a source of richness and diversity (Ray Croc of McDonald's is reported as saying 'if two members of a Board agree about everything, one of them is redundant'). Differences can usually be resolved constructively, provided we bring our creative skills, particularly *Creative Behaviour*, to bear on the issues. We do not have to agree on how the world is, but we do have to reach agreement on how we will deal with the situation we are facing.

I am conscious that debating is much loved in the academic world, where it is believed that it is a way to arrive at Truth. De Bono[4] attributes this belief to the influence of Aristotle 'with his word-based inclusion/exclusion logic. Each side claims the truth and seeks to attack the other claim. This way we are supposed to arrive at the truth through triumph or synthesis'. Whether he is right to attribute responsibility to Aristotle (aided and abetted by Plato and Socrates) is not for me to judge. We know that, today, better alternatives exist, as described below.

Resolving conflict creatively

Creative Problem-Solving (particularly the Synectics model) has four characteristics that combine to maximise the chances of inventing a win-win outcome:

1. A positive field/climate
2. The concept of ownership
3. High quality communication
4. Generating a wide variety of ideas.

I would like to examine each of these in more detail before going on to describe how they map on to the variety of situations which may arise.

1. *A Positive Field/Climate*: Creative problem solving works because it establishes an environment in which participants feel free to speculate and generate ideas which are not yet feasible solutions, without fear of rejection by critical judgement. In brainstorming, the field is created by the basic rule 'suspend judgement when generating ideas'. The Synectics model extends this protection to alternative ways of looking at the problem, wishes, and associations, so that participants feel free to voice any connections and embryonic ideas that occur to them. The use of a skilled facilitator, who sets and monitors the observation of appropriate behavioural rules, ensures that the positive field is maintained. *Excursions* (idea-getting strategies that take a brief holiday from the problem to generate fresh material) also reinforce the positive field, because they involve taking mental and emotional risks together. Participants find it a bonding process, as barriers are lowered, both in their minds and between them.

Synectics also extends the protection against rejection to the convergent 'idea development' stage, during which responsibility for selecting avenues to explore, evaluating ideas and setting the target for further ideas, is vested in one individual, the *problem owner*. That individual must follow a strictly enforced protocol, with three components, to sustain the positive field:

- 'understand before evaluating' - the problem owner must paraphrase the idea and check with the idea-giver that the paraphrase correctly captures the idea intended (as often as not, it does not)
- 'find value in every idea' - specify all the potentially attractive aspects of the idea, giving it the benefit of the doubt and also, incidentally, illustrating the qualities the problem owner is looking for in the solution
- 'convert negatives to a direction for improvement' - we do not want to know what is wrong with an idea (this is *not* a plus/minus evaluation) but rather how it needs to be improved to achieve a solution.

2. *The Concept of Ownership*: As described above, the problem owner has the responsibility for evaluating ideas constructively, so that when a solution is reached it will have the commitment of the person who will have to implement it. The underlying philosophy is that judgements and opinions of individuals are truths about themselves, not truths about the world. Given that we all have had different experiences in our lives, we are likely to see the world differently. The differences need to be respected and used as a source of possible enrichment for both parties. If I can listen to and understand your view of the world, maybe I can find something in it that I can incorporate into my view, but the choice is mine, not yours. To try to force someone to change their view, by argument and persuasion, infringes their ownership of their life and is in fact disrespectful. 'I see it differently' is respectful; 'You're wrong' is not!

Only on questions of *fact* can one party be right and another wrong; if a disagreement is identified as a question of fact, an agreed decision can be made to check the facts or investigate the situation in some way (if it is sufficiently important). If the facts cannot be verified, it may be necessary to agree to differ and explore the implications of *both* alternatives.

But most arguments are not about facts but about the future (and there are, by definition, no future facts[5] - only probabilities of various degrees). So the arguments are about matters of opinion, often the likely outcome of a course of action, which cannot be known. Even though the action may have been taken before, there is no guarantee that the outcome will be the same - circumstances may have changed or different people may do it differently. And people can legitimately hold different views on the likely outcome; neither is right or wrong until the action is implemented.

Or the disagreement may stem from different values about matters of morality or ethics. Again, it is not a matter of right and wrong but of holding *different* sets of values. It is not, in my experience, very fruitful to try to persuade anyone to adopt a different set of values; the energy is much better used in trying to invent a course of action that might be acceptable to both parties.

3. *Care with communication*: Misunderstandings are much more common than is generally believed because we *assume* we have understood, without checking that our understanding is correct. Only when understanding is checked by means of a paraphrase (playing back the listener's understanding of what has been said) does the frequency of misunderstanding become apparent. My experience of applying paraphrase in the context of Synectics

meetings suggests a misunderstanding rate of 50% (some communications researchers put it higher).

In the context of argument, checking understanding becomes even more vital than in less emotionally charged situations. In the heat of debate, participants are often not listening to understand; they are listening for flaws or opportunities to score debating points. Not surprisingly, there are many misunderstandings - in fact a common debating trick (among politicians especially) is deliberately to misunderstand and misrepresent the opposing point of view, to make it easier to discredit it! By insisting on a paraphrase which satisfies the speaker that his or her point has been understood, we can eliminate such dirty tricks! The process also usefully slows down (and calms down) the discussion.

Moreover, taking the trouble to check your understanding of what someone has said is a way of demonstrating *respect* for that person. It says 'I value you and what you have to say - that's why I want to make sure I have understood it'. Whether this message is successfully delivered can depend on how the paraphrase is made: to make it in an incredulous tone of voice, for example, does just the opposite! It has to come over as a genuine attempt to restate the other's point in one's own words, to show that it has been 'taken on board', even though it may or may not be agreed with.

So the use of paraphrase in the context of differences of view has a double benefit; one functional - it removes the danger of misunderstanding – the other as a contribution to maintaining a positive field.

In addition to paraphrase, other communication skills encouraged in creative problem solving are:

- headlining - putting the main point first, as in a newspaper headline, without build-up or justification which are not needed in a protected environment
- open-minded listening - a way of listening that filters out judgmental reactions to focus on understanding
- crediting - the acknowledgement of the value of another's thought
- building - using one person's contribution as a stepping stone to a new thought
- clarifying the purpose behind a question - questions are often used adversarially, to put the other party at a disadvantage. Stating why you are asking ensures that only 'clean' questions are asked!

All of these contribute to the maintenance of the positive field/climate.

4. *Generating a wide variety of ideas:* When people argue, they are usually in a binary frame of mind; they are either 'for' or 'against' a proposition or 'for' one proposition, against an alternative. There is an implicit assumption that these one or two propositions are all that exist (or all that are worth discussing). Switching into the creative problem solving mode of working forces participants to generate and consider many alternatives, some perhaps previously known, some still to be invented. It compels them to engage in *plural* rather than *binary*

thinking and to shift from a closed-minded, adversarial mindset into an open-minded, co-operative one.

To make the switch, it is necessary to take a step back from the propositions under discussion and look at the objectives they are trying to achieve. The propositions are set aside, temporarily, while the protagonist and some colleagues (they will probably need help with the shift!) use their creative skills to come up with a variety of alternatives, some of which they will develop into alternative propositions. These are then evaluated constructively along with the original ones to see if an agreed solution can be achieved.

While there is no guarantee that it can be, the chances are good because the creative process has broadened the agenda; there is a wider and richer range of options in play. More importantly, the protagonists will have experienced a co-operative and mutually respectful activity that will have enhanced rather than damaged their relationship.

The pre-conditions for creative resolution of conflict

Any creative problem solving session needs careful planning, but in the case of conflict, the need for planning is particularly strong. Its purpose is to establish that the preconditions for successful conflict resolution exist, namely:

- the protagonists are motivated to resolve the conflict, if possible - there is no vested interest in prolonging the conflict, or belief that they have no need to resolve the conflict because they can win the argument
- there exists some common ground between them, in terms of ultimate goals and objectives
- the protagonists are prepared to enter the session with open minds and a willingness to follow the disciplines specified by the facilitator.

Planning involves individual in-depth interviews with each of the protagonists to find out their perception of the situation and their ideas for a solution, i.e. their starting position. The opportunity can also be used to encourage them to start visualising a future state when the conflict no longer exists. In this way, the facilitator can build his or her own map of the territory to be covered and decide on the most appropriate process to use.

The planning interviews are a critical stage of the process. The facilitator needs to be listening for hidden agendas and to challenge any apparent inconsistencies in what the respondents are saying. Done well, they can get the whole process off to a flying start and begin to establish a relationship of trust between the facilitator and the protagonists. They can also ensure that the whole process is terminated if there is no reasonable chance of success.

A model for the creative resolution of conflict

Although conflict situations will vary in their nature and consequently require different methods to deal with them, it is possible to identify a basic model, from which variations can be made as necessary. The following model, derived from the Synectics Creative Problem-Solving Model, is described from the perspective of a facilitator charged with managing the process of a conflict resolution session - following a series of successful planning sessions with each of the participants. It divides into four phases:

1. Climate setting
2. Information sharing
3. Mutual evaluation
4. Idea generation and solution development.

Climate setting: Any of the wide range of techniques used for creative problem solving sessions can be used, depending on the degree of risk-taking the facilitator judges to be acceptable to the group. There need to be some personal introductions; if participants already know one another, the introductions can become a creative exercise by asking them to imagine they are different people, animals, plants etc. and introduce themselves as such. Other 'right-brain' activating techniques, such as drawing, collage making, story telling can be used to advantage - provided the group is willing to 'play' briefly.

It will also be necessary to brief them on the behavioural ground rules for the session and obtain their agreement to operate accordingly; not difficult, if the rules make sense. The facilitator's role as a neutral referee needs to be understood and accepted by all.

Information sharing: Each party in turn outlines their basic position briefly. The 'opposition' are then asked to paraphrase their understanding of it as objectively as they can (without judgement or evaluation, explicit or implied). The speaker checks that the paraphrase correctly expresses his or her position; if it does not, he or she identifies in what respects it is correct and how it needs to be modified to be 100% accurate. The listener plays back the new understanding with another paraphrase and the process is repeated until both parties are satisfied that they have mutual understanding.

This process may seem laboured and time-consuming, but it is fundamental. When people are in conflict, they tend to listen judgementally and react emotionally; the danger is that they hear their own prejudice rather than what is actually being said. And the slowness is an advantage - it helps to calm people down. Successful completion of the paraphrase ensures a shared understanding of the issues and introduces the participants to the (possibly unfamiliar) experience of agreeing with each other!

Evaluation: Having established a shared understanding of one anothers' positions, we can move on to the exchange of opinions - in the most constructive way possible. Each party makes a constructive evaluation of the other's position, identifying all the aspects they agree with/can accept, in as much detail and as generously as possible (giving the benefit of the doubt). This process articulates the common ground between the parties and puts issues in a different perspective from a normal argument, where the focus is on differences only. My experience is that 90% of the emotion is about 10% of the content.

It is then necessary for each party to identify the issues they have with the other's position, but they must express them not as negatives but as problems to be solved: 'we would need to find a way to...' overcome the problem. The list of the issues so generated becomes the agenda for the creative phase of the session, in which everyone tries to generate ideas to solve them, one at a time.

Idea generation and solution development: This is familiar ground to the creative problem solver and any techniques can be used as appropriate to the situation. Synectics excursions can be particularly valuable, because they enable participants to explore contentious issues by metaphor and analogy, which may be less threatening than discussing them directly. And the excursions can have a bonding effect.

Responsibility for directing the development of the solution rests with the 'owner' of the issue under discussion, but the solutions will need to be acceptable to the other parties.

There is, of course, no guarantee that all the issues can be resolved, but in my experience if the creative abilities of all parties have been successfully harnessed, the chances of achieving a win-win consensus are quite good. Even if it is not achieved, the group will have experienced working co-operatively, rather than adversarially and will have a far better understanding of one anothers' positions than they had originally. They will also have developed a greater respect for one another and improved their personal relationships. So even if a win-win solution cannot be achieved, the chances of reaching an acceptable compromise are greatly enhanced.

The model may sound long-winded, but in practice events can move very quickly, owing to the positive dynamics involved, for example:

- a skilled facilitator ensures that the discussion is clearly structured and each participant knows what kind of contribution is required at each stage
- each type of transaction-information exchange, expression of opinions/ judgements, idea generation and decision-making is handled separately, so that the group is working in the same mode at any time
- understanding is checked out by paraphrase and check, and not assumed
- judgements are suspended while ideas are being generated
- judgements are made constructively at the appropriate time and by the appropriate person
- the group's creative skills are harnessed to ensure that a wide range of options is available
- an emotionally safe climate is created by application of all the creative behavioural rules of a creative problem solving session.

Argument and conflict signal an opportunity for the application of creativity. The message is 'invent your way out of conflict, rather than try to fight your way out of it!'.

References

1 I first came across the expression in *The Practice of Creativity* by George Prince (Harper & Row, 1971).
2 Edward de Bono, 'Away with the Gang of Three'. *The Guardian*, 1997.
3 Deborah Tannen, *The Argument Culture*, Virago Press, 1998.
4 Edward de Bono, *op cit.*
5 From the Latin 'factum' - that which has been done.

Jon-Chao Hong, Ming-Yueh Hwang, Chan-Li Lin

How to shape the innovative culture in your organisation

Introduction

The Chinese have a saying: 'Three cobblers with their wits combined equal Chuge Liang the mastermind', meaning teamwork can often achieve better results than individual effort. However, it is not uncommon to see in real life a single talented individual leading millions of ordinary people. The difference between the gifted and the mediocre often lies in their ability to detect and solve problems. In other words, the wits of three cobblers may equal Chuge Liang if the problem is directly related to cobbling, whilst with plotting tactics, even the combined wits of a few more cobblers may not match that of Chuge Liang. In addition to their expertise in cobbling, the only areas where they may perform better are probably limited to Chuge Liang's 'blind spots', such as the topographic features of places Chuge Liang himself has never seen or read about whilst one of the cobblers has been to and actually knows about. However, such knowledge may need further integration and application to create more value, at which Chuge Liang again excels.

This may hold true for the relationship between highly talented and below-average people. However, when the highly talented are competing with those who are also above-average, three together may have a very good chance of defeating a single genius. For example, when basketball superstar Michael Jordan plays with ordinary people, his victory is almost guaranteed, whilst with other strong opponents, such as Vince Carter or Kobe Bryant, he will probably have little chance to beat three of them together single-handedly. This explains the power of teamwork. However, if the three players are suspicious of each other and do not work as a team, Jordan might still win. Hence, in team building, members' mutual trust and open discussion during problem solving are essential to corporate innovation (Ahmed, Kok & Loh, 2002).

The OK theory and a trusting culture

Harrison's OK theory of trust (2001) can be applied to the discussion of both members' intentions and competences. But what is the basis of trust? What makes one member trust another? To develop mutual trust, two conditions are essential: OK intentions and OK competences of both parties. When one party suspects the other's intentions, mutual trust fails. Likewise, when one party has doubts about the other's competence, the basis for trust becomes shaky.

Chart 1 is an adaptation of Harrison's OK theory describing the interaction and sharing between team members. The following results can be derived from the various combinations of 'OK' and 'not OK' intentions of both parties:

1. I am OK + You are not OK = No trust in the other party
2. You are not OK + I am not OK = Each party has its own agenda
3. I am OK + You are OK = Mutual trust
4. You are OK + I am not OK = Plotting against the other party or having reservations.

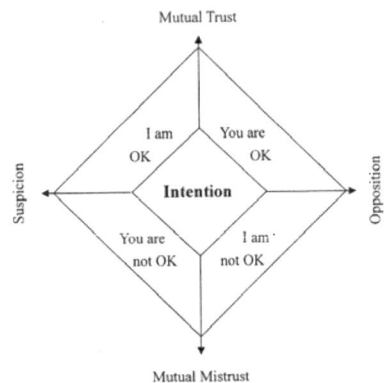

Chart 1 On Intention of Human Interaction (Adapted from Harrison's OK Theory)

However, intention alone does not determine the result of member interaction. The respective competences and decision powers of all parties involved are also important. Therefore, the OK theory should be modified to describe also the competence levels and decision powers of team members.

In chart 2, 'OK' refers to high competence levels, while 'not OK' means a lack of competence. Possible combinations are listed below:

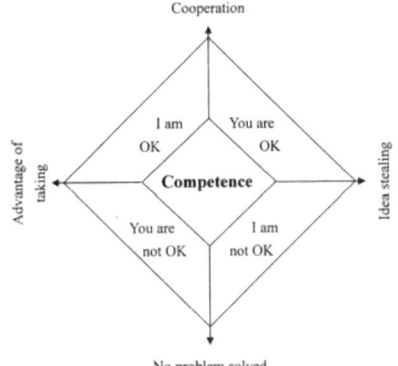

Chart 2 On Competence of Human Interaction (adapted from Harrison's OK Theory)

1. I am OK + You are not OK = Feeling being taken advantage of
2. You are not OK + I am not OK = No hope for the problem to be resolved
3. I am OK + You are OK = Working together to resolve the problem
4. You are OK + I am not OK = Stealing others' ideas

The OK theory can be further applied to members' decision power during negotiations, with 'OK' referring to the party fully authorised to make decisions and 'not OK' to the party without real decision power. The results from various combinations are as follows:

1. I am OK + You are not OK = Conclusion is not final; ratification is required
2. You are not OK + I am not OK = Meaningless discussion
3. I am OK + You are OK = Conclusion is immediate and final
4. You are OK + I am not OK = Requesting for approval before further negotiation

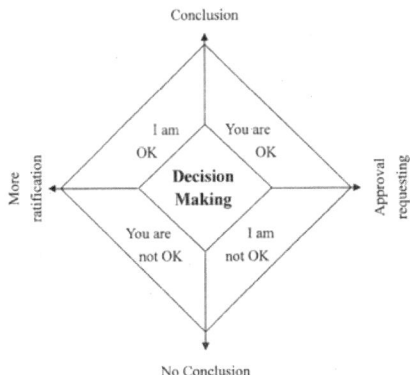

Conclusion

I am OK

You are OK

Decision Making

You are not OK

I am not OK

More ratification

Approval requesting

No Conclusion

Chart 3   On Decision Power of Human Interaction (adapted from Harrison's OK Theory)

In short, whether it is intention, competence or decision power, the OK theory suggests that mutual 'OK' intentions and competences are required for trust to develop between both parties and mutual 'OK' decision powers are indispensable for any negotiation to be meaningful. Of the three elements, competence and decision power are rather explicit. Even when one party has no prior knowledge of the other's level of competence and decision power, a few encounters can make this information easily known to the other. Intention however, is more implicit and often mercurial. Some people tend to think that their intentions are OK while the others' are not. This is either because they believe they can only advance when their counterpart retreats and therefore they try to make their rival suffer or find fault with every detail through complaints or outright attacks. We have all seen stray puppies fleeing on the sight of a person crouching down, believing that the person is about to pick up a pebble to throw at them. People with persecution complex are exactly like that because they have been conditioned by previous experience to think that others are always ill-intentioned.

On the other hand, some people tend to think that they deserve more than they already have due to excessive anxiety over gaining and losing. They 'worry endlessly about gaining anything before they actually do and about losing once they have it', and are unappreciative of the philosophy of 'to give is to take' (Lao-tse, B.C. 300-400). Although they sometimes defend their behaviours as taking firm positions, in fact they are simply afraid of being taken advantage of. However, to cooperate, both parties must have a thorough understanding of their own intentions and competences before they make any judgement about their counterpart. In other words, each party has to evaluate others' opinions, circumstances and conditions in an objective way and try to avoid unnecessary generalisation or assumptions in assessing others' intentions in order to create an 'I am OK and you are OK' atmosphere. Furthermore, only with objectivity and critical thinking can both parties truly embrace fair criticisms about their drawbacks and from there generate self-esteem. Self-esteem is about not feeling offended even when one knows that one is being taken advantage of. In other words, both parties have to first allow for 'lose/lose' situations to bring about 'win/win' results and to boost effective knowledge sharing.

Intention and competence are interrelated. Internally, if one is competent while the other person is not, the competent one will gradually become suspicious of the intention of the incompetent. Contrarily, the incompetent person will feel that he or she is a drag on team progress. In other words, competence can affect intention, and can also affect members' intention. Therefore, it is often the biggest challenge for a team leader to recognise both team effort and individual contribution appropriately. For example, in the Bulls Dynasty, Jordan has been the most highly regarded player and often given the most responsibility, the highest pay and most applause. In the meantime, Jordan attributes his success to the critical support of his team mates such as Pippen and Rodman. By allowing equally competent members to develop compatible intentions, Jordan has helped build a successful team in basketball. In other words, people at similar competence level should be able to tolerate each other in order to develop compatible 'OK' intentions. One way to ensure mutual tolerance between talented people is to assign each talent a different task with the more capable taking on greater challenge and receiving more rewards upon mission accomplishment. In short, each member should have a distinct role to play and responsibility to shoulder under a 'fair and just' rewarding system. This is how members' mutual trust can be developed and sustained.

A team of both 'OK' intentions and competences can best tackle challenges head-on. This also holds true for business entities. When facing external challenges, the stronger the team, the greater the chance to succeed. The strength of a team is often defined by its ability to detect problems and solve them creatively. To generate creative ideas however requires knowledge sharing. Hence, if the three cobblers can share knowledge among themselves and jointly formulate a plan more comprehensive than that of Chuge Liang's, they can accomplish even impossible missions. The process of knowledge sharing in Johari's Window refers to the increase of the pane that is known both to self and to others. That is, the larger the pane, the closer the competence levels and the less suspicion. With an open mind and free exchange of information and ideas, team members will be drawn closer together to achieve both 'OK' intentions and competences.

Johari's Window and an innovative and open culture

Johari's Window (Luft & Ingham, 1969) contains four window panes with each representing a specific human interaction, which can also be used to categorize knowledge sharing as discussed below:

Known to self   Unknown to self

	Known to self	Unknown to self
Known to others	Arena	Blind spot
Unknown to others	Facade	Unknown

Chart 4   Johari's Window

1. *Arena*: The arena is an area where information is open to oneself as well as to others. For example, when someone puts on a new outfit to attend a social function, he or she is in fact providing information for sharing. Enlarging this particular pane will help boost mutual trust.
2. *Blind Spot*: The blind spot is an area where information is only known to others. A good example is when required to respond to an issue, a new member not familiar with the rules of the game is most likely to simply force a smile.
3. *Façade*: The façade is an area where information is only known to self. For example, senior members often hold back their views when sharing knowledge with newcomers, fearing that familiarity will breed contempt and that they will lose their authority, get hurt, or be taken advantage of.
4. *Unknown*: This area is where information is unknown to self and to other members. Corporate culture or business philosophy for example is often implicit. Members are affected by it but unable to define it. According to Freud (1926) such information is in the unconscious of members and often goes undetected.

The knowledge sharing modes mentioned above can further develop into four interaction states as members give (telling their own feelings) and receive (listening to others) feedback (see Chart 5) (Hanson, 1973).

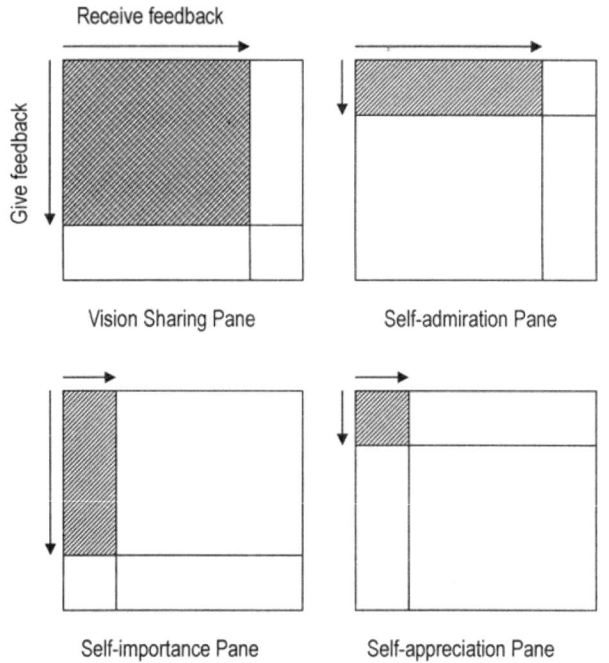

Vision Sharing Pane   Self-admiration Pane

Self-importance Pane   Self-appreciation Pane

Chart 5 Four Knowledge Sharing Characteristics of Johari's Window

1. *Vision sharing pane*: This pane happens when free interaction increases, meaning the member shares knowledge on the basis of honesty and trust, instead of suspicion. As the top left window in the above chart shows, both arrows of feedback receiving and giving extend longer. This type of member interaction can best create a harmonious organisational culture and ensure best results of knowledge sharing.

2. *Self-admiration pane*: This pane happens when the façade (hidden) area is far larger than other areas with the basis of knowledge sharing (for even non-confidential information). As the top right window in the above chart shows, when the person cares only about his or her own interest, he or she takes feedback (longer arrow), but gives little (shorter arrow). Sharing knowledge with this type of person can often make people feel not worth it or even insecure.

3. *Self-importance pane*: This pane happens when the blind spot outweighs any other areas. During knowledge sharing, because this type of person talks too much and is too eager to show off, he tends to ignore others' ideas or rights. This is partly the person's nature to think that he is more important than others and to enjoy showing off and denying others, and partly has to do with the

person's lack of the ability to listen and observe. As the bottom left window in the above chart shows, this type of person receives little feedback (shorter arrow) and gives too much (longer arrow).

4. *Self-appreciation pane*: This pane happens when the unknown area is larger than other areas. The sharing of knowledge is based on insufficient, but self-appreciated, knowledge. This type of person does not like to give or receive feedback (both arrows are short) as shown in the bottom right window of the above chart. Since the person knows little and is too afraid to be seen through, he tends to be suspicious and jealous of others. The sharing of knowledge will gradually lose strength, and the atmosphere within the organisation soon becomes 'dead'.

When knowledge sharing encounters difficulty with members being extremely selfish or suspicious, the team leader may employ interaction exercises to cultivate Lao Tse's thinking of 'the more you give, the more you have' (Lao-tse, B.C. 300-400). If the problem is with members' strong desire to express themselves and strong self-confidence, the exercises should be aiming at cultivating their ability and patience to listen, observe, and understand the world around them. The Johari's Window can be useful too in terms of helping members assess and improve. For example, all participants can mark the number of feedbacks given and taken (evaluated by others) during the previous sharing and then review the results in order to have a clearer understanding of their own type and of others'. If the result shows a member has given and taken little feedback (two short arrows), at the next meeting (usually 45 minutes per meeting) one should guide this particular member to better participate in the discussion and create a balanced member interaction by making sure each participant is both contributing to and gaining from the meeting. (The chairperson can certainly use the evaluation result as a tool for guidance). The Johari's Window evaluation chart is a nine-point scale on axes. When the total score exceeds nine points for both feedback giving and receiving, proportionate numbers can be used (e.g. 16:12 can be expressed in the chart as 8:6) as shown below.

Jacob (2001) believes that the transformation process of team thinking not only increases the occurrence of 'I don't know (forget) that I know', but also the chances of 'I don't know that I don't know' and 'I know that I don't know', from the ideas raised by others. In other words, the process of team thinking itself often stimulates the generation of more ideas. If these ideas can be collected, collated, and then forwarded to relevant personnel, they can further generate, construe, evaluate, and transform or reflect on concepts to ensure the thinking is comprehensive and forward-looking. In other words, the management of innovation is in effect the process of making ideas a shared property, and thus effective management can ensure both the inevitability and innovation happen faster, more frequently, and in better quality.

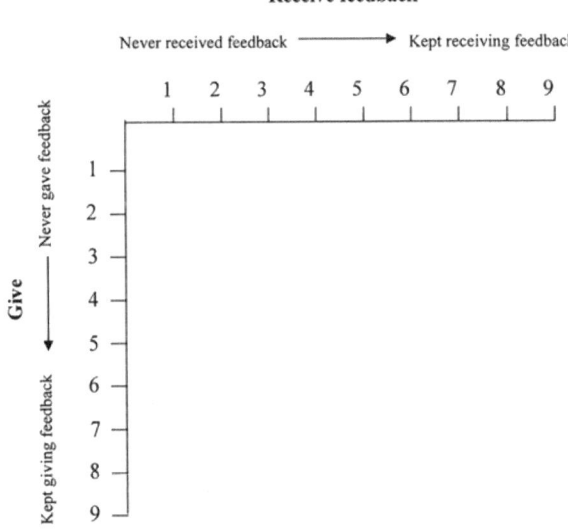

Chart 6 Knowledge Sharing and Feedback

Promoting a knowledge sharing mechanism

To ensure an enlarged 'arena' area in Johari's Window, an OK intention or the 'to give is to take' mindset is required. When one member starts to open himself up to others, the other members will also gradually open up. But what is a good way to start the first step to open oneself up without having doubts about whether others will respond accordingly? Passively, each member may start by convincing himself of the usefulness of even the laymen's ideas. In other words, each participant has to stop judging others before giving them a fair chance to fully express themselves in order to elicit more ideas. To examine if negative attitudes exist among members, the following ten reminders proposed by *Liu Shao* of the Wei Kingdom during the Age of the Three Kingdoms can be used (Hui-Nan-Tse).

To enlarge the 'arena' pane and facilitate knowledge sharing, team leaders may encourage members to speak up immediately after they come up with an idea. However, this principle should not be others' shortcomings because they may be hurt and the harmonious sharing atmosphere may be ruined. So, members should learn to use suggestions instead of criticism during team dialogue. In other words, members' good command of the 3-step team dialogue principle of 'commending others, self-criticising (may or may not be applicable) and proposing a new idea for reference' (Hong, 1998) is prerequisite if members are to be encouraged to speak out their ideas immediately and to increase the 'arena' pane for knowledge sharing. In the West, speaking one's thoughts is part of the culture. However, in the East, people still believe that 'silence is golden'. In other words, ideas are only worth money if they are kept to oneself. The downside, however, is that the idea may die prematurely or lack perspective and comprehensiveness; and carrying out ideas all by oneself can often lead to failure. Therefore, three cobblers brainstorming for ideas may come up with a much more refined plan than a mastermind formulating a plan on his own. This is why team leaders usually make speaking up a requirement for quiet members and hope that it will help force them to change their way of thinking and to start participating in knowledge sharing.

No.	During a dialogue, you believe others would think the following of you
1	You know little about the subject if you don't talk
2	You are pompous if you raise your voice and object
3	You know nothing if you insist on own opinion
4	You lack perspective if you commend only on one single idea or person
5	You are competing with them if you oppose their ideas
6	You are asking credit for an idea if you speak of an idea before they do
7	You are looking for trouble if you keep raising new ideas
8	You simply don't know enough if you point out the areas they overlooked
9	You are showing off if you spend some time to get to the point
10	You lose focus if you know too may exotic or abstruse things

Table 1 Checklist for Innovation Obstructing Attitudes (Hui-Nan-Tse)

Idea generation and a sharing culture

Chart 7 depicts the differences in ways of thinking during knowledge sharing. Dewulf & Baillie (1999) describe the process of innovation as continuous transformation of either individual or team thinking, which includes idea generation, explication, evaluation and application. The construction of a knowledge innovation platform thus helps boost the efficiency and effectiveness of the transformation process. Another important key to efficient and effective transformation is taking note of the process of transformation (difficulties and breakthroughs) and learning from mistakes. Chart 7 summarises the transformation process of idea generation and sharing.

The transformation process usually starts with the surfacing of a problem. In seeking the causes of and possible solutions to the problem, some ideas will emerge. The transformation then takes place in two directions. With individual thinking, the next step will be to construe the ideas and evaluate their adequacy and feasibility. If adequate and feasible, the idea will be applied to solve the problem and the results will then be evaluated. Of which, the process of construing ideas usually includes the analysis of idea value as well as types.

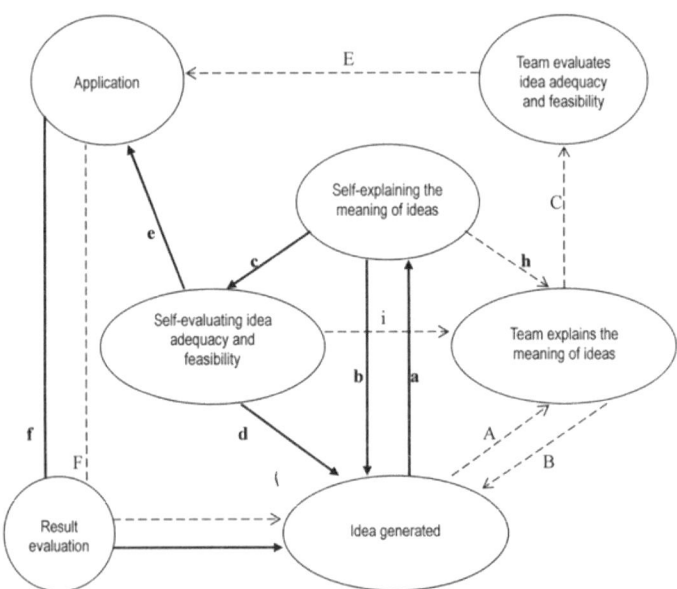

Chart 7 Transformation Process for Idea Generation and Sharing

When self-explanation is not satisfying, the person will go back to generate other ideas (the a-b loop indicated in the chart). If the idea can be satisfactorily explained, the person will then evaluate its adequacy and feasibility. (In terms of problem-solving, it refers to the adequacy of causes and the feasibility of solutions.) The next step is to prioritise the ideas for application (the a-b-c-e loop). If the evaluation the ideas are either inadequate or unfeasible, the person will again go back to generate other ideas (the a-c-d loop). With application, if the results are poor, the person will start over again with idea generation (the a-c-e-f-g loop).

Both with team knowledge sharing (discussion) and individual thinking, the transformation process forms a big continuous circle. However, conservative members tend to make sure the ideas are explainable before presenting them to the team (the a-h-B loop). Some will not even raise their ideas until they have completed the process of both self-explanation and self-evaluation in order to make sure that the ideas are not completely off target (the a-c-i-B loop). However, this can often restrain thinking.

In addition to the 'face-sensitive' culture of the East, a corporate culture that is dictatorial or that highly values seniority can result in repeated inner loops (self-explaining and evaluating), particularly with lower-ranking personnel. In other words, the flatter the organisation structure, the more open the knowledge sharing process. Other factors that affect members' choosing of inner or outside loops include members' department and self-image. For instance, the sales department tends to more of the outside loop than the manufacturing department, and risk-averters tend to more of the inner loop than risk-lovers (see Table 2).

Attribute	Inner loop	Outside loop
Department	Manufacturing	Sales
Power Structure	Dictatorial	Flat
Personality	Risk-averting	Risk-loving
Age	Old	Young
Background Culture	East	West

Table 2 Culture Attributes and Thinking Process

As far as business development is concerned, at the beginning stage of a business entity, members tend to share a common fortune and the organisation is often flat. Knowledge sharing at this stage is relatively open with strong ability to innovate (Tidd et al, 2001). However, as the organisation grows and individual ability varies, the less capable tend to lose motivation to share for fear of making mistakes, or because the supervisor judges people by their rank or is unwilling to listen. To make sure the egalitarian culture continues through later stages of the organisation, a fair and just reward and disciplinary system should be established as early as possible. Such a system can effectively reduce suspicion among members during times of success. In other words, an uninterrupted egalitarian culture for knowledge sharing is necessary if an innovative team is to be built, and the 'silence is gold' principle is to be replaced with an 'open and responsive' culture. In fact, having something to say is a process of self-realisation. It is a realisation of the fact that making mistakes is not unacceptable and that others' comments are helpful for making corrections. In short, it is a culture of 'inter-dependence'. When such an inter-dependent culture is developed, the area of the 'arena' in Johari's Window will grow, which in turn will help enhance the organisation's knowledge capital as well as the support for domain-specific innovations. Hence, knowledge sharing should be aimed at producing better team results through stimulation and transformation of individual ideas (the outer circle). As the chart below shows, the thinking transformation process has to surpass both departmental and hierarchical barriers to ensure a continuous process, and to avoid creating a knowledge island (see chart below).

To boost egalitarian knowledge sharing and remove the pressure from emphasis on seniority, the NGT (Nominal Group Technique) (Harvey, 2003) can be a useful tool, as it allows each member to express their own ideas (on paper or over the Internet) anonymously, and employs an assistant as the idea catalyst to read out the ideas or to check them over the Internet. In addition to NGT, other team thinking techniques such as TRIZ and the KJ Method are also useful for promoting knowledge sharing among team members (Terninko, Zusman & Zlotin, 1998).

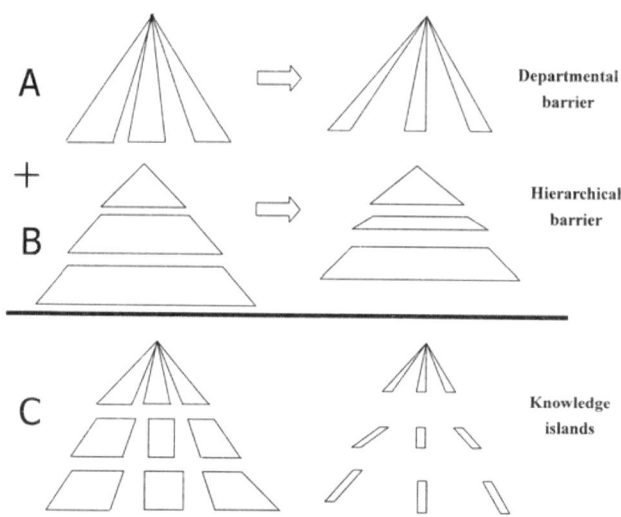

A ⇒ Departmental barrier

+

B ⇒ Hierarchical barrier

C Knowledge islands

Chart 8 Knowledge Sharing and Organisational Change

Conclusion

Teamwork usually generates better results innovation than individual effort. Therefore, to boost organisational innovation, a team knowledge sharing culture is necessary. To ensure the effectiveness of knowledge sharing however (Ahmed, Kok & Loh, 2002), an egalitarian culture is important in order to relieve members from unnecessary pressure and to encourage them to speak freely and fully. In other words, an effective knowledge sharing mechanism can best serve as a platform for organisational innovation.

Tidd et al (2001) stress the importance of shaping a trusting, open, self-realization and mutually supportive corporate culture (Gibb, 1978) to the acceleration of the inevitability of innovation. Based on such corporate culture, supervisors should then create successful leadership and members should learn how to continue to grow for the enhancement of organisational innovation and R&D results.

References

Ahmed, P. K., Kok, L. K. & Loh, A. Y. E. (2002) *Learning Through Knowledge Management*. Boston: B. H.

Dewulf, S. & Baillie, C. (1999) Creating is science and engineering. *EACI the 6th Conference 1999*, Dec. 12-15. Lattrop, the Netherlands.

Freud, S. (1922) *Introductory Lectures on Psycho-Analysis*. Trans. Joan Riviere. London: Allen.

Gibb, J. R. (1978) *Trust: A new view of personal and organizational development*. Los Angeles, CA: Guild of Tutors Press.

Hanson, P. C. (1973) The Johari Window: a model for soliciting and giving feedback. In J. E. Jones and J. W. Pfeiffer (Eds.) *The Annual Handbook for Group Faeilita*, Lim. Assoc. Inc.

Harrison, J. S., Hitt, M. A., Hoskisson, R. E. & Ireland, D. R. (2001). Resource complementarity in business combinations: extending the logic to organizational alliances. *Journal of Management*, 27, 679-690.

Harvey, J. (2003). http://www.icbl.hw.ac.uk/ltdi/cookbook/nominal_group_technique /index.html#endhead. 2003/12/27.

Hong, J.C. (1998) *Head Start with Creativity*. Taipei: Teacher Chang Cultural Publishing.

Huai-Nan-Zi (B.C. 200-300) Huai Nan Zi.

Jacob, I. (2001) The transfer of innovative practices. *EACI the 7th Conference 2001*, Dec. 9-12. Enschede, the Netherlands.

Lao-Tse (B.C. 300-400) *Dao De Jing*.

Luft, Joseph (1969) *Of Human Interaction*. Palo Alto, CA: National Press.

Sugiura S., Kinoshita T., Shiratori N. & Munemori J.(1988). A proposal of an evaluation method IPL for effects of individual quantity of domain knowledge on an intuitive classification in a distributed and cooperative KJ Method and its application. *Proceedings of the 13th International Conference on Information Networking* (ICOIN '98).

Terninko, J., Zusman, A. & Zlotin, B. (1998) *Systematic Innovation: an introduction to TRIZ*. St: Lucie Press.

Tidd, J., Bessant, J. & Pavilt, K. (2001) *Managing Innovation: Integrating Technology, Market and Organizational Change*. New York: Wiley & Sons.

Martin Shovel and Martha Leyton

Metaphor and creativity

Imagine you are settling down to a long train journey. You reach into your bag and pull out the novel you are reading and just as you are about to take up the story the stranger sitting opposite starts talking to you. You have plenty of time on your hands so you welcome the chance to begin a conversation with her. But how would you respond if she were to start by describing *the song of her life* or by explaining *the painting of her life* or even, perhaps, telling you about *the recipe of her life*? Her behaviour might seem very strange and you would probably feel a growing sense of discomfort and confusion.

Now rewind the tape and start again. This time she begins by telling you *the story of her life*. Now the experience of listening to her feels comfortable and familiar, and both the content and structure of what she is saying make sense to you. Story is the medium through which we understand and experience our lives and the lives of other people. Stories give our lives their structure and meaning. They help us make sense of the world around us by transforming the constant flux of experience into meaningful patterns. Without stories our existence would be chaotic and ineffectual.

In their influential study of metaphor Lakoff and Johnson (1980) write that, 'the essence of metaphor is understanding and experiencing one kind of thing in terms of another' (p.5). In Western society, for example, life can also be understood and experienced as a journey. It is not always a *smooth ride*, sometimes you can *take a wrong turn* and *lose your way*, but if you *keep going* you will find *the right path* and get to your *destination* in *the end*. To return to our friend on the train, life is not conventionally understood and experienced as a painting. But it could be a creative and valuable exercise to look at a number of different paintings, select one that strikes you in some respects as a metaphor for your life and then produce some statements along the lines of, 'my life is like this painting because...' In the process you may well uncover insights about your life that were hidden when you made sense of it through the more conventional, and therefore largely unnoticed, metaphor of *life as a story*. As Lakoff (1993) puts it, 'metaphor is not just a matter of language, but of thought and reason' (page 5).

The key point is that life is not just *like* a story, it *is* a story. The metaphor of *life is a story* encapsulates the essential nature of the experience of living one's life in Western society. Moreover, if we lived in a culture in which the metaphor that structured our experience of life was quite different, then our experience of life itself would be qualitatively different too. Another example will help to clarify the point. In Western societies the structuring metaphor for argument is *argument is war*. Most of us are unaware of this structuring metaphor and its all-pervasive influence on our day-to-day experience of argument and debate, but the evidence for it is reflected in a wide variety of everyday expressions. Arguments are *lost* or *won*; *positions* are *attacked* or *defended*; *opponents* can *destroy* or *demolish* our arguments. Claims can be *indefensible*, while arguments can be *shot down* and so on. Lakoff and Johnson wonder just how different our experience of argument would be if the structuring metaphor for argument were, instead, *argument is dance*. 'In such a culture, people would view arguments differently, experience them differently, carry them out differently and talk about them differently. But we would probably not view them as arguing at all: they would simply be doing something different' (ibid.).

To summarise and elaborate on this way of understanding metaphor, we can say that:

- metaphors mediate and structure our experience of the world
- metaphors constitute a necessary framework for creating meanings out of the constant flux of experience – they enable us to function by restricting the potentially overwhelming amount of information that constantly assails our consciousness
- metaphors operate at the horizon of our conscious awareness - we are mostly unaware of their influence on the way we frame our experience of the world
- metaphorical frameworks function by highlighting certain aspects of experience and concealing other aspects - they construct our 'point of view'
- metaphors reflect and reproduce the culture they exist in and are culturally and historically specific
- individuals living in a particular culture have a unique relationship to metaphor which is personal and idiosyncratic and reflects all aspects of their personal history - their needs, desires, fears, aspirations and so on
- metaphors are not only expressed in language, but also visually, aurally and as imaginative representations - sensed in the body and communicated through movement, gesture, tone of voice and so on
- we can explore the nature and influence of *the metaphors we live by*, by attending to our everyday use of language – both verbal and non-verbal.

What does all this have to do with creativity? Following the approach to metaphor pioneered by writers such as Lakoff and Johnson, we would like to explore ways in which the language people use to talk about creativity shapes their experience and understanding of creativity itself. Lubart (1999) suggests that, 'The Western definition of creativity as a product-oriented, originality-based phenomenon can be compared with an Eastern view of creativity as a phenomenon of expressing an inner truth in a new way, or of self-growth' (page 347). With this idea as our starting point, we begin by drawing attention to some of the metaphors used in the language and literature of creativity with which we are familiar; and suggest how these metaphors might shape the way we understand creativity and the creative process.

De Bono (1995) compares the working of the human mind to rain falling on a landscape, which 'will eventually form streams, rivers, and valleys. Once these have formed, future rainfall is channeled along these rivers and valleys, which then affect the way future rain is collected and organised' (page 10). The purpose of creative/lateral thinking is to *side-track* the channels/patterns that the rain/experience creates over time. De Bono's methods are designed to help us 'to escape from the *main track* in order to increase our chances of getting to the *side-track*' (page 15). His main purpose is to bring about change. Lateral thinking is the '*set of systematic techniques* used for changing *concepts* and *perceptions* and *generating* new ones' (page 54).

Similar metaphors are used by other writers. For example, Von Oech (1983) says that creativity is released when you apply the necessary *tools* and *techniques* as a *key* to open the *mental lock* that prevents your natural flow. For Michalko (1998), creativity is something that has to be *cracked*. The *tools* and *techniques* will *generate* the *ideas* and *creative solutions* you need in your business and personal life. Others (e.g. McLeod and Thomson, 2002) regard creativity as primarily a *rational combinatory process*: that is one in which you combine previously unconnected ideas, information and elements to make something new. Many of these ideas stem from Poincaré's influential description of the creative process as having four stages: preparation, incubation, illumination, and verification (Poincaré, 1908). In this model, creativity has a certain linearity, a beginning and an end, a producer and a product, presaging Henry Ford's production line. This cannot be said of some non-Western characterisations of creativity.

Broadly speaking, the Western concept of creativity is characterised by concern with what the creative process *produces*, and it requires that the *end products* of the creative process, the creative *output*, should be both useful and original. Not surprisingly, Western metaphors for creativity tend to be industrial, system-based, cognitive, solution-focused, systematic, individualistic, rational and functional. In a Western capitalist culture, it could be argued, the structuring metaphors for creativity present it as a tool, or set of tools, for originating innovative products that get the job done more efficiently and more profitably.

In many non-Western cultures the emphasis appears to be on *process* rather than *product*. Creativity is linked to enlightenment - it is about development rather than innovation. Lubart (1999) cites a number of studies suggesting that in many such cultures, creativity is about re-interpreting traditional ideas and about revealing and re-activating what is already latent in the unconscious. Traditional artists often practise meditation in order to connect with the 'essence' of an object or event and try to make manifest what they find within.

It has been suggested that a culture's concept of creativity may derive from its creation myth, in which case it would be interesting to look for parallels between the various concepts of creativity and their mythic counterparts in terms of the metaphorical structures embedded within them. There is no single Hindu myth of origin, but the many classic creation myths of Hinduism are all expressions of a belief in time as cyclical, with no beginning and no end. There is no first stage of primeval nothingness and no final end to come. Instead, there are four successive periods, called *yugas*, which deteriorate progressively until the universal deluge, after which a new golden age begins and the universe recycles itself again. This provides a marked contrast with the Judeo-Christian creation myth in which an almighty being creates order out of nothing (or chaos), completing the task in six days. It is surely no coincidence that the modern Western concept of creativity is also based on the idea of the production of something from nothing by an individual involved in a linear process with a definite beginning, middle and end. Equally, the Hindu concept of creativity appears to place far less emphasis on originality than the Western, and instead sees the artist as involved in re-creation and re-interpretation. We live in a world where cultures - and their metaphors - clash, collide, cross-fertilise and mingle. So it is no surprise that the language of creativity increasingly reflects this and many Western writers, teachers and practitioners are adopting models and metaphors drawn from non-Western sources, such as Taoism and Zen Buddhism.

One such writer is Claxton (1997) who advocates the cultivation of a state of what Buddhists call 'mindfulness' in order to allow the 'undermind' to deliver up its riches. He explores the phenomenon of 'incubation' - the effect of leaving ideas 'on the back burner' or 'allowing the mind to lie fallow'. Here we have metaphors taken respectively from the life-cycle, from cookery and from agriculture, all attempting to convey the same thing: the idea that creativity involves an element of trust in the natural course of events. Each metaphor carries with it a separate set of entailments, which both enable and limit its meaning. Putting an idea *on the back burner* entails turning down the heat, leaving the pot alone, turning the attention away. However, it requires that there is a cook taking the decision and a heat-source that can be controlled. Cookery is a deliberate human activity involving knowledge, practice and the following of some basic rules. Similarly, *lying fallow* could be said to entail a deliberate intervention in the natural process of soil fertility, but it also implies a return to the natural state and perhaps a more radical potential for the germination of new life. The metaphor of *incubation* carries different entailments: like cookery, incubation involves the application of heat, but unlike it, the heat is usually gentle body heat and the outcome is new life. There may be no human or conscious decision involved: bacteria and diseases can incubate all by themselves. While each of these metaphors has distinct entailments and implications, they also have much in common. The emphasis in all three is on leaving things alone, on letting things happen by themselves - a notion quite at odds with the industrial process metaphor for creativity which is employed by many in today's 'creativity industry'.

Cameron (1995) employs an eclectic mixture of metaphors drawn from a wide selection of cultures and religions. One of her central tenets is that 'creativity is our true nature, that blocks are an unnatural thwarting of a process at once as normal and as miraculous as the blossoming of a flower at the end of a slender green stem' (page xiii). In Cameron's model, blocks can be 'dissolved' through the 'willing use of the tools' provided by her book. But despite the use of metaphors associated with chemistry and plumbing, Cameron's is not a mechanistic or scientific model. She also believes that 'creativity is a spiritual experience' and that 'when we open ourselves to our creativity, we open ourselves to the creator's creativity within us and our lives' (page 3). Interestingly, the link between these two metaphorical themes is provided by the underlying structure of her approach, which is based on her experience as a recovering alcoholic. Like the programme offered by Alcoholics Anonymous, Cameron's book offers a twelve-stage process, each described as an aspect of creative 'recovery', with prescribed 'tasks' for the reader to perform along the way and a 'check in' to end each stage. Here are metaphors of detoxification, of the sacred and of tool kits, all rolled into one package - which we might perhaps call *spiritual plumbing*.

This brief foray into the literature of creativity can only give a taste of the different ways in which the idea of creativity is characterised and experienced within Western society. In our view, for example, the success and appeal of de Bono's *lateral thinking* in the corporate environment is clearly linked to the development of his method within a framework of Western business and organisational metaphors. In contrast to more esoteric and artistic approaches to creativity, de Bono *gets down to business* by avoiding 'semi-mystical' approaches and being logical, serious, systematic and deliberate. He writes:

> I regard creative thinking (lateral thinking) as a special type of information handling. It should take its place alongside our other methods of information handling: mathematics, logical analysis, computer simulation, and so on. There need be no mystique about it. A person sitting down with the deliberate intention of generating an idea in a certain area and then proceeding to use a lateral thinking technique systematically should represent a normal state of affairs (*op. cit.* Introduction).

De Bono is obviously operating within a metaphorical frame very different from that of Claxton or Cameron. He wants his readers to think of the creative process as something practical, measurable and systematic – quite the reverse of the mysterious, even magical associations called upon by Cameron through the metaphors she chooses.

As we have already seen, each metaphorical frame brings its own set of entailments, which put constraints on the kinds of meanings that can be produced. An example of this is the metaphor of *problems and solutions* which poses a specific – and limited – way of thinking about creative problem solving. Many practitioners of 'corporate creativity' talk in terms of *problems and solutions*, and in doing so risk limiting the scope of their endeavours. An analogy helps to demonstrate this: if your kettle is broken and you want to work out a way of either repairing or replacing it, the metaphorical frame of *problems and solutions* will serve you well. But if you decide to use the broken kettle as a starting point for thinking about wider questions such as 'do I really need a kettle?' and 'what would happen (to me, the tea/coffee industry, the world...) if I changed other aspects of my life so that I no longer use a kettle?', then you would have moved beyond an everyday concern with *problems and solutions* and begun to explore and challenge the metaphorical frame of *problems and solutions* itself. You would have set in motion an experiential and cognitive process that results in your having a fundamentally revised understanding of both yourself and the world. This level of creative thinking is open-ended, playful, often risky. It moves beyond the realm of simple creativity and learning to one where learning and creativity can be described as *generative*. This wider perspective enables an exploration of the limitations of the metaphorical frame itself, and this in turn can lead to changes in world view and self image.

Generative creativity moves us into new areas of thinking; everything is open to question, nothing is taken for granted.

It could be argued that commercial constraints prevent certain questions (such as 'should we be doing this at all?') from being raised within a corporate metaphorical frame, and that generative creativity should perhaps be applied with caution in the corporate context. However, we believe that because of the accelerating speed of change in today's world, it is even more urgent that we focus on generative creativity and learning in all walks of life. All the approaches to creativity we have looked at here are concerned with change and difference - whether it be changed states of being or transformative change in the material world. Creativity is essentially concerned with these things, and it is vital that we keep our options open. The forces of globalisation threaten to homogenise cultures and differences, and we risk ending up in a world in which the range of metaphorical frames is diminished and our creative choices are curtailed as a consequence. However, like the rainforest, which contains countless unclassified species of flora and fauna with the potential to cure disease and transform our lives, the diversity of our cultural and linguistic heritage provides us with a rich resource and repertoire of survival strategies, which, if lost, would diminish the creative potential of humankind.

References

Cameron, J. (1995) *The Artist's Way*. London: Pan Books.

Claxton, G. (1997) *Hare Brain Tortoise Mind*. London: Fourth Estate.

De Bono, E. (1995) *Serious Creativity*. London: HarperCollins.

Lakoff, G (1993) The contemporary theory of metaphor. In A. Ortony (Ed.) *Metaphor and Thought*. Cambridge University Press.

Lakoff, G. & Johnson, M. (1980) *Metaphors We Live By*. University of Chicago Press.

Lubart, T. I. (1999) Creativity across cultures. In R. J. Sternberg (Ed.) *Handbook of Creativity*. Cambridge University Press.

Michalko, M. I. (1998) *Cracking Creativity*. USA: Ten Speed Press.

McLeod, F. & Thomson, R. (2002) *Non-stop Creativity and Innovation*. London: McGraw-Hill.

Poincaré, H. (1952) The foundations of science. In B. Ghiselin (Ed.) *The Creative Process*. University of California Press (work first published in 1908).

Von Oech, R. (1983) *A Whack on the Side of the Head*. New York: Warner Books.

Yuichiro Kubo

Challenges for creativity in Singapore and Japan: Confucius' influence and professionalism

This paper presents a general view of cultural similarities and differences between Singapore and Japan on the basis of Confucius' influence and professionalism. I will briefly touch on Confucianism first. Then I will discuss Confucius' influences in Singapore and Japan. I will also consider how the influences reflect upon professionalism in the two countries. Finally, I will attempt to predict some coming challenges for creativity in Singapore and Japan.

Introduction

Singapore and Japan are both in Asia and share certain values in their cultures, but at the same time significant differences can be observed. I would like to take a look at Confucius' influence in the two countries first and consider how the philosophy has made an impact on their current values. The most striking difference between Singapore and Japan lies in the experience of World War II. The former became independent from Malaysia after the people experienced the occupation by the Japanese Imperial Army, whereas the Japanese invaded the island in the name of liberation from colonisation by Western countries. I do not intend to go into the details of history, but it must be pointed out that the historical experience of the war and the confidence in one's own culture have had a big impact on Confucius' teaching and led the two countries into different modes of national mentality.

Singapore has been steered by a trusted and effective government and has implemented quick, realistic and practical strategies for the ongoing economic survival game in the world; while Japan, although economically the second strongest country, has shown a slow administrative change and reformation of the government structure in the current world-wide economic downturn. Singapore has striven to make full use of its strengths, weaknesses, advantages and threats and has been successful in education as well as economy, whereas Japan has had difficulties in adjusting itself to so called global standards.

Understanding these issues and differences helps us realise the key elements of traditional values in a modern context; and how these values affect the ways of thinking and creativity. Traditional values operate unconsciously in thinking and we need to be careful about this kind of thinking. Thus, we must be vigilant in thinking when it comes to creativity. Especially in this new millennium, we must solve a lot of big and small problems professionally, not only on a local level but also on a global one. Confucius presents us with a simple way of forming an ideal society and world.

Confucianism

The essential teachings of Confucius and Neo-Confucians consist of the principles of humanity (ren), righteousness (yi), prosperity (li), and wisdom (zhi), as explained by Lu (1983). They were believed to be bestowed by heaven in those days. The Confucianists taught people to develop their inborn moral qualities fully and then to extend them to others and communities, through love and consideration. They regarded the *family* as the basic social unit and emphasised that filial piety must be learnt; and genuine kindness and goodwill must be brought into a society.

Another simple but intriguing teaching of Confucius is to take a middle path. Extreme views of matters and events cannot solve issues and problems in themselves and instead pour oil on a burning fire. Taking the middle path can be rephrased as thinking and acting in a balanced way. To put it differently, unbalanced views divert from reality. It has been said that a balance is inevitable in any ecosystem. This brings us to a holistic view where we can pay attention to present environmental problems and issues in the world.

One might think it ridiculous to say that Confucius' view is related to an ecological view since Confucius did not foresee the environmental destruction on Earth. However, the middle path approach can warn us of human-centric thinking and behaviour.

Confucius' influences in Singapore and Japan

Singapore, being a young and multi-racial country, has shown the world that a small island can make it this far, even though some people thought Singapore could never achieve this level of success upon its independence. This success could not be achieved without excellent leaders, hard working people and racial harmony. In the Confucian core teaching, one of the key concepts is humility (ren) which requires one to be honest with one's inborn moral qualities and extend them to others. This is exactly what Singaporeans have put into action. The importance of humility can be equally shared in other major religions in Singapore, that is, Buddhism, Islam, Christianity and Hinduism.

Confucius' emphasis on filial piety can also be shared in the other faiths. It is straightforward to maintain that the family unit is the very basic unit of a society and must be the first educating ground for honesty and love to one's own family. But, it is observed that in a Chinese family, too much emphasis on family tends to restrict love only to one's own family and close friends. In theory, love is not only bound to one's own family and close friends. Because leaders made right decisions at the right times and gained trust from fellow citizens, Singaporeans are proud of their achievements and government and trust their senior leaders. This is exactly the case of Confucius's government. In other words, leaders must be good examples to the people. In a sense, Singapore's success proves the reliability of Confucius' philosophy. What is to be noted here is that the philosophy is the very core teaching of all faiths in the world and the largest ethnic group in Singapore is Chinese and they happen to call it Confucian values. As far as the core teaching is concerned, it can sometimes be called Asian values.

Now consider the case of Japan. As pointed out in Varley's *Japanese Culture* (2000), the Japanese native religion, Shinto, does not mention a code of personal ethics, but it puts stress on sincerity. From about the mid-6th Century, Buddhism and Confucianism were imported from China. Since the core teaching of Shinto is co-existence, the Shinto philosophy can be said to absorb the religions without any conflict or confusion. Co-existence is considered as harmony, non-violence, righteousness, filial respect and love to others.

However, the Japanese culture drastically changed after the end of the Edo Era (around the end of the 19th Century) and Japanese people forced themselves to follow Western culture and went blindly into colonialism. As a result, the Japanese invaded and colonised neighbouring countries in World War II. This was the very turning point of Japanese Confucianism because government officials began to take wrong steps and made people in most Asian countries, as well as their own people, suffer. From then onwards, Confucius' presupposition did not stand for Japanese people. After WW2, the Japanese traditional teachings that seemed to lead Japanese people into the war were weeded out and were taught at school as *not* correct. This caused a generation gap in attitudes toward their own traditions and culture between pre- and post-war Japanese people. The gap has widened between those who experienced WW2 and the post-WW2 second generation. Generally speaking, with the increase of individualism in Japan, filial piety has gradually weakened due to the mistakes that the grandfather generation had committed in the war.

We have to consider another reason also. Confucianism is transferred from the older generation to the younger in village culture. During higher economic growth, most of the younger generation moved to the city. They became nuclear families. There is no person who teaches Confucianism to the children.

How the influences reflect upon professionalism

Singapore has implemented national education to make the younger generation know and learn how the former generation built their own country, facing various difficulties, and overcoming the challenges with great effort. In addition, National Service ensures Singaporean men are patriotic to their own country through their own contribution. Consequently, they take pride in building a successful country. This mentality helps Singaporeans to work with pride, trusting the Singapore government and educational systems as successful. They can proudly follow their traditions and culture at work as well as at home. Hence, Singapore is based on the right presupposition of Confucianism of respected leaders and older generations. Consequently, they are sometimes apt to stick to top-down management owing to meritocracy, and bureaucracy is by and large respected in management and administration. What is noticeable here is that this bureaucracy can be changed into a more flexible one through effective feedback and assessment systems.

A superficial glance at Japanese professionalism may give you an impression of similarity to Singapore's professionalism. However, this is not the case. Since WW2, Japanese people have had no confidence in their traditions and older generation. Before this, the Japanese professional tradition of Shu-Ri-Ha had been passed down from generation to generation, but it is now dwindling. Shu-Ri-Ha is written in Chinese characters and the three Chinese characters literally mean Follow - Stay away - Break. This encourages professionals to innovate in following three steps, that is, following their traditions, thinking independently and innovation. Thus, the post-WW2 first generation did their best in catching up with new technologies and skills and indeed some of their products became internationally valued and contributed to world technology developments in some way or other. The achievements looked as if post-WW2 education in Japan had no problems. Yet it can be said that the post-war first generation were engrossed in American culture and did not pay much attention to their own respectable culture. This attitude of parents after the war tremendously accelerated the erosion of the Japanese traditional mentality in the second generation and led to a world of individualism, liberalism and feminism.

Thanks to Westernisation and the traditional way of innovation, Japan revived as, economically, the second strongest country and could enjoy the luxury of materialism. This success has made the first generation believe in their way of working effectively and established their ways of management and administration as a system, which implies their presupposition is to follow the existing rules and to keep the system as a norm. Thus, the system is not very flexible and not fast to change. The system change is rather slow, but steady in improvement and innovation.

We have to differentiate three kinds of system:

1. The system in the organisation (company), which is flexible and fast to change;
2. The system in government (welfare, education, university, environments, etc.), which is now changing greatly, for example, all national founded universities will soon become semi-private universities.
3. The system in politics (politician, bureaucrat, trader), which is hard to change (politician, bureaucrat and trader made up the 'Iron Triangle' for their interests, not for the people).

When it comes to professionalism, people think about someone who is at work. But, traditionally, that is not true in Japan. Home management was one of the inevitable factors for building a successful country. Thus, being a skilled mother used to be highly respected by the older generation. From the traditional point of view, Japanese women played an important role in the family and were respected by Japanese men for their dedication and devotion to taking care of children of the next generation. There used to be a harmonious co-operation between male and female professions on the basis of each one's characteristics and potential. Housework was regarded as equally important as working for a company, although the contribution by the housewife was not very obvious. This can be said to be one of Confucius' core teachings for a healthy country. Nowadays, it is unlikely that the younger generation will consider work at home, such as home management and raising children, as the foundation of human development and education, even in Japan.

Challenge in future

Some of the future major challenges for Singapore and Japan may be of the same kind, but one can help the other in facing the challenges. First of all, the two countries need to take into account the seriousness of environmental problems since they consume a lot of materials and energy for daily and business activities. Even though ecological movements and campaigns are observed, it will be necessary to seriously reconsider our lifestyles and try to be good examples for neighbouring countries. Among possible ecological solutions, the most challenging is energy conservation. Urgent attention must be paid to the excessive use of energy and water, because these are closely linked to air and water pollution. Otherwise, pollution by current generations will be detrimental to future generations who are not directly responsible for them.

The second challenge will be how to keep national and cultural identity in this torrent of variegated information and pop cultures. As Singapore is a young and multi-racial country, Singaporeans regard National Education as playing an important role in the education system. A number of educational programmes and exhibitions have been created for this purpose. This can be a good example for Japanese people, but before following it, they have to solve historical issues related to WW2 because they cannot implement such a programme as national education without understanding their own traditions and culture. In particular, younger generations in the two countries need to discuss and exchange their opinions about world and Asian history. Thinking in the other's shoes will enable the younger generation to find good keys and solutions to our present issues and problems.

The third challenge will be related to the second in the sense that family issues have something to do with national and cultural identity. Logically speaking, the basic unit of a nation is a family unit. If parents of nuclear families work during the first stage of childhood and let maids take care of their children, the absence of parents can affect the child's cognitive and personality development. A Japanese saying tells that what a child has acquired by three years old will persist until death. That is why Japanese women were culturally encouraged to take care of their own children personally with love. These days, it has been argued that a fatherless home can affect a child's cognitive and personality development since there are a number of juvenile delinquencies all over Japan and they are seen as a big social problem. For over two generations, this problem is said to be slowly and invisibly growing, with the help of hard working fathers who work overtime willingly for the benefit of their companies. Moreover, it can be added that filial piety has been decreasing for over 50 years. Having observed this, the Japanese should warn other countries of the dangers of the absence of parents for a baby and the significance of each role of the parents. Fortunately, Singaporeans have been increasingly aware of the problems of working parents and are looking for the best solution to this particular issue. Maybe, it will be good for both of the countries to collaborate on the effects of working parents.

The fourth challenge will be how to make a breakthrough in the current success and what to learn from past mistakes. A spirit of constant improvement is essential for genuine innovation. To put it differently, there is also some room for improvement in any system. As everything changes very rapidly these days, we must keep up with the changes in latest technologies and must be vigilant to unforeseen problems in future. In this sense, both success and mistakes are treated equally as we can learn from both extremes. People are supposedly easily susceptible to successful cases and not very enthusiastic about studying mistakes and failures. However, it is worth remembering that it is the governing system that determines whether a solution is successful or not. If problems persist in the system, the cause must be the very presupposition of the system.

Reviewing the presupposition is regarded as neither accusing nor despising those who were involved in the system. It does not mean to let someone lose face. When a problem surfaces, the person in charge will really lose face. In conjunction with this, management teams must have listening ears to solve and improve our system. Sometimes, top-down management can be a hindrance to holistic improvement, given that the management refuses to listen to subordinates' frank feedback and keeps pushing their plans at their own convenience. Holistic improvement literally takes everyone's objectives into account. Taking a close look at past mistakes and failures can help us to find a new path to finer improvement. Thus, we should not be haunted by past grace of success and bitter memories of mistakes and failures, and must have courage and love to overcome them and strive for a more harmonious and peaceful society.

The fifth challenge concerns spiritual issues. While keeping a sustainable economy in this competitive world, it can be said that it is almost impossible to continue to work just for materialistic ends. As far as this issue is concerned, it is high time to reconsider the role and meaning of the family and contemplate the meaning of life. It appears that a great number of people are now wondering why they are so stressed and suffering from health problems, in order to make a living and contribute to their country. If you look around, you see many babies are dying from hunger in poorer countries, whereas food is wasted in the diets of richer countries. This unbalanced situation in the world raises a question: Is being economically or materialistically successful our aim of life? As Confucius says, after easing hunger, we can start to educate people. Singapore and Japan are now in the stage of implementing a holistic education of the people and the main objective is to nurture people of balanced minds and guide other neighbouring countries. This effort will hopefully lead us to a world free of conflict and war, by solving current complex problems.

To achieve such a dream, we need to take realistic steps to the ultimate goal. As a start, we have to change our mindsets and subconscious use of words, as pointed out in Kubo (1999a & b). Interestingly, Bohm (1994), the founder of quantum physics, maintains that cognition can be governed by proprioception that is reinforced by thinking and feeling, and de Bono (1983, 1998) emphasises simplification of our existing systems by re-examining and re-evaluating the rationales behind them. We must be very careful about pitfalls in the existing systems in the world and scrutinise the origins and hidden histories of current systems. To see and think properly, I propose (Kubo, 2001) a reviewing process of the system in terms of light logic. Light logic can lead us to think and act in a balanced way because balancing the three basic colours of mind settings reminds us to reconsider the presupposition, the underlying assumption and dualistic distinctions in a system. Metaphorically speaking, the mind settings of state, process and result act as lighting primary colours, namely, blue, green and red, so that the composition of the three colours (mind settings) affects our perception of the world. What dualistic distinctions means here is that we cannot always make a conclusion in terms of yes/no or black/white. In reality, it all depends on yes and no, or grey (black & white), but not all-or-nothing. Medical treatment is a good example. An extreme dualistic approach to sickness encourages a doctor to cure a patient externally, whereas a non-dualistic doctor cures a patient internally and externally alike.

Thus, light logic gives us a hint to solve our problems and issues on the basis of a non-dualistic approach. Just following the latest theory and trends and getting qualified, can be considered as a kind of extreme approach to problem solving. It is essential to attain mental calmness first and think intuitively and creatively. To be creative, one needs to achieve equanimity and equilibrium first and observe what has to be improved next. Consequently, this holistic view will guide us to a holistic sound education system where education begins at home, at school and in the community.

References

Bohm, D. (1994) *Thought as a System*. Routledge.

De Bono, E. (1993) *Water Logic*. Viking.

De Bono, E. (1998) *Simplicity*. Viking.

Kubo, Y. (1999a) Synergy in language and brain: Towards holistic linguistics. Paper presented at the *12th World Congress of Applied Linguistics*, Tokyo, Japan, Aug. 1-6. (AILA99 CD-ROM publication).

Kubo, Y. (1999b) A 3-D cognitive model for language and creativity: Towards light logic. In Cumming, G. et al. (Eds.) *Advanced Research in Computers and Communications in Education*, Vol.1, pp.236-239. IOS Press.

Kubo, Y. (2001) Applying light logic to problem-based learning. In M. I. Stein (Ed.) *Creativity's Global Correspondents–2001*, pp.169-176. Winslow Press.

Lu, M. (1983) *Confucianism: Its Relevance to Modern Society*. Singapore Federal Publications.

Varley, P. (2000) *Japanese Culture* (4th edn). University of Hawaii Press.

Alice Lee

Creative Southeast Asians

I would like to begin by referring to a published PhD thesis entitled, 'Why Asians are less creative than Westerners' by Dr Ng Aik Kwang (2001). This Singaporean explains that Asians are hierarchical, tightly organized and collectivist, emphasizing social order and harmony and gaining the social approval of one's group. They have a more negative view of conflict in society. On the other hand, Westerners are loosely organized in the sense that they have few social rules and norms to adhere to. They are individualistic and egalitarian, emphasizing open and democratic exchange of ideas between individuals to develop their creative potential. They have a less negative view of conflict in society. Therefore, Asians are less creative. Since globalization began, this picture of the differences between East and West may be too simplified. As Dr Ng says in a caveat: 'East is not East and West is not West'.

This is true of the Asians presented here who are at home in East and West. They include two Southeast Asian Write Awardees, one from Indonesia and the other from the Philippines. The other two are a Malaysian Chinese Professor who specializes in EQ building and an Indian (who has made Singapore his home) who specializes in brain-building.

Saini Kosim Karnamisastra

Saini Kosim Karnamisastra stood out from among 224 million Indonesians in 2001 when he received the Southeast Asia Write Award presented by Thailand. He has lived up to his name, for 'karnamisastra' means having an ear for literature. The SEA Write Award is an honour given to Southeast Asians for outstanding writing and productivity. Saini has written more than 30 plays, four anthologies of poems, essays and novels.

Born in Sunda in 1938, Saini comes from a family of poets and musicians as well as rebels. His grandfather was a pioneer in the struggle for independence and he was imprisoned by the Dutch for three years. His father was a freedom fighter who fought the Dutch during the War of Independence (1945-1949). As he informed the writer: 'So, there is a tendency of being a rebel in my blood. I think it is this tendency that made me a playwright'. He is also an introvert and was painfully shy when he was young. Even now, socializing is a kind of burden to him. From a young age he used to weave stories in his head which he wrote down later. Saini has spent most of his life as an educator in Bandung. He has taught drama and poetry at both college and university level as well as the Philosophy of the Arts in a Catholic University. He was Director of the Academy of Dance in Bandung. From 1995 to 1999, he was Director of Arts in the Department of Education and Culture. He is known as the Father of Creativity in Bandung literary circles because of his life-long contributions to literature. He is noted for his plays, which are presented as comedies, tragicomedies and tragedies. He admits to being influenced by Brecht. He deals with crucial issues in Indonesia in his humanist–humanitarian way in his plays, poetry and novels.

His *Family of the Pure* is a play that throws light on fanaticism and religious violence in Indonesia. Apparently, some Indonesians are so inclined to learn about Islam that they spend their holidays studying the religion. This happened to two friends who joined a sect to learn about Islam. However this sect happened to be a fanatic group. Realizing their mistake, the two friends wanted to quit. But it was the rule of the sect to execute deserters in case the sect was betrayed to the government. One of the two friends was killed. Finally the fanatic group was suppressed.

A House in Argentina, which won an award, is based on the anti-Chinese riots of 1971. A Chinese family decided to buy a house in Argentina to escape from Indonesian violence. But it did not materialize when the head of the family decided to stay on because of his friendship with an old Indonesian army general whom he had once helped.

Who says I am Godot? presents the plight of a poor Indonesian couple who migrated from Jakarta but returned to it, homeless. Subsequently they were murdered. As ghosts they returned to this world with other ghosts wandering around because they could not find either Heaven or Hell. They realized their religious quarrels were meaningless. The title of the play is taken from the speech of a character who told the others that an annoyed member of the audience who wanted to watch a delayed demonstration of the martial art on stage had asked him 'Godot, why do you make us wait?'. The reply was, 'Who says I am Godot?'. Saini's plays were performed during the Saini Drama Festival held in Bandung in October 2002.

His works have been enriched by his knowledge of foreign languages and he is quite at home in Eastern as well as Western culture. He has four anthologies of poems: *The House of Mirrors, The Ten Delegates, Songs of the Motherland* and *The Red Rose*. The first and the fourth have been greatly influenced by Rainier Maria Rilke, the religious German poet whom he considers as one of the great poets of the Twentieth Century.

One of his favorite themes is his existential agonies concerning theological problems. As told to the writer, 'God is so elusive... I need him badly in my daily struggle as a person and citizen of my turbulent country'. In the poem, *The Old Man Whose Name is also Zacharias* he referred to a country ruled by a forged signatory where women sell their flesh and men their souls. It ends with advice to nail one's dream to the cross of reality. *The Ten Delegates* deals with the social-political problems of Indonesia. *Songs of the Motherland* are odes to his 'formerly beautiful and rich country'.

His anthology, entitled *The Red Rose,* blooms with 30 love poems focussing on the thrills, hopes, sorrows, longings and doubts of love. Here is one example, which shows the influence of Rilke's 'Autumn Day' and other poems:

A CLEAR POOL

Looking in the mirrors of each others' eyes
Thinking that we found something. That's the beginning
Finding something that gives meaning
To our lives. But what is it? What is it?

'God smiles at us.' You said to me, touching my hand,
'Just be grateful.' Still my excited heart asks:
How, while regulating all the galaxies, he still
Has the grace to place us in this Pavilion of Dreams?

As if looking into a clear pool
And though we know that this miracle will be erased
By the ripples when Summer forces a leaf to fall,
We have been here My Love, in one of His lovely dreams.

Saini's essays discuss the philosophy of the arts. They include his views on the theatre, the dramatist and the responsibilities of writers in presenting Truth. As a rebel, he also writes about social protest in literature. For almost half a century he has agonized over and written about life, love and God in all genres, ending triumphantly as SEA Write Awardee for 2001. It is a well deserved award for the Father of Creativity from Bandung.

Dilip Mukerjea

Dilip Mukerjea's father studied in Oxford (1939-1945) and his career was in management. It required him to travel a fair bit. Thus, since he was one year old, Dilip has been travelling the world. Familiar with the cultures of both East and West where he has lived and worked extensively, he has travelled to well over 30 countries. He is now Owner and Managing Director of the Buzan Centre, Singapore, where he has been based for the past ten years.

During his marine engineering course, he secured first place in the UK for the 1979 final examinations in this field, winning two internationally acclaimed awards for securing top marks in all his subjects. Eight years ago, he switched from being a marine engineer to a researcher and trainer in building brainpower. Nevertheless, he is still the technical director of a company. It enables him to engage in freelance marine consultancy work in conjunction with the training of technical, sales, marketing personnel and other department staff members of various organizations. His widespread experience of management has led him to believe that all personnel can excel through the development of their mental resources. Consequently they benefit not only themselves but also the institutions they represent.

As he informed the writer, creativity is his passion. Since he is dedicated to it and the advancement of Mental Literacy, his focus is directed on developing intellectual capital for the knowledge economy via strategies encompassing Creative Problem Solving and Solution Finding, Mind Mapping, Speed Reading,

Memory Enhancement and Lifescaping. He is the Regional Master Trainer for the Buzan Techniques and publicly acclaimed by Tony Buzan as 'easily one of the world's top ten Master Mind Mappers'. He has also undergone training from Dr Betty Edwards in Perceptual Skills in Drawing, learning to draw and drawing to learn. According to him, 'Anyone can draw as long as one learns how to see'. He believes that left and right modes of brain hemispheric activation are aimed at achieving cortical balance. Dilip calls this skill *Visual Intelligence*. He teaches it to members of corporations and society at diverse levels in the belief that verbal and visual skills dynamically complement each other.

Asked about the influence of culture on creativity, he replied, 'In brief, culture does have a significant impact on the emergence of creativity but not on inherent creativity. More open societies encourage creative output; paranoid societies stifle the slightest urge towards idea generation. The East was prolific in its creative output prior to the Industrial Revolution, following which the West whooshed off into the lead. The issue is attitudinal, not aptitudinal'. In his extensive travel, he also noticed creativity in action in the poorer sections of Thailand, Malaysia, Indonesia, India, Iran, Afghanistan, Bahrain, Pakistan, etc.

Dilip's personality could be described as fun-loving, cheerful, proactive, adventurous, creative, meticulous, insatiably curious and shaped by motive forces which include recognizing opportunity, developing focus and confidence, and having convictions and a philosophy of life. He loves jokes, reading, sports and martial arts, as well as learning in general across multiple domains.

He enjoys writing on brain skills for the 21st Century with immediate and multi-purpose application which is the prime aim of every skill. His best selling books, such as *Superbrain* and *Brainfinity*, have gone into several reprints. *Superbrain* has been written for those from '5 to 105', focussing on the fundamentals of Mind Mapping, Speed Reading and Memory Boosting. *Brainfinity* takes one on to much higher levels of Mind Mapping and Critical Thinking Skills. *Braindancing* is a metaphor for the joy of learning, the ecstasy within creativity and the innate genius of the reader.

His latest book, *Surfing the Intellect*, includes jokes like this one from Winston Churchill who was reputed to have said: 'There are only two things more difficult than making an after-dinner speech... one is climbing a wall that is leaning towards you and the other is kissing a girl who is leaning away from you'. The book tries to help the reader with creative problem solving, mental gymnastics, the training and development of memory, and peace of mind. Dilip is now writing seven books: *Brain Symphony, Brainchild, Lifescaping – Inspiring the Human Spirit, Brainaisssance, Primary Genius, The Transcendental Rickshaw Puller* and *Cash in Blood* "the last of which is being co-authored with Peter Ho, a Malaysian Chinese New Zealander.

Dilip's accomplishments have been recognized and included in the Millennium Edition of *Who's Who of the World* and *The Baron's 500: Leaders of the New Century*.

Felice Prudente Santa Maria

Felice Prudente Sta. Maria stood tall, sophisticated and elegant as the SEA Write Awardee in 2001, the chosen one from among 81 million Filipinos. It is a much deserved award for a life dedicated to service to her country and to Asia, as a writer, lecturer, photographer, cultural advocate and administrator.

In an autobiographical note sent to the writer she recalled, 'At the age of five in 1955, the public library across my kindergarten was quickly becoming a favourite spot. It was at the edge of the University of California where my father was taking his PhD in political science.' Her early American education of half a dozen years is probably an important factor that has influenced her to major in speech and drama for her BA in the University of the Philippines. She had also attended special courses in magazine publishing and management, and selected photography courses in New York City from 1976 to 1978. She is also experienced in radio and television scripting, announcing and programming, advertising, conceptualization and institutional PR writing.

When asked about how culture has influenced her creativity she replied, 'Cultural issues trigger my creativity.... The surroundings influence my adjectives and metaphors: *papaya red sunsets*; *as pure as coconut water fresh from the nut*. My culture offers me the liberal atmosphere to think. I have had strong doses of family life, different styles of living from conservative to truly not'. Her one page reply ends with 'My culture of no bounds is still forming me, concerning me, calling me'. She has found that one has a responsibility to fathom, choose a path and mature according to where that path leads.

Let us follow her path by looking at her personality test from *Colour your Life* by Howard and Dorothy Sun. She was told 'Blue is in your first position. You are soft, gentle and peaceful.... Your essence works on a spiritual level valuing qualities like truth and honesty'. Besides being interested in the above, she also had strong doses of formal Christian religion, both the Methodist and Roman Catholic kind. This religious influence may be observed in a poem, *The Lord's Hand on my Forehead* which she wrote at 4.30 am. It ends with:

The palm of the Lord wipes away all doubt...
making the heart rejoice in truth.
The mantle of care is a river of light...
and the Lord's voice is the first birdcall of the new day.

This poem was sent to the writer in response to a query whether she goes through the process of preparation, incubation, illumination and verification. She replied that she did not. She just sat down and wrote what she thought on the spur of the moment. According to her, the creative process can start with illumination.

Her versatility as a writer is seen in the wide range of topics in her essays on socio-political events, art and aesthetics, culinary history and cuisine, sociology, cultural environment development and values education. She has written exhibition text for major art exhibitions at the Metropolitan Museum of Manila. Her pioneering advocacy of Filipino language text for museum exhibitions with

English adaptations has found followers in the Philippine museum section including national institutions. She promoted the understanding of photography as art by supporting foreign exhibitions on loan by major photographers such as Cartier Bresson. She began the first travelling exhibition using local photographs for the simultaneous teaching of aesthetic and values education in the 1980s and 1990s. She is still supporting the growth of photography for arts and social development. Recently, she started a column in a newspaper for readers interested in cuisine and culinary skills. She is advocating good food for good health and life too.

She is a cultural administrator. When the National Commission for Culture and the Arts was created by Congress in 1992 she became the first Commissioner for Cultural Heritage. Since 1993 she has been Commissioner, UNESCO National Commission of the Philippines. Her first initiative was to provide a social and human science framework of major concepts, situational basis and heritage properties for the teaching of social studies and citizenship education and cultural policy leadership. As a leader in cultural policy formation she had to get others interested in understanding the need to rank historical sites and other tangible cultural assets and how to create laws related to tangible and intangible cultural properties. As founding member of the Asia Pacific Network for International and Values Education she offers technical advice and support to UNESCO towards establishing peace, human rights and democracy.

In the Philippines, she is a catalyst for cultural development. In 1988 she introduced the first teacher's aid, relating to a coffee table book of photos of ethnic communities by Eduardo Masferré and sponsored by Mobil-Philippines. It was a pioneering bilingual aid. She wrote the first coffee table book that is an adult civic education aid for Filipino democrats in 1998, entitled *Visions of the Possible*. It values cultural action as civic action and clearly cites gains made from the Philippine Revolution which are often overlooked by the focus of historical chronology.

Her book, *A Cultural Worker's First Manual: Essays in Appreciating the Everyday*, is the first guide book attempted for cultural workers in the Philippines. It includes definitions of basic working terms and answers to some of the common questions cultural workers are likely to ask. It helps cultural workers better understand that they are responsible for helping people handle and cope with change. The book emphasizes that cultural development impacts on human development. For Felice, cultural development raises the standard of being in contrast to the standard of living.

She sets very high standards for her writing as can be seen in the awards she has won. Awards were given her for her books: *Household Heirlooms and Antiques, Dynamic Partnerships: a Fusion of Power and Vision, Discovering Philippine Art in Spain, Visions of the Possible: Legacies of Freedom, The Eldest Child* (fiction for children), and *In Excelsis: The Vision and Mission of Jose P. Rizal, Humanist and Philippine National Hero*. A recent laurel was the National Book Award in the Reference Book Category presented by the Manila Critics Circle in September 2002 for her book, *A Cultural Worker's First Manual: Essays in Appreciating the Everyday*.

Other awards accorded to her include Dangal Ng Haraya (freely translated as Tribute to Imagination), the highest recognition of the National Commission for Culture and Arts for Cultural Management. It is a lifetime achievement award being given for the first time. She received the Women of Distinction Award in Cultural Education, University of the Philippine Alumni Association Outstanding Professional Award in Arts and Letters and the Philippine Centennial Commission Award. She was awarded the French Knighthood, (Le Grand Orde des Arts et Lettres) for her cultural work as president of an art museum and as an opinion page columnist advocating cultural awareness. This award, together with her work for UNESCO and other organizations, has made Felice Prudente Sta Maria internationally known.

Professor Leonard Yong

At the tender age of five, Leonard Yong learned to be resourceful when his father passed away in 1957. He helped his family to earn a living. Less than forty years later he rose from poverty to be promoted as one of the youngest professors in the University of Malaya. He was the founder-director for the Centre of Continuing Education there from 1998 to 2002. He is now Management Consultant for an international consultancy group based in the United Kingdom. He has clients from all parts of the world.

Much of his success could be attributed to his personality. According to his own LEONARD Personality Inventory (Let's Explore our personality based on Openness, Neutral, Analytical, Relational and Decisive behavioral tendencies) his is the *Accomplisher Profile*, comprising neutral and decisive preferences. His neutral tendency (which equates with agreeableness in the Big Five Model) is outstanding. He is very cool and calm in handling problems. He is decisive in whatever he wishes to accomplish for himself and others. His proactive creative intelligence makes him 'work smart' cheerfully each day. He is noted for his interpersonal intelligence and diplomacy. Professor Yong, who is a member of our Malaysian Psychological Association as well as the American Psychological Association, uses psychology effectively. Angry clients who consult him leave their anger behind when they leave his office.

He started his career as a Mathematics and Chemistry teacher in St. John's Institution in Kuala Lumpur before becoming a lecturer in the University of Malaya in 1981. In 1984 he started his PhD thesis to research on the creativity of 16 year old students in Malaysia. One of his findings was that the creative abilities of the students in the study were comparable to American students of similar age. Another finding was that the social-economic status of the pupils had no bearing on their creativity. His three-way analysis of variance using sex, SES (social economic status) and cognitive levels as the independent variables makes use of seven components of creativity (figural originality, flexibility, fluency and elaboration; verbal originality, flexibility and fluency). Taking account of home environment and overall figural and verbal creativity, he found that boys are significantly more creative than girls. In the early 1990s he compared the creativity of Malaysian, Japanese and American children based on the Torrance Test of Creative Thinking (TTCT). Very interesting examples are found in his book, *The Joy of Creativity*, based on his findings.

Professor Yong was awarded a Fulbright Scholarship in 1992 to study the creativity of Americans. He noted that they value and display originality. In 1993 he was awarded the Japan Foundation Research Fellowship to study the creativity of the Japanese. He found that their main characteristic is elaborative creativity, that is, they tend to improve on existing products. According to Professor Yong, Southeast Asians also tend to display a similar type of creativity to the Japanese. In 2000, he was appointed Senior Research Fellow for the European Studies Programme in Bocconi University, Italy where he conducted personality research and found that the Italians demonstrate a high openness to new ideas.

Professor Yong has been consulted for a number of projects on Innovation and Creative Thinking in Malaysia. One of his earliest was when he served as a psychological and research consultant for market survey companies, as well as the quantitative research consultant for the National Productivity Centre, Ministry of Trade and Industry, Malaysia. He has also been a consultant for countries such as Papua New Guinea, Singapore and Indonesia. For the last seven years his focus has been to help corporate managers become more creative through profiling their personality with the LEONARD Personality Inventory. Therefore he could help them improve their creative behaviors from their understanding of what was lacking in their creativity. His Inventory, published in 2000, has 16 personality profiles ranging from the Creative Imaginator to the Versatile Person.

He has served as External PhD Examiner for the National University of Singapore and the University of Brunei. He is Honorary Adjunct Professor for the University of South Australia's Doctoral Program in the International Graduate School of Management. Based on his LEONARD Personality Inventory and the LP1 Software and its use in helping individuals to develop their *emotional intelligence* and creativity, Professor Yong has addressed groups in many countries - in America, Australia, Europe, the Middle East and Asia. His students include Associate Professor, Dr Ananda Kumar, one of Creativity's Global Correspondents and Dr Chia Chee Fen.

Professor Yong has co-authored *The Creative Teacher* (published in Malay) with Fulbright Visiting Professor Karen L. Biraimah who was in Malaysia in 1994. His most recent book is *Creative Malaysians* which he co-authored with his research assistant, the writer. This book includes a linguist who knows almost 30 languages, a writer who can write well in all genres of literature, an artist who can paint four paintings almost simultaneously, a brilliant scientist, and other outstanding Malaysians. His articles have appeared in journals such as *Perceptual & Motor Skills*, *The Journal of Creative Behavior* and *Education Quarterly*.

The above study is a follow-up to the study of *Creative Malaysians*. It draws its inspiration from writers like Howard Gardner, Edward de Bono, Tony Buzan and Joyce Chapman. I would like to thank all of them and my four subjects who patiently answered all my questions, as well as Dr. Ng Aik Kwang whose book helped as a launching pad for this chapter.

References

Buzan, Tony (2000) *Head First. 10 Ways to Tap into your Genius*. London: Thorson.

De Bono, Edward (1992) *Serious Creativity*. London: Harper Collins.

Gardner, Howard (1997) *Extraordinary Minds*. New York: Basic books.

Ng Aik Kwang (2001) *Why Asians are Less Creative than Westerners*. Singapore: Prentice Hall.

Tan, Dawn (2002) *Daughters of Asia. Inspiring Stories of Southeast Asian Women Leaders*. Singapore: Flame of the Forest.

Yong, Leonard and Lee, Alice (2002) *Creative Malaysians*. Kuala Lumpur: Leonard Personality Incorporated.

Yong, Leonard (2000) *The Leonard Personality Inventory*. Kuala Lumpur: Leonard Personality Incorporated.

Zulfi Hussain

Synergy of East and West for greater creativity

Introduction

There has been a great deal of interest in creative thinking within the business world over the last couple of decades. Almost all businesses, large and small, consider themselves to be creative, but too often they only pay lip service to the importance of creativity. The same applies to many governments and educational institutions around the world.

However, creativity has been the real driving force over the ages, behind the development of technology, the economy, the arts and culture. This chapter examines creativity from historical, religious, cultural and technological perspectives and explores how the synergy of East and West has contributed and no doubt will continue to contribute to greater creativity. It is fair to say that the understanding and definition of creativity may differ between Eastern and Western cultures. The traditional Eastern culture is more conservative, while the modern culture of the West is more liberal. But in terms of creative thinking, their influences and contributions are equally significant. However, the contribution of the East is often underplayed and at times totally sidelined or forgotten.

Religion and creativity

Religious beliefs both in the East and West have made a significant contribution to the creativity debate. For example, the Hindus translated their concept of nothingness into 'zero'; the Muslims determined exactly the phases of the moon so as to worship Allah correctly; the Christians of Europe charted the passage of the seasons and their holy days according to the rotation of the Earth around the Sun. The daily lives and religious beliefs of these culturally diverse people have led to the use of wisdom and creativity to chart the passage of time.

In the 7th Century, c. 622 AD, Islam emerged from the arid sands of Arabia. It is a religion so progressive in its philosophy and dynamic in its scope and creativity that it revolutionised society at that time, and changed the world forever. Soon, this new religion powered its way into the deepest interiors of Africa, Asia and Europe not by the sword but by the power of ideas. So vigorous was its impact that today, almost one-quarter of the world's population claims adherence to it. The unfolding history of Islamic civilization has been, without doubt, one of humanity's grandest achievements. To a far greater extent than Western records might suggest, it was Islam that laid the cultural and scientific foundations on which the modern world is based. The Muslim scholars reclaimed the ancient wisdom of the Greeks, while Europe languished in the Dark Ages. It was the Muslim scholars who sowed the seeds of the

Renaissance, 600 years before the birth of Leonardo da Vinci. From the way we heal the sick to the numerals we use for counting, cultures across the globe have been shaped by Islamic civilization. All this began with the life of a single ordinary man and a profound message he proclaimed that would change the world forever. Mohammed (may peace be upon him) the Prophet of Islam and Messenger of God said that:

The ink of the scholar is more holy than the blood of a martyr.

One hour spent thinking about (contemplating) the works of the Creator is worth more than seventy years of prayer.

One learned man gives more grief to the Devil than a thousand worshippers.

Seek new knowledge even unto China.

The powerful message of the Prophet placed great emphasis on learning, thinking and creativity as illustrated by these quotations. For example, China was a long way from Arabia, where travel was almost impossible across a land of savage scarcity.

The West owes a substantial debt of gratitude to the Islamic world for its preservation of, expansion upon and transmission of the Hellenistic sciences, including philosophy, astronomy, medicine, logic and mathematics. However, there are seismic transformations that took place within the Islamic world-view which made possible the acceptance and assimilation of Greek thought that are very rarely discussed and hence little understood. With the establishment of the Abbasid Empire in the early Eighth Century, and the relocation of the caliphate and capital from Damascus to Baghdad, Muslim rulers and thinkers began what was to become an extraordinary feat of translation and appropriation of the great texts of ancient and classical learning.

Historically throughout the Muslim World, the search for knowledge, science and creativity was undertaken in an effort to improve Society as a form of worship. This creative approach resulted in the development of medicine, the construction and provision of hospitals, the building of hundreds of schools and libraries, the planting of countless beautiful gardens and green parks, and so much more, making the Muslim World an oasis of light in a dark surrounding. Islam's stress on creativity, excellence and its search for perfection was crucial to the progress of its civilisation. This explains the advanced levels of knowledge that the Muslims reached in astronomy, surgery, ophthalmology and map making. It also explains how the Muslims managed to develop the empirical method, mathematics and physics, produce extremely accurate instruments and write scientific and scholarly works of the greatest detail, precision and excellence.

The same fervour and faith that propelled Muslims to spread Islam across the world was also found in learning and education with creativity at its heart. When so many individuals – a whole society – are motivated for betterment and are animated by such faith and fervour to learn, invent and create, it is no surprise that a great civilisation, characterised by science, art and scholarship rapidly came into being in a huge and unequalled explosion.

Creativity – East v West

In the West, many artists and creators view creativity as something to do. This leads to the perception that only hard work is required to create the best works. Yet, we all know that there are many great artists that don't need to overwork to succeed, while others need to work very hard.

A person's creativity is often influenced by their individual viewpoint on creativity which suggests that one way to increase creativity is to understand how we view creativity itself and especially how it works for each one of us. Therefore, we cannot teach creativity to a group of people and expect them to perform similarly. This seems so obvious, but creativity is rarely taught in that way. Hence we need to revisit the traditional way of teaching creativity and develop new and innovative tools and techniques.

The Eastern philosophies such as Buddhism and Taoism have some components relative to creativity, which suggest that we cannot create adequately from the control and illusion of the mind. It is believed that we must go beyond it, beyond its power and just let the mind be free to express anything it wants. We need to learn to loosen control and let the mind be, because as soon as we try to create, i.e. 'to do it', we start controlling. Instead of forcing anything, we need to let it come, or more appropriately, we must give it a chance to come. It is fair to say that this does not always work for everyone.

If we look at the 5000 years of Chinese history, we can find many illuminating examples of creativity and inventiveness. These include the invention of paper, gunpowder, printing and the compass. We can also find outstanding works of great thinkers like Confucius, Mencius, Lao Zi and Zhuang Zi. Despite all these achievements, there has been no similar breakthrough for the last 1000 years. The cause of this stagnancy is linked to the historical traits of a very long period of feudalism of some 2000 years and the rigid and deeply entrenched Imperial Examination System.

By comparison, the feudal period in Europe was much shorter and was followed by over 200 years of the Renaissance, a movement spurred on by the call to revive the arts of classical Greece. This was seen as a revolution in intellectual thought and inventiveness. The Enlightenment and the Industrial Revolution that followed caused a tumultuous transformation as a result of Europe shaking off its feudal shackles in ideology and social systems. This led to Europe producing many new creations and inventions in the realms of art, science, music, architecture and so on.

If we turn to the United States, we find that in the last 200 years many new opportunities for self-development have been created. The favourable conditions offered by the US have attracted many high calibre immigrants from around the world. The amalgamation of Eastern and Western cultures and thinking has resulted in many new ideas being unearthed and breakthroughs being achieved in economics, science and culture, making the US the only superpower in the world today. On the whole, the historical circumstances in the West over the past few centuries have provided very favourable conditions for creativity and inventiveness. Many of the new scientific ideas and theories have come about as a result of the clash of Eastern and Western cultures and the resolution of this conflict. Whether it is Hegel's idealism or Engel's materialism, they all converge at a common point: the resolution of conflict. Creativity, in my view, is a multi-level and complex thought process, involving many different factors. I passionately believe that gleaning the best from both the East and West to resolve the conflict is the best and most fruitful way forward.

In order to understand Western culture and its effect on creativity, we need to look at its characteristics. Western culture from a scientific viewpoint is reflected in making bold hypotheses followed by meticulous search for evidence. The scientific experiment is used to verify the soundness of the hypothesis and/or to improve or expose it. It is due to these cultural traits that Westerners are more used to making bold hypotheses. As a result, many important and revolutionary discoveries have been made over the years. The downside to this approach is that some of these new ideas and hypotheses may not have solid foundations, but this is a minor drawback where creativity is concerned.

From my personal experience and research I have found that another distinct characteristic of Western culture is the emphasis on individual contribution. This trait is manifested in the idolisation of individual heroes in Western culture and creativity. The individual's heroic exploits and contributions are placed above collective effort. The advantage of this is that it can spur people on to greater heights. The downside is that it results in self-centred individualism, which indirectly affects creativity.

The traditional Eastern system places great emphasis on building a solid foundation, and then building up the basic knowledge step by step. However, in my view, Eastern tradition places too much emphasis on foundations. The insistence on rote learning, for example, has robbed people of the initiative to make bold hypotheses about new situations and new problems. Another very distinct and obvious trait of Eastern culture is humility in learning.

As we move forward we will no doubt witness an explosion of human knowledge and technology. Individuals will no longer know everything about anything. Under these circumstances, the unique and innovative ideas that creativity requires, as well as the grasp of new ideas and new situations, will be difficult to come by. Humility and prudence in my view will prove invaluable for sorting out the thought process and assisting creative innovators as they move forward on the voyage to new discoveries.

I have also found that the relationship between Eastern and Western cultures and creativity is multi-faceted and has much to offer. I believe that if we synergise the essence of Eastern and Western cultures, and seek a new direction amidst the clashes and contradictions, we can achieve a greater breakthrough in creativity for the mutual benefit of both East and West.

What can I do to increase my creativity?

I believe the short answer is to use the power of the subconscious and just relax or simply take a walk. Just think how many of the great ideas have been born when people have been sitting around, walking, jogging, bathing or driving? Our subconscious mind is constantly processing the ideas and stimuli received consciously. I find that a useful technique is to actively work on a problem before going to sleep and then allow the subconscious to take over. Then review and record any ideas when you awake.

I don't believe that there is any sure way of guaranteeing success in creating great ideas. A structured approach can be good but can be a stumbling block for many. True inspiration is not physically measurable, nor tangible in any concrete way. Creativity cannot be limited, and therefore anything which limits cannot contain creativity.

Conclusions

It is clear that both Eastern and Western cultures and civilisations have made outstanding contributions in areas such as art, culture, mathematics, science and technology. These continue to influence our thinking and the way we live today. Much of this contribution has its roots in religion, be it Buddhism, Christianity, Hinduism or Islam.

If we have a creative and scientific age today, it is because of the Muslim scholars of the middle ages. If we have advances in the arts, culture, medicine, space exploration, computer science and technology, then it is down to the creativity of the Muslims and their gift of knowledge to the West.

There is a great deal of synergy to be found in the thinking and creativity of the East and West. By drawing on the essence of Eastern and Western cultures, and seeking a new direction amidst the clashes and contradictions, we can achieve a greater breakthrough in creativity for the mutual benefit of both East and West.

Kathy Goff

Women's creative development

Traditional tests have neglected the competencies important to real-world performance, thereby neglecting the competencies of most women. The intelligence testing movement originated in attempts to predict the academic competence of men and so concerned itself with the prediction of school performance. Using familiar situations with prior knowledge and reasoning may be sufficient in school and on intelligence tests, but it is not very effective in solving real world problems or meeting the challenges of everyday life.

Daily we are required to use our creativity to deal with the unexpected and ever changing world. We know very little about the creative processes of everyday life. Most creativity research has focused primarily on men and on exceptional or extraordinary creativity, not the kind we use every day. Consequently, we know very little about the creativity used every day to navigate life and survive. And we know very little about the creativity of women.

Creativity

Creative thinking is much more than using our imaginations to invent lots of new ideas. Creative thinking is a lifestyle, a personality trait, a way of looking at the world, a way of interacting with others and a way of living and growing. Living creatively means developing our talents, tapping our unused potentials and becoming what we are capable of becoming through self-discovery and self-discipline. Anytime we are faced with a problem or dilemma with no learned or practiced solution, some creativity is required (Torrance, 1995). It takes courage to be creative.

Creativity is a vital ingredient in meeting the challenges of a continuous life cycle, a cycle in which growth and change are the norm from conception throughout life. A life filled with growth and change requires a conscious effort to think creatively; it takes practice. To develop creativeness, the mind needs to be exercised, as well as filled with materials out of which ideas can be formed. The richest fuel for ideation is first hand experience (Osborn, 1963).

Creativity is the ability to see a situation in many ways and continue to question until satisfaction is reached. This satisfaction can be defined in as many different ways as there are people experiencing it, but it basically boils down to personal satisfaction and how you choose to define satisfaction.

The creative process can involve tiny creative leaps or giant breakthroughs in thinking. Both require that an individual go beyond where she has gone before, embracing the unknown, the mysterious, the change, the puzzling, without fear. Creativity involves risk-taking. Whether it's a small risk or a huge risk, it takes courage to take a risk and be creative.

Creative potential is the ability to respond constructively and in non-habitual ways to change and stress. A substantial body of evidence indicates that males and females perform at similar levels on tests designed to measure creative potential (Torrance, 1983). Creativity measures are consistently better predictors of women's creative achievements than are measures of intelligence (Torrance, 1972). As IQ tests are based on learning cultivated and valued by men, traditional learning settings are generally not the best learning environments for females (McCracken, 1997).

Creativity and women

A balance of feminine and masculine intellectual and personal qualities appears basic to creative endeavors (Helson, 1973). Our overemphasis or misplaced emphasis on sex roles is a serious block to the development of many talents, especially creative talents (Torrance, 1995). Creativity, by its very nature, requires sensitivity and independence. In our culture, sensitivity is a feminine virtue, while independence is a masculine virtue. Girls are encouraged to speak quietly, avoid math and sciences classes, defer to boys, and value neatness over participation and appearance over intelligence (Sadker & Sadker, 1994). Rarely do women become scientific discoverers, inventors or composers. Very few women have made contributions to theories of creativity.

There is little doubt that society's attitudes towards, and treatment of, girls and women influences their creative development and behavior (Torrance, 1972). Many areas of experiences are placed off limits to girls, which interferes with their natural gifts and what they might become as women (McCracken, 1997; Torrance, 1965). Helson (1996) compared highly creative women with less creative women and found the former were:

- more ambitious
- confident
- had a stronger sense of purpose
- needed partners and relationships that support creativity.

In Maslow's study of positively healthy, self-actualizing people he changed his ideas about creativity. Maslow (1987, p.159) described one woman as uneducated, poor, a full-time housewife and mother who was not creative by traditional standards, yet was a marvelous cook, mother, wife and homemaker. With little money, her home was somehow always beautiful. She was a perfect hostess and her meals were banquets. Her taste in linen, silver, glass and furniture was impeccable. She was original, novel, ingenious, unexpected and inventive in all of these areas. He just had to call her creative. He learned from her and others like her to think that a first-rate soup is more creative than a second-rate painting, and that generally cooking, parenthood and/or making a home can be creative, while poetry can be uncreative.

Creative innovation is facilitated by certain social roles that are not usually available to women (Helson, 1978). Creativity investigators have concerned themselves only with creative men and masculine areas of interest or with the question of why women are not creative (*ibid.*). Male judges of creative contributions tend to favor work similar to their own. Women's contributions do not customarily receive the same recognition. Pohlman (1996) suggests that creativity may be more of a social process, dramatically affected by social environments and institutions, than simply a psychological trait inherent in individuals.

Until recently, most publicized and depicted roles for women were those of tradition – housewife, secretary, nurse, etc. Only lately have women begun to reach levels of recognized success in roles previously off limits to women – professional basketball player, CEO of a Fortune 500 company, senator, investment broker, doctor, governor, etc. These successes will contribute to changes in the history we teach our children.

By excluding women from the textbooks we study and the stories we tell, women have been relegated to a second class citizen status. The perception is that women must not have contributed to Wall Street or scientific discoveries. Women become invisible and are perceived as being incapable of such contributions. Despite the increasing number of women entering the public arena, they remain relatively rare in the elite levels of the arts, sciences, letters, finance, politics and ranks of the eminent (Noble, Subotnik & Arnold, 1999).

Women and learning

In general, women are relational learners whose motivation to learn depends upon how relevant it is to their lives. Most of women's valued lessons are learned with friends, colleagues, via life crises, transitions and community involvement. Women tend to place emphasis on relevance and personal meaning in what is taught and how we feel about that information. For many women, the truth is personal, particular and grounded in first hand experience (Belenky, Clinchy, Goldberger & Tarule, 1986). However, most school environments place emphasis on inanimate facts and figures, with no opportunities to personalize the learning.

Human experience has traditionally been defined using the patterns of the male experience. Male attributes are valued, studied and articulated, while those associated with the feminine tend to be ignored. The analytical, masculine styles of most school and work environments generally do not encourage nor foster relational learning, thereby denying many girls and women equal opportunities for learning. Kaplan (1995) indicates that new ways of seeing girls and women and human possibilities can come from women bringing to light their own unique ways of operating.

Generally, men and women approach learning differently. The feminine approach to learning focuses on: negotiation, feelings, understanding, personal relationships and intuitive, other oriented, win-win outcomes. A growing body of literature on women's development has begun to illuminate issues regarding women's learning styles (Belenky, Clinchy, Goldberger & Tarule, 1986; Gilligan, 1982, 1993; Goldberger, Tarule, Clinchy & Belenky, 1996; McCracken, 1997).

Women have grown up with historically and culturally ingrained definitions of womanhood in which women, like children, should be seen and not heard. The majority of voiceless students in typical college classrooms are women (Sadker & Sadker, 1994). Women in college and university classes speak less and are interrupted more (Reis, 1998). Many women fear that others will condemn or hurt them if they speak, that others won't listen or understand, that it is better to be 'selfless' and give up their voices to keep the peace (Gilligan, 1993). By not speaking, women are giving up a powerful instrument and channel that connects the inner and outer worlds.

Women typically approach adulthood with the understanding that the care and empowerment of others is central to their life's work (Belenky et al., 1983). Tradition teaches a woman that getting something for herself is selfish and will deprive others, since her role is that of caretaker and nurturer who sacrifices her needs for those of her family and others. In everyday and professional life, women often feel unheard or discouraged from pursuing unfeminine work or roles. Only with the help of mentors have women been encouraged to pursue creative achievements or to think of themselves first.

Most women have cooperative and collaborative learning styles which value experience and connecting with others (Gilligan, 1993). Belenky et al. (1986) believe that connected knowing comes more easily to many women than does separate knowing. Girls respond well to working cooperatively in a relaxed atmosphere with hands-on experiences (AAUW Report, 1995). For many girls and women, successful learning takes place in an atmosphere of collaboration and opportunities for exploring diversity of opinion. Pearson (1992) cited that most women prefer:

- collaborative, intimate learning settings
- learning experiences which integrate theory with practice
- cognitive processes which utilize feeling, empathy and thought.

Learning is more than the accumulation of new knowledge; it is a process where many basic values and assumptions, by which we operate, are changed through our learning processes (Mezirow, 1978). Increasing awareness of gender related differences will increase levels of understanding and awareness. Learning environments that are collaborative, creative and caring provide the support that many girls and women need to excel. Creative work and personal happiness come through finding environments which celebrate success and individual differences (Reis, 1998).

Development

As children, before we begin our traditional learning experiences, we are expert learners who use all our senses and motor capabilities to learn. We learn by experiencing, such as sticking a crayon into our mouths, ears or noses. We learn by seeing what the crayon can do, such as drawing, mashing, eating or crumbling it. We learn by comparing the crayon to other things that mark or are colorful. All of us begin life as experiential and relational learners. It seems logical then to believe that education must validate these processes of learning in order to meet the needs of all learners, not just those who do well on pre-determined standards.

Children are experts in creative ways of learning and self-expression. They have considerable experience in questioning, inquiring, searching, manipulating, experimenting, creating, exploring and playing. However, as children enter school, many restrictions are placed on their manipulativeness and curiosity. Schools target the cognitive and intellectual areas for development, with the areas of intuition, affect and self-expression being left to develop on their own. As a consequence, many children do not learn to express themselves or their creativity and do not learn to deal with personal difficulties in a healthy manner.

One of the most consistent findings in creativity research with children is that discontinuities in creative development often result in loss of interest in learning, increased behavioral problems and more emotional disturbances (Torrance, 1977). These periods are at times so extremely stressful that an individual's creativity is inhibited, reduced or unnecessarily lost as she or he ages. As children age into adulthood there are more obstacles to the development of their creativity and self-expressiveness. These obstacles include pressure to conform, ridicule of unusual ideas, the drive for success and rewards based on others' demands and standards, and intolerance of a playful attitude. It is far too common for people to grow up and lose touch with their creativity and inner potential.

Learning by doing should not be left to chance, but should be part of the guidance we give to learners of all ages. We need to offer opportunities for learners to explore and examine core subjects creatively. Creative thinking and learning involve such abilities as evaluation, redefinition, analysis, divergent production and problem solving abilities. Creative learning is a natural, healthy human process that occurs when people become curious or excited about understanding or knowing more.

A model

Although development is a continuous process, discontinuities or pauses do occur in the developmental flow. These can occur in childhood and continue throughout life. Due to societal enculturation and expectations, creativity tends to develop differently in women and men. The following model supposes that creativity is an innate ability whose development occurs in stages.

The model of women's creative development below is based on the works of Maslow and Torrance. Maslow's hierarchical model of development is a broad based triangle with self-actualization at the highest but smallest peak; in this model, an individual is not likely to engage in creative activities (self-actualization) until s/he has met all the other needs. Whilst my model of women's creative development is similar to Maslow's conception, it has an open-ended V depicting self-actualization as limitless. Encasing the developmental stages in a V rather than a closed triangle is a better reflection of how creative development occurs. The V formation indicates the infiniteness of self-actualization and proportional amounts of creativity needed at each stage of development. The broken lines of the model represent the transitional and flexible nature of creative development.

Needs

Self-actualization
--- --- --- --- ---
Esteem needs
--- --- --- ---
Social needs
--- --- ---
Survival
needs

Stages

Survival needs are our physical needs including food, clothing, shelter, safety, health, care and nurturing. These basic needs must be satisfied first. Many single women head of households find themselves here trying to feed, clothe and keep a roof over the heads of their families. The creative process, at this stage, is focused on 'making do with what we have', i.e. surviving.

Once the survival needs are being met, we progress on to meeting our social and emotional needs. This second stage involves using creativity to meet these needs. Social needs include developing relationships with neighbors, family, friends, groups, communities, etc. This involves the development of human connections to outside supports. Meeting our social needs involves the development of empathy, the empowerment of others, and rewarding external relationships. The creative process, at this stage, is expressed in terms of a group process, such as fundraising, art shows or civic activities. At this stage, creativity may be focused primarily on benefiting and caring for others, roles which are generally acceptable and available to women.

The esteem needs focus on self-confidence, self-worth, self-discovery and the mental needs of life. Personal validation is a major factor at this stage of development, involving the identification of personal, inner strengths. Many women do not know what their strengths are because they have never stopped to think about themselves in terms of their personal ideas, dreams and abilities. Meeting esteem needs involves developing the courage to express individual ideas in the face of ridicule and rejection.

Meeting spiritual needs comprises the fourth stage of creative development or self-actualization. Maslow (1959) developed the concept of self-actualization and defined it as an ongoing process of making growth choices. Self-actualization involves the full use and exploitation of talents, capacities, potentialities, abilities, etc. Maslow found that creativity is a universal characteristic of self-actualizing people. Self-actualizing creativeness involves boldness, courage, freedom, spontaneity, integration and self-acceptance. Maslow (1987) described self-actualizing creativity as being almost synonymous with health and humanness.

Steps

My conception of creative development is synonymous with learning. Each stage depicted in the above model involves three developmental steps (as in Torrance's *Incubation Model of Teaching*, Torrance & Safter, 1990). These steps are 1) Awareness of a problem dilemma, challenge or a curiosity to learn more. This step involves the creative spark or idea; 2) Acceptance of the need to learn. This involves inquiry, investigation, research etc. and 3) Incorporation of what has been learned. This involves understanding and using this new learning in our lives. It is characterized by action, practice, experimentation and integration and is concerned with personal relevance, meaning and satisfaction.

An individual may be on any step or at any stage of development at any given time since creative development involves transitions and is multi-dimensional. Because of society's attitudes towards, and treatment of females and because many areas of experience have been traditionally off limits to them, it is necessary to have a better understanding of their creative development.

What can be done to help?

Education can help by emphasizing (Belenky et al., 1986, p229):

- understanding and acceptance over assessment
- collaboration over debate – most women find the experience of being doubted debilitating rather than energizing
- respect – and allowing time for knowledge that emerges from firsthand experience.

Various strategies have been used to enhance and foster women's learning. One approach is that of mentoring and a second is an instructional model, the Torrance Incubation Model of Teaching, used successfully by women in learning environments.

Mentoring
Mentoring of female students by women scientists (Association for Women in Science, 1993) may be particularly crucial for attracting and retaining women in science because women are socialized to value connection (Rosser, 1997). The model for fostering women's learning advocates a connected approach to learning where life experiences are valued (Merriam & Caffarella, 1998). The connected approach to learning involves support and nurturance of every learner; where learners develop their own voices and see themselves as capable of being constructors of knowledge rather than just recipients (ibid.).

Most women have different learning needs than most men, who represent the dominant and traditional culture (Tisdell, 1995). Recognition of women's talents by a teacher or another significant person in their lives is vital to their development as both people and artists (Kirschenbaum & Reis, 1997). Mentoring has proved to be a powerful vehicle for women in developing their creativity and confidence and appears to be an essential element of successful programs for recruiting and retaining women.

Instructional model
Torrance's Incubation Model of Teaching (Torrance & Safter) was first published in 1990. Torrance had researched the model for 22 years before publishing it. This three-stage model has been used successfully in planning courses and lessons, developing instructional materials and making instructions more effective for students and adults of all ages (Torrance & Safter, 1990). According to Torrance (1965, 1979, 1987), many things can be learned more economically and effectively if they are learned in creative ways rather than by authority.

In 1990, the Incubation Model was used to develop an interdisciplinary, innovative curriculum that was delivered to older adults in rural settings. Evidence indicated that this increased participants' creativity scores significantly when experimental and control groups were compared (Goff, 1992).

Torrance's model has proven to be very effective in teaching adults as well as children. In courses with only women enrolled, this model was used successfully in instructing the students and in the development and delivery of lessons by the students. The Incubation Model is an effective method for transforming traditional curricula into a more women-friendly format.

Conclusion

There continues to be an unequal ratio of successful women to men in creative fields. This can easily be seen in the large numbers of highly successful, recognized creative men in traditionally feminine pursuits, such as fashion design, hair styling, art, interior design, cooking, etc. The reverse is not true. There are very few successful, recognized creative women in traditionally masculine pursuits, such as politics, law, medicine, business, etc. (Noble, Subotnik & Arnold, 1999).

Why is this? Women have been enculturated to stay in the background and follow the male lead. Women tend to attribute their success to luck, while men attribute their success to ability (Kerr, 1994). The longstanding tradition of excluding women from public life has meant that women's experiences have been largely overlooked in research and theories of talent development (Noble, Subotnik, & Arnold, 1999). Women have as much work to do within themselves to break down stereotypes, self-defeating attitudes and negative self-talk, as they do in the outside world.

Educational emphasis must be placed on nurturing the creativity of girls and women. According to Sadker and Sadker (1994, p14), 'if the cure for cancer is forming in the mind of one of our daughters, it is less likely to become a reality than if it is forming in the mind of one of our sons. Until this changes, everyone loses'. Creativity is not a gender specific ability, but its recognition, acknowledgement and development are.

References

AAUW Report (1995) *How Schools Shortchange Girls*. New York: Marlowe & Co.

Association for Women in Science (1993). *A Hand Up: Women Mentoring Women in Science*. (D. Fort, Ed.) Washington, DC: Author.

Belenky, M. F., Clinchy, B. M., Goldgerger, N. R. and Tarule, J. M. (1986) *Women's Ways of Knowing*. New York: Basic Books.

Gilligan, C. (1982) *In a Different Voice*. Cambridge, MA: Harvard University Press.

Gilligan, C. (1993) *In a Different Voice*. Cambridge, MA: Harvard University Press.

Goff, K. (1992) Enhancing creativity in older adults. *Journal of Creative Behavior*, 26 (1), 40-49.

Goldberger, N., Tarule, J., Clinchy, B. and Belenky, M. (1996) *Knowledge, Difference and Power*. New York: Basic Books.

Helson, R. M. (1973) Heroic and tender modes in women authors of fantasy. *Journal of Personality*, 41, 493-512.

Helson, R. M. (1978) Creativity in women. In J. A. Sherman and F. L. Denmark (Eds.) *The Psychology of Women: Future Directions in Research,* 555-604. New York: Psychological Dimensions, Inc.

Helson, R. M. (1996) In search of the creative personality. *Creativity Research Journal*, 9, 295-306.

Kaplan, K. L. (1995) Women's voices in organizational development: Questions, stories and implications. *Journal of Organizational Change Management*, 8 (1), 52-90.

Kerr, B. A. (1994) *Smart Girls Two: A New Psychology of Girls, Women and Giftedness*. Dayton, OH: Ohio Psychology Press.

Kirschenbaum, R. J. and Reis, S. M. (1997) Conflicts in creativity: Talented female artists. *Creativity Research Journal*, 10 (2 & 3), 251-63.

Maslow, A. H. (1959) Creativity and self-actualizing people. In H. H. Anderson (Ed.) *Creativity and its Cultivation*, 83-95. New York: Harper & Brothers.

Maslow, A. H. (1987) *Motivation and Personality* (3rd Ed.) New York: HarperCollins.

McCracken, J. L. (1997) *Women Who Invent: Examining the impact of formal and informal education on their creativity*. Doctoral dissertation, Oklahoma State University.

Merriam, S. B. and Caffarella, S. R. (1998) *Learning in Adulthood* (2nd Ed.) San Francisco: Jossey-Bass.

Noble, K. D., Subotnik, R. F. and Arnold, K. D. (1999) To thine own self be true: A new model of female talent development. *Gifted Child Quarterly*, 43 (3), 140-49.

Osborn, A. (1963) *Applied Imagination* (3rd Ed.) New York: Charles Scribner's.

Pearson, C. S. (1992) Women as learners: Diversity and educational quality. *Journal of Developmental Education*, 16 (2), 2-4, 6, 8, 10, 38-39.

Pohlman, L. (1996) Creativity, gender and the family: A study of creative writers. *Journal of Creative Behavior*, 16 (2), 1-24.

Reis, S. M. (1998) *Work Left Undone: Choices and Compromises of Talented Females*. Mansfield Center, CT: Creative Learning Press, Inc.

Rosser, S. V. (1997) *Re-engineering Female Friendly Science*. New York: Teachers College Press.

Sadker, M. and Sadker, D. (1994) *Failing at Fairness: How our Schools Cheat Girls*. New York: Touchstone.

Tisdell, E. J. (1995) *Creating Inclusive Adult Learning Environments: Insights from Multicultural Education and Feminist Pedagogy*. Information Series, No. 361. Columbus, OH: ERIC Clearinghouse on Adult, Career & Vocational Education.

Torrance, E. P. (1965) Developing women's natural gifts. *Women's Education*, 4 (1), 1, 7.

Torrance, E. P. (1972) Creative young women in today's world. *Exceptional Children*, 597-603.

Torrance, E. P. (1977) *Discovery and nurturance of giftedness in the culturally different*. Reston, VA: Council for Exceptional Children.

Torrance, E. P. (1979) *The Search for Satori and Creativity*. Buffalo, NY: Creative Education Foundation.

Torrance, E. P. (1983) Status of creative women: Past, present and future. *Creative Adult and Child Quarterly*, 8, 135-44.

Torrance, E. P. (1987) Part two: Recent trends in teaching children and adults to think creatively. In S. G. Isaksen (Ed.) *Frontiers of creativity research*, 204-15. Buffalo, NY: Bearly Limited.

Torrance, E. P. (1995) *Why Fly? A Philosophy of Creativity*. Norwood, NJ: Ablex Publishing Corp.

Torrance, E. P. and Safter, H. T. (1990) *The Incubation Model of Teaching*. Buffalo, NY: Bearly Limited.

Joanna Kwasniewska

The role of gender in creativity[*]

The study aimed to determine the impact of gender-role on creative ability in artistic performance. 106 students from the Academy of Fine Arts, who were considered to be more creative, and 134 engineering students from the Warsaw Politechnic, assumed to be less creative, answered questions on the Bem Sex Role Inventory (Polish version). It was hypothesised that more creative students would evaluate themselves high both on femininity and masculinity scales (androgynous gender-role type), while less creative students would tend to ascribe to themselves their own gender characteristic only (stereotypical gender-role type).

Results indicate that the more creative group scored significantly higher than the other group on the femininity scale only. However, it appears that there are important differences within the creative group. Women in that group are relatively more masculine and men more feminine than the participants in the less creative group. One explanation may be that creativity in fine arts is mainly stimulated by female traits. Possibly, traits connected with masculinity stimulate in women the independence and strength necessary in creative work, while female attributes such as sensitivity and delicacy are developed in artistically creative men's personalities. Theoretical and practical implications of these and other results are discussed.

Introduction

On accepting the assumption that creativity is generally available but only selectively observed (Kozielecki, 1997), the question about the causes of this phenomenon arises. Why don't all potentially creative people use their abilities? The answer to this question would undoubtedly be a great discovery, allowing our species to develop faster, to solve problems great and small in a more creative manner, and would render itself to art as entertainment rather than to the addiction of popular culture and television. Many researchers try to analyse the creative personality by looking back at the individual's earliest years of life, considering development in childhood and early adolescence. In these periods people shape the basis of their ego, acquire a basic trust in the world and in other people, learn to be independent and gain knowledge. This knowledge is organised in schemas (Maruszewski, 1996). Thanks to them we can both think

---

[*] This paper is based on the unpublished Masters Thesis: *The role of gender in creativity* [Znaczenie plci psychologicznej w tworczosci].

about the world surrounding us and understand it. However, schemas do not always make it easier to perceive reality adequately. Some of them, called stereotypes, can even disturb this process (Wojciszke, 2000). One kind of stereotype, gender stereotype, markedly mis-shapes and limits our perception of sex-related behaviour because they are closely connected with evaluative judgements and negative or positive emotions (Kwiatkowska, 1999). Stereotypes influence individuals' performance by building boundaries between what is commonly accepted and what is not. Therefore, an important question is: do gender schemas have an impact on individuals' performance in the other areas of their lives as well? Do they also influence a person's creative potential? Does this connection exist at all? If so, what is its characteristic and mechanism? A vast array of studies both in psychology and other social disciplines has been aimed at answering these questions.

The data from some of the research imply that femininity is the factor stimulating creative behaviour. Hammer (1964) found that, within a group of artists, creative men accept female aspects of their personality without the feeling of gender conflict. It makes them more open to emotions and more aesthetically sensitive. Femininity was also found to be a factor stimulating creativity in the group of women. In an investigation of female scientists (Helson, 1967), a prestigious group of mathematicians was compared with another group of female mathematicians judged as having more average ability. The creative group received similar judgements on the characteristics typically ascribed to women, but they were often less 'masculine'.

Considerably less research pertains to male features in the mental processes of individual creativity and data in this case is rather ambiguous. The investigation carried out by Lukasik (1999) showed that in tests measuring various components of the creative process, creative men received significantly higher scores than women did. The participants' gender traits were not measured in this experiment. Nevertheless, assuming that most participants had adequate gender traits for their sex, it could be supposed that 'masculine' features stimulate information processing fluency, data synthesis and generation of original and useful ideas. In addition, interestingly, men generated more original ideas. The author of the research considers that these results could be the outcome of designating women and men to qualitatively different tasks in our culture.

The majority of researchers consider that the combination of 'male' and 'female' characteristics, so-called *androgyny*, enhances the development of a creative personality. What is androgyny, though? Sandra Bem has argued (1996) that feminine and masculine traits are related to each other orthogonally and are positive domains; one is not the absence of the other. She has stated that adherence to the traditional sex-role orientation has produced anxiety and maladaptive behaviour for males as well as females. Therefore, she has proposed a construct of psychological androgyny.

To determine empirically which individuals were psychologically androgynous, sex-typed or sex reversed, Bem and her associates developed the Bem Sex-Role Inventory (BSRI) (Bem, 2000). The aim of this tool was to identify several gender options and to operationalise these in questionnaire form. People completing the questionnaire could then determine their psychosexual identity. They had to read a list of traits presented and then decide on the suitability of each trait as a self-description.

Bem's study resulted in a concept of gender schemas describing four main configurations of psychological traits connected with gender, which could be ascribed to the following gender options:

1. Sex-typed individuals who can be characterised by psychological traits suitable to their sex (feminine females and masculine males). According to Bem's theory, a sex-typed person is the one who acquires and processes information as well as regulates her or his behaviour on the basis of social definitions of femininity and masculinity. Bem argues that which traits an individual possesses is not of prime importance. The key thing is the extent to which the self-concept and behaviour are organised according to gender schema and not to other dimensions.
2. Androgynous individuals who are equally high in feminine and masculine traits, independent of their actual sex.
3. Undifferentiated individuals who are equally low in feminine and masculine traits, independent of their actual sex.
4. Cross-sex-typed individuals who can be characterised by psychological traits suitable to the other sex (masculine females and feminine males). Like the sex-typed individuals, these people create self concepts on the basis of socially defined gender schema.

Numerous authors have investigated the connection between androgyny and creativity, although different terminology has been used. Freud defined the creative personality as full of contradictions (Rosinska, 1985). An artist, according to Freud, uses logic based on free associations and emotions and is often bisexual. The psychoanalytical term bisexuality is close in meaning to the concept of androgyny – it joins what is feminine with what is masculine. Jung went even further in developing the concept of bisexuality (Hall and Lindzey, 1994). He argued that each individual is actually bisexual. Each man owns the feminine aspect of personality. It has been conveyed to him through ages in the form of archetype, called *anima*, and was built by continual contact between men and women in our culture. Similarly, women possess masculine aspects of personality, which are called *animus*. Jung argued that a woman is the embodiment of life itself, but in her development she should fight against inactivity and lack of confidence. A man embodies life-shaping - giving form and shape to the life energy. Jung believed that everybody should be aware of the elements of the opposite sex which exist in his or her personality. The harmonious connection of all opposing elements is the only way that can lead individuals to wholeness. This is the optimal way to become really creative as well (Dudek, 1996; Jacobi, 1996).

According to Strozewski (1983), creativity can be described by 32 pairs of antinomies. Although the author does not distinguish femininity and masculinity as significant contradictions, he lists certain traits which in our culture are assigned to a particular sex. The following pairs of extreme traits necessary for creative behaviour are mentioned: submission-domination, casualness-rigour, and improvisation-calculation. It seems that creativity is possible only when the 'boundaries of tension' between the poles of antinomy are used consciously or intuitively. This may initiate the creative process, providing creative activities with energy and determining the final form of creative work. In this example of dialectic reasoning, contradiction is the motivating power of all changes and improvements (Necka, 1994).

Maslow (1970) shares the opinion about the need for connecting the elements which are apparently mutually exclusive, arguing that the harmonious connection of contradicting personality traits is typical in creative people.

In contemporary psychological literature, further data about the relationship between creativity and androgyny can be found (Solowiej, 1997). Studies on this topic have been carried out by IPAR, the Institute of Personality Assessment and Research. The subjects, chosen by experts as distinguished in their field of creativity, were asked to complete numerous tests and were observed during both deliberately-induced problem situations and informal social meetings. The control group consisted of less effective representatives of the same professions. Altogether 600 subjects took part in this study. After the two groups were compared, the personality characteristics of distinguished creative subjects were defined. According to this study, one of the most prominent features of creative people is that they possess stronger than average qualities of the opposite sex. It was noticed that creative men are more emotional and self-conscious, while creative women have high levels of achievement motivation. Referring to Bem's typology, it is difficult to determine if these subjects were androgynous or cross-sex-typed as there is no information about the traits tied to their own sex.

On the basis of the research carried out, Richardson and Crichlow (1995) argued that art students differ from nature students. Subjects from the first group had a higher need for autonomy and scored higher on a femininity scale, while the others appeared to have the tendency to dominate.

The research conducted by Jeanne Flyntz De Joseph (1977) indicates that androgynous individuals tend to have untypical interests and are inclined to undertake non-traditional professions. In the androgynous group 3.6% of subjects chose fine arts as their future job, while among all the subjects only 2% chose art as their future career. These results could mean that androgynous people, more than the others, are interested in creativity in the field of art.

Dakowicz's research (Dakowicz, 2000) about the relation between gender and self-actualisation suggests that the highest level of self-actualisation tends to be achieved by androgynous individuals, just above cross-sex-typed women and sex-typed men. Rufflin-Rahal, Barin and Combus (1998) have obtained similar results. Although self-actualisation is not the synonym of creativity, in humanistic concepts it is considered to be one of the main ways to become truly creative.

Finally, investigations by Torsten Norlander and Ann Erixon (2000) indicate a strong correlation between androgyny measured by BSRI and creativity. In Modeus, Stahlbrost, Wester and Orgen's test, which consisted of nine squares depicting incomplete drawings which subjects had to complete in 15 minutes, similar results were found. Androgynous participants were evaluated significantly higher than sex-typed and undifferentiated participants. No significant differences were found in the level of creativity between androgynous and cross-sex-typed subjects, although androgynous participants' work was evaluated a little higher.

No clear conclusions can be drawn from the above research. It seems that the majority of authors agree that androgyny stimulates creative behaviour. However, should the domain of creativity be considered then numerous doubts appear. Therefore, this study assesses only one domain of creativity – art. Art was the subject of interest for a few of the authors mentioned above. Both Freud and Jung analysed creativity in art, arguing that it requires the connection of contradictory traits. Moreover, Norlander and Erixon's research could be regarded as concerning art, since picture completion was chosen as the indicator of creativity. The researchers concluded that creativity is closely connected with art. And, as mentioned above, in the correlation study by Jeanne Flyntz De Joseph, it was found that androgynous individuals tend to choose professions connected with art more often than others do. Still the connection between androgyny and creativity is not clear enough and requires further research.

The hypothesis of the present study suggests that androgyny may be a vital factor in artistic creativity. In other words, creative men and women will be very feminine and masculine at the same time. To test these hypotheses, two groups differing in the level of potential creativity were selected. Since it was important to avoid the mistake of measuring creativity in one activity only (which is what would happen if a creativity test were used) it was assumed that students from art profiled schools, in general, tend to be more creative than the students from non-art profiled schools. This assumption may be supported by the fact that the art schools' entrance exam is a kind of creativity test, selecting the most creative individuals, whereas exams for non-art profiled schools only assess level of knowledge. The distinguished groups were expected to exhibit differences in gender type. It was hypothesised that at the art profiled school there would be significantly more androgynous subjects than at the non-art profiled school; and more sex-typed subjects at the non-art profiled school than at the art profiled school.

Method

Subjects

240 subjects recruited from two Warsaw universities participated in the study. The universities were chosen on the assumption that students from art profiled schools are more creative than students from non-art profiled schools. The first of the schools was the Warsaw Academy of Fine Arts, where 106 students (40 men and 66 women) participated. The second school was the Warsaw Politechnic, where 134 students (83 men and 51 women) took part. The average age of participants was 21.59 (SD=1.78, age range = 18 to 29). The subjects from the Warsaw Academy of Fine Arts were a little older (M=21.9. SD=2.07) than students from the Warsaw Politechnic (M=21.3, SD=1.48).

Instruments
The tool used in this research was the Polish version of BSRI construct by Alicja Kuczyńska (1992). The Polish inventory (Inwentarz do oceny Płci Psychologicznej – IPP) is a new instrument, based on theoretical assumptions elaborated by S. L. Bem, but constructed due to a recent, more economical procedure. The IPP (see Appendix) is a 35 item paper and pencil instrument which consists of 15 feminine, 15 masculine, and five psychologically neutral personality characteristics. An individual rates herself/himself on a five point scale on each characteristic. The results are obtained by summing the points assigned to the feminine, masculine and neutral scales, separately.

Design
The variables of the study were:

1. femininity level indicated by the general score on the femininity scale (score range: 15 to 75). The following items of IPP were aggregated: 2, 5, 8, 11, 12, 16, 17, 19, 20, 21, 22, 23, 29, 30, 34
2. masculinity level indicated by the general score on the masculinity scale (score range: 15 to 75). The following items of IPP were aggregated: 1, 3, 6, 7, 10, 13, 15, 24, 25, 26, 27, 28, 32, 33, 35
3. artistic creativity level indicated by the kind of university the participant attends. Participants from the Academy of Fine Arts were assumed to be more artistically creative than those from the Warsaw Politechnic.

Operational hypotheses
On the basis of this background, seven operational hypotheses are presented:

1. Average femininity level measured both for men and women together tend to be higher at art profiled school than at non-art profiled school
2. Average masculinity level measured both for men and women together tend to be higher at art profiled school than at non-art profiled school
3. Females from art profiled school tend to have a higher average level of femininity than females from non-art profiled school
4. Males from art profiled school tend to have a higher average level of femininity than males from non-art profiled school
5. Females from art profiled school tend to have a higher average level of masculinity than females from non-art profiled school
6. Males from art profiled school tend to have a higher average level of masculinity than males from non-art profiled school
7. There is a significant difference in the number of participants with particular gender types between schools. There are more androgynous individuals at the art school and more sex-typed individuals at the non-art profiled school.

Procedure
240 participants were recruited during regular lectures and seminars held at their universities. The lecturer's permission was previously obtained. It was explained to participants that the study involved different aspects of personality-related questions, that the questionnaire would take 15 minutes maximum to

complete and that the tests were anonymous. On agreeing to take part, the participants were informed about how to complete the test and were asked to do this individually. Once all the data were gathered and analysed, subjects were informed of the general results.

Results

Femininity level analysis revealed the results predicted. As Fig 1 shows, femininity level at the art profiled school was higher than at the non-art profiled school, t(233) =1.68, p=0.047. Equal proportions for this analysis were vital so

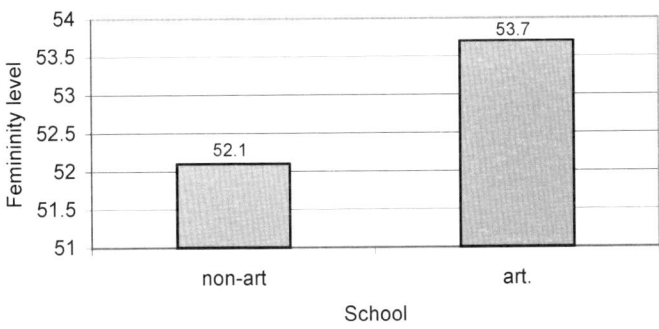

Fig 1. Comparison of femininity level between the subjects from non-art profiled school and art profiled school

before the test was performed the observations had been weighted by appropriate factors to equalise the number of subjects in each group. Factor values used were as follows: non-art profiled school for female subjects k=1.173 and for male subjects k=0.723; art profiled school for female subjects k=0.909 and for males k=1.497.

However, the difference in the level of masculinity between subjects from art profiled school and non art profiled school was not statistically significant, t(233) =0.594, ns. In this case the data had been weighted before the analysis as well. Average scores on masculinity scales appeared to be similar in both groups. This did not confirm the hypothesis that creative people are simultaneously more masculine.

Although there was no significant difference in femininity level between females from the two schools (see Fig 2), the difference in femininity level between two groups of males has been revealed, t(120)=1.477; p=0.071. However, the difference was significant only on tendency level. What is more, independent-sample t tests performed on students' scores revealed significant differences between males and females in femininity level, t(233)=4,726; p<0.001. Mean femininity level for female subjects was 55.00 while for male subjects 50.55. This result is the confirmation of test validity.

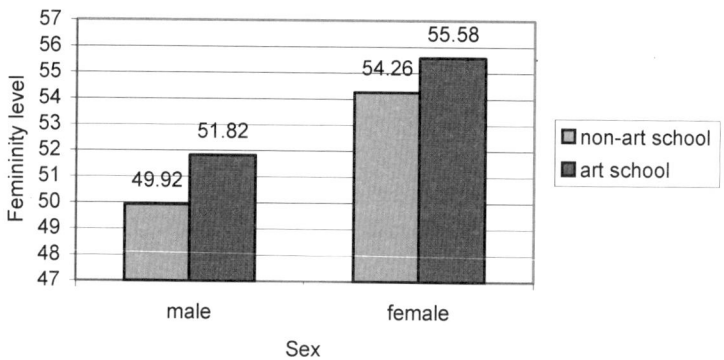

Fig 2. Comparison of femininity level between female and male subjects from both schools

Analogously, the level of masculinity has been analysed. The difference on the masculinity scale between female and male participants scores is depicted in Fig 3. Statistical analysis revealed that men from the non-art profiled school scored more on masculinity (M=51.56) than men from the art profiled school (M=50.77). Although this result was not significant it appears to contradict the hypothesis. On the other hand, the differences in the level of masculinity between female subjects from the two groups tend to follow the hypothesis. It was revealed that women from the art profiled school were more masculine (M=49.45) than women from the non-art profiled school (M=47.32). Also in this case independent-sample t tests were computed to assess the relation between masculinity and participant's sex. On average, men scored 51.31, women 48.53. These results were statistically significant, t(234) =2.639; p<0.01. However, it is worth emphasising that in masculinity level the difference between 'creative' females and males was smaller (1.32) than between females and males in the less 'creative' group (4.24).

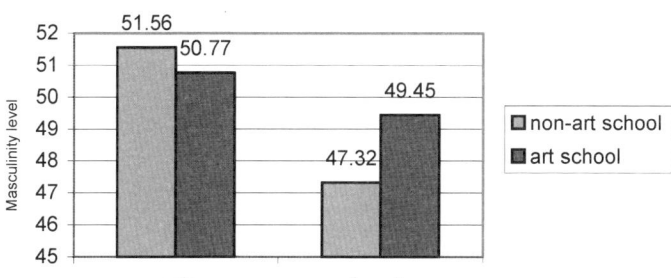

Fig 3. Comparison of masculinity level between male
and female subjects from both schools

To determine whether the two variables "sex" and the 'kind of school' interact
with each other in the impact on femininity and masculinity scales, one-way
analysis of variance (ANOVA) was conducted. As expected the main effect of
sex was revealed and appeared significant in both cases: for femininity $F(1,
231) = 17.174$, $p < 0.001$ and for masculinity $F(1, 232) = 6.491$, $p < 0.05$. Neither
main effect of the 'kind of school' nor interaction effect was revealed.

The main objective of this study was to determine whether the number of
students with each gender type differs from one school to the other. To answer
this question a test of association was conducted. Analysis revealed that there
are no significant differences in the number of androgynous and sex-typed
subjects between schools. However, other interesting tendencies have been
uncovered (see Fig 4).

Firstly, among the art profiled school students there were more androgynous
subjects (29%) than among the non-art profiled school students (22%).
Secondly, there were fewer sex-typed participants at the art profiled school
(31%) than at the non-art profiled school (36%). No differences in the number
of cross-sex-typed subjects could be seen. But, analyses were computed for
each sex separately (Table 1). It was found that the percentage of cross-sex-
typed female subjects at the art profiled school was higher (20%) than at the
non-art profiled school (12%) and the percentage of cross-sex-typed male
subjects was higher at the non-art school (18%) than at the art profiled school
10%). The percentage of undifferentiated subjects was higher at the non-art
profiled school (24%) than at the art profiled school (21%). This general
tendency seems to confirm the hypothesis, although it was not significant.

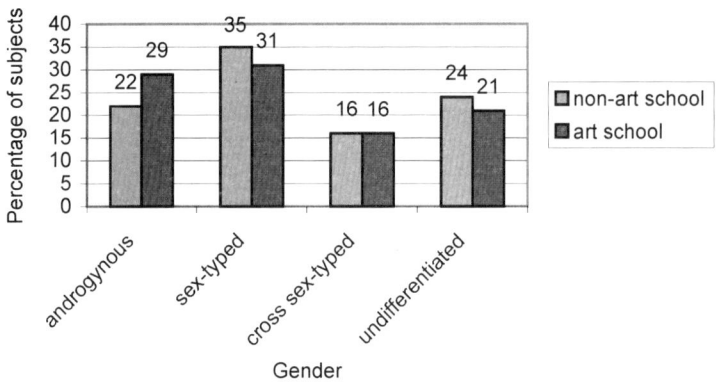

Fig 4. Percentage of subjects with particular gender type at non-art profiled and art profiled school

Sex	Type of school	Androgynous subjects	Sex-typed subjects	Cross sex-typed subjects	Undifferentiated subjects
Female	Non-art profiled	22%	41%	12%	18%
	Art profiled	29%	32%	20%	15%
Male	Non-art profiled	22%	31%	18%	28%
	Art profiled	30%	30%	10%	30%
All	Non-art profiled	22%	35%	16%	24%
	Art profiled	29%	31%	16%	21%

Table 1. Percentage of female and male subjects from art school and non art school and gender type

Discussion

This study assessed the relation between gender type and creativity. It was hypothesised that more creative people, particularly in art domains, would be more androgynous which means, according to Bem's concept, that they would be more feminine as well as more masculine. This hypothesis was not fully confirmed, since it was revealed that although more creative people are more feminine, they are not more masculine. These results applied to creative people as a whole group without distinguishing sex. The study suggests that masculinity in creative people stays at a certain level, which is similar for both women and men. On performing the analysis for women and men respectively, it was revealed that creative women could be characterised by masculine traits to a higher than average extent. Interestingly, creative and less creative women did not differ significantly in the reported level of femininity. What is more, the results suggest that femininity level in creative men was much higher than in less creative men.

The analysis of gender types did not uncover significant results, which could have been caused by a too small number of participants in each cell of the chi-square test. Some tendencies are worth discussing. Among creative people there seemed to be more androgynous subjects and less sex-typed subjects, as predicted. However, it is hard to corroborate why among creative male subjects there was a higher percentage of cross- sex-typed men than in the less creative group. Maybe, in our culture, men need to be very courageous to exhibit feminine behaviours (Miluska & Boski, 1999). As numerous studies show (Necka, 2000, 2001), creative people are likely to be non-conformist, which gives them strength to behave in a socially unacceptable way. These results require confirmation through further studies.

To conclude, it could be stated with high probability that feminine traits are vital for creativity. Possibly, they help artists access their own feelings and use emotions as directions in the creative process. It is difficult to determine the role of masculine features in creativity. Some of them may give strength (May, 1994) which motivates people to reach for ambitious goals. However, is art performance considered an ambitious activity in contemporary society? Probably for some yes, for the majority no. The results suggest that women need masculine ambition and strength to be creative. Conversely, to be creative, men have to resign from the qualities tied to their sex and develop features which are not compliant to the schema of their gender role. Therefore, the differences in the level of masculinity between creative men and women decline.

The data obtained in this study are close to existing results (Hammer, 1964; Richardson & Crichlow, 1994). These researchers drew similar conclusions about the stimulating impact of femininity on male creativity. Moreover, my findings are consistent with those of IPAR, who analysed creativity in domains other than art. They argued that creative men are more emotional and self aware, while women have high levels of achievement motivation. Also correlation research conducted by Flyntz (1977) suggests that androgynous people tend to choose art professions. Freud's and Jung's concepts of creativity and gender are not based on empirical research, so it is difficult to assess what they meant by connection of contradicted traits. They could mean androgyny as well as cross-sex-typed individuals. However, Lukasik's research can still lead to opposite conclusions. How can these divergences be explained?

Firstly, it should be taken into consideration that art creativity, except for a few features in common with all kinds of creativity, has its own characteristics (Necka, 1999). Art possibly requires femininity, while creativity in general is connected with an increased level of traits tied to the opposite sex. Different results might be the effect of not determining the kind of creativity analysed.

Secondly, various indicators of creativity have been used in each research project. This could mean that each study measured something different. Some of the creativity tests concern cognitive processes, some manual skills and others literal abilities. For instance, in the IPAR research, test results and judges' evaluations were indicators of creativity. In Norlander and Erixon's research, the level of creativity was assessed by picture evaluation. The creativity indicator in my study omitted this problem in a way. Neither kind of creativity was favoured, although it was assumed that a certain group was more creative than the other. The main drawback of such a solution was the lack of information about creativity level for each participant. Certainly a lot of interesting data about differences within the groups have been omitted.

Thirdly, divergences between this study and the others could result from certain methodological problems in this research. Replies to the IPP test items could have been influenced by the need for social acceptance. Although individuals from the non-art profiled school knew that the surveys were anonymous, they could have evaluated their features higher to 'look better from a psychologist's perspective'. Subjects from the art profiled school were probably less likely to raise their scores, since creative people are generally more non-conformist. Therefore, this uncontrolled variable could have diminished the difference between scores of people from both schools, which made for a decreased statistical significance of the results.

In future research on this topic, gender as well as creativity level should be empirically assessed. Moreover, creativity indicators should be chosen more carefully to make it certain what is being measured. This task, however, appears to be very sophisticated as it is difficult to find objective creativity indicators. Various indicators might be favourable for creators in particular domains. On the other hand, use of different indicators for each creativity domain would make comparisons between groups impossible. Therefore, it seems that the opinion of competent judges, professionals in various disciplines, who could determine the level of creativity appropriately, would be the only adequate creativity indicator. The gender assessment should be conducted in a way which would eliminate the disruptive influence of the need for social acceptance. Only then could it be determined whether the connection between androgyny and creativity really exists and if there are any interactions between such variables as the domain of creativity, creativity itself, femininity and masculinity. Although the realisation of further studies proposed here might be difficult for practical reasons, such as inducing creative individuals to participate, the conclusions which could be drawn would certainly be interesting from both a scientific and social viewpoint. It could be found that a perfect educational system would not force children to keep to the rigid rules of gender role schema, but would rather stimulate development in various aspects of personality independent of sex.

References

Bem, S. L. (1977). Androgyny and sexual identity. In: P. G. Zimbardo, F. L. Ruch (Eds.), *Psychology and Life* (pp.435-438). Glenview, Illinois: Scott, Foresman and Company.

Bem, S. L. (1993). *The Lenses of Gender: Transforming the Debate on Sexual Inequality.* Yale: Yale University.

Dakowicz, A. (2000). *Gender and Self-actualisation [Plec psychiczna a poziom samoaktualizacji].* Bialystok: Wydawnictwo Trans Humana.

Dudek, Z. W. (1996). *Jung's Integral Psychology [Psychologia integralna Junga]*. Warszawa: Wydawnictwo Psychologii i Kultury Eneteia.

Flyntz, D. J. J. (1977). *Selected Correlates of Androgyny*. Utah: Utah University Press.

Hall, C. S. & Lindzey, G. (1978). *Theories of Personality*. New York: John Wiley and Sons.

Hammer, E. F. (1964). Creativity and feminine ingredients in young male artists. *Perceptual and Motor Skills*, 19, 414.

Helson, R. (1967). Sex differences in creative style. *Journal of Personality*, 35, 214–233.

Jacobi, J. (1959). *C. G. Jung' Psychology [Die Psychologie von C.G.Jung]*. Dusseldorf & Zurich: Patmos Verlag GmbH & Co KG.

Kuczynska, A. (1992). *Sex Role Inventory Professional Manual [Inwentarz do oceny plci psychologicznej. Podręcznik]*. Warszawa: Pracownia Testow Psychologicznych PTP.

Kozielecki, J. (1997). *Transgression and Culture [Transgresja i kultura]*. Warszawa: Wydawnictwo Akademickie „Zak".

Kwiatkowska, A. (1999). The power of tradition and temptation for change - the thing about sex stereotypes [Sila tradycji i pokusa zmiany, czyli o stereotypach plciowych]. In: J. Miluska & P. Boski (Eds.), *Masculinity-feminity in Individual and Cultural Perspective [Meskosc - Kobiecosc w perspektywie indywidualnej i kulturowej]*. (pp.143–172). Warszawa: Wydawnictwo Instytutu Psychologii Polskiej Akademii Nauk.

Lukasik, A. (1999). *The External Limitations of the Creative Process [Zewnetrzne ograniczenia procesu tworczego]*. Rzeszow: Wydawnictwo Wyzszej Szkoły Pedagogicznej.

May, R.J (1994). *Odwaga Tworzenia [The courage to create]*. Poznan: Dom Wydawniczy Rebis.

Maruszewski, T. (1996). *Cognitive Psychology [Psychologia poznawcza]*. Warszawa: Znak, Jezyk, Rzeczywistosc. Polskie Towarzystwo Semiotyczne.

Maslow A. (1970). The creative attitude. In: W. R., L. Mooney, T. A. Razik (Eds.), *Exploration in Creativity*. New York: Harper and Row.

Miluska, J., Boski, P. (1999). *Masculinity-feminity in Individual and Cultural Perspective [Meskosc-Kobiecosc w perspektywie indywidualnej i kulturowej]*. Warszawa: Wydawnictwo Instytutu Psychologii Polskiej Akademii Nauk.

Necka, E. (1994). *TROP... Creative Problem Solving [TROP...Tworcze rozwiazywanie problemow]*. Krakow: Oficyna Wydawnicza „Impuls".

Necka, E. (1999). *The Creative Process and its Limitations [Proces tworczy i jego ograniczenia]*. Krakow: Oficyna Wydawnicza „Impuls".

Necka, E. (2000). Creativity [Tworcosc]. In: Strelau J. (Ed.), *Psychology. The Academic Manual [Psychologia. Podrecznik akademicki. Psychologia ogolna]* (Vol.2, pp.783-807). Gdansk: Gdanskie Wydawnictwo Psychologiczne.

Necka, E (2001). *Psychology of Creativity [Psychologia tworczosci]*. Gdansk: Gdanskie Wydawnictwo Psychologiczne.

Norlander, T., Erixon, A. (2000). Psychological androgyny and creativity: dynamics of gender-role and personality trait. *Social Behaviour and Personality*, 28 (5), 423-436.

Richardson, A. G., Crichlow, J., L. (1995). Subject orientation and creative personality. *Educational Research, 1,* 17-33.

Rosinska, Z. (1985). *Psychoanalytical Approach to Art [Psychoanalityczne myslenie o sztuce].* Warszawa: Panstwowe Wydawnictwo Naukowe.

Ruffing-Rahal, M. A., Barin, L. J., Combs, C. J. (1998). Gender role orientation as a correlate of perceived health, health behaviour, and qualitative well-being in older women. *Journal of Women Ageing,* 10 (1), 3-19.

Solowiej, J. (1997). *Psychology of Creativity [Psychologia tworczosci].* Gdańsk: Wydawnictwo Uniwersytetu Gdanskiego.

Wojciszke, B. (2000). Knowledge structures and understanding of social world [Struktury wiedzy i rozumienie swiata społecznego]. In: Strelau J. (Ed.), *Psychology. The Academic Manual. [Psychologia. Podrecznik akademicki.]* (Vol.3, pp.27-45). Gdansk: Gdanskie Wydawnictwo Psychologiczne.

Strozewski, W. (1983). *Creativity Dialectics. [Dialektyka tworczosci].* Krakow: Panstwowe Wydawnictwo Muzyczne.

Appendix

Items from the Polish version of BSRI (Bem Sex Role Inventory) constructed by Alicja Kuczyńska. In the original Polish version the subjects were asked to describe themselves on the following scale placed next to each item:

1 – *Never or almost never true*   4 – *Usually true*
2 – *Usually not true*   5 – *Always or almost always true*
3 – *Occasionally true*

1. Dominating*
2. Sensitive**
3. Independent*
4. Responsible***
5. Caring**
6. Competitive*
7. Success oriented*
8. Concerned for others**
9. Friendly***
10. Forceful*
11. Gentle**
12. Susceptible to flattery**
13. Makes decisions easily*
14. Truthful***
15. Arrogant*
16. Taking pride in her/his appearance*
17. Economical**
18. Tolerant***

19. Aesthetic**
20. Grumbler**
21. Tender**
22. Affectionate**
23. Sensitive to the feelings of others**
24. Athletic*
25. Witty*
26. Strong personality*
27. Self reliant*
28. Self-sufficient*
29. Altruist**
30. Soft-spoken**
31. Nice***
32. Extravert*
33. Experimenting in sex*
34. Gullible**
35. Smart*

* Masculinity scale   **Femininity scale   ***Neutral scale

Kenichi Yumino

Education reform and fostering creativity in Japan

Introduction

Japan has learned a lot of things from the European and American worlds since the Meiji Era (which began in 1867). These included science, technology, medicine, politics and democracy. After World War 2, Japan imported these things mainly from the USA. The main purpose of education was to teach these things to the students. To achieve this, the Ministry of Education indicated 'Guidelines for Learning'. Based on these guidelines, textbooks of all subjects were edited. And Manual Books for Teachers were published by several companies. The main role of the teachers was to teach the students, precisely and efficiently, the contents of textbooks, referencing the Manual Books.

In such situation, the students were recommended to learn the textbooks faithfully. Students who memorised and understood the textbooks got higher grades. Fostering creativity was not so important a goal in ordinary public schools, as in a small number of private schools and attached schools of the Faculty of Education.

However, many environmental, social, informational, educational, humanistic and moral problems occurred when Japanese society had matured and the differences between Japan and the European/American countries had diminished too much.

In some small academic areas, for example science and technology, there is less and less dependence on the models learned from these countries. Japan has to make new models. Therefore, Japan is now requiring to foster 'creativity' in education.

In order to solve the problems, a new national curriculum was introduced in all of Japan's public education in April 2002. It includes a 'Period of Integrated Study' that has no textbook and no guideline. The teacher has to make an original curriculum that fits each student.

Purposes of national curriculum standards reform

The following goals for reforming national curriculum standards are stated by the Ministry of Education HP (www.mext.go.jp/english/news/1998/07/980712. htm):

(1) To help children cultivate rich humanity, sociality and identity as a Japanese living in the international community

Children will be encouraged to cultivate well-balanced rich humanity and sociality. Rich humanity includes sympathy, the mentality to respect each other and live together in harmony, respect for life and human rights, sensibility in appreciating beauty and the environment, volunteer spirit, the mentality to make efforts to achieve one's own goal and the like. High value will be set on moral education which helps children acquire social rules and basic morality, a sense of norms, public morals, justice and fairness, sound judgment, strong will and ability to take action, awareness of responsibility, autonomy, self-control and the like. In addition, children's healthy development and physical strength are also emphasised for them to lead vigorous lives.

Children will be encouraged to deepen their understanding of national as well as local history, culture and tradition, and to develop a love of those matters. They will also be encouraged to appreciate different cultures open-mindedly, and to cultivate the mentality of international cooperation and the identity as Japanese living in the international community.

(2) To help children develop the ability to learn and think independently

There was a tendency for school education to emphasise volume of knowledge. Now however, school education is focused on the children's standpoint and places a high value on the development of children's intellectual interests and inquiring minds. It also emphasises the importance of motivating children to learn and helping them develop abilities to learn, reason, judge, express, discover and solve problems; and to create and cope with social changes independently. Besides, to aim at children's successful self-realisation, it is essential to relate knowledge to real life. This entails promoting hands-on learning and problem-solving approaches.

(3) To help children acquire basic abilities and skills and grow their own individuality by allowing ample scope for educational activities to develop

Schools will effectively help children acquire the selected educational content thoroughly by conducting educational activities without pressure of time or stress. They will also encourage children to study independently what they are interested in.

The common contents of compulsory education will be closely examined so as to consist of the very basics necessary for social life. Education for growing children's individuality will also be focused on. Thus, considering children's interests, schools need to promote children's independent learning and to further develop individualised instruction.

In addition, the elective course system will be introduced to the fifth graders and older pupils at elementary school, and there will be more elective subjects for higher graders at lower secondary school. At upper secondary school, elective subjects will take the most part of the curriculum and common subjects will be minimized.

(4) To encourage each school to show ingenuity in developing distinctive educational activities

The national curriculum standards will be clearly specified and more flexible so that individual schools will be able to show ingenuity in developing unique educational activities to make the school distinctive. Specifically, each school will be able to make its own timetable and curriculum in accordance with the actual situations of the community, school and children.

In addition, the number of elective subjects will be increased and the 'Period of Integrated Study' will be established to further promote each school's unique educational activities.

Moreover, schools will be encouraged to establish a good relationship with families and communities and to be more open to them.

(5) To encourage moral development

Schools will be encouraged to develop distinctive approaches suitable to the stage of child development in accordance with the actual situations of the community, school and children. Schools are also expected to positively adopt a hands-on learning approach and practical activities, such as volunteer activities and hands-on learning activities in the environment.

In particular, preschool children and lower graders of elementary schools need to be given the basic discipline and repeatedly taught what they should not do as a human being, what is right and what is wrong until they understand thoroughly.

Responses

Internationalisation

Children will be inspired to be proud of and to feel love for Japanese history, culture and tradition, as well as to deepen their understanding of these. At the same time, they will be encouraged to appreciate different cultures open-mindedly and to develop capabilities in English and the ability to live in harmony with people of different cultures and from different customs. Elementary schools will be expected to provide hands-on learning activities to expose children to foreign language.

Information-oriented society

Consistent and systematic information education through every stage of school will require the positive use of computers in virtually every subject. Elementary schools will employ computers for children's learning activities in the 'Period of Integrated Study'.

Environmental issues

Children will deepen their understanding of environmental and energy issues and will develop respect for the environment. They will be encouraged to develop practical minds and abilities to voluntarily take action to preserve the environment and make it better.

The aging society
Children will deepen their understanding of the aging society and will develop practical minds to voluntarily take actions for the elderly.

The 'Period of Integrated Study'

The newly established, tentatively named 'Period of Integrated Study' will encourage each school to show ingenuity in conducting interdisciplinary and comprehensive courses, such as: international understanding/foreign language conversation, information education, environmental education and welfare education, in accordance with the actual situation of each community and school.

The Period of Integrated Study:

- aims to help children develop the capability to discover and to properly solve problems by themselves. It also aims at developing children's minds to voluntarily cope with problem-solving activities and/or inquiring activities depending upon their own interests. Additionally, it emphasises that a child needs to learn thinking process and reasoning, including ways of getting information, examining, summarising, reporting and debating.

- emphasises the need to employ hands-on learning and problem-solving approaches as in experiential activities in nature, and social activities like volunteer activities, experimentation and observation, inquiring, creative and other productive activities.

- is defined, in elementary and secondary schools, as educational activities other than formal subjects and will be established for third graders and older elementary school pupils. It will also be a requirement in upper secondary school and a discussion will be given on this matter.

- comprises 2-3 credit hours per week; third grade in elementary to third grade in senior-high school.

Psychological goals of the new national curriculum

(1) Cultivate 'zest for living' amid 'room to grow'
'Zest for living' is the ability to identify problems for oneself, learn for oneself, think for oneself, make independent judgements and actions and solve problems well. These are its important pillars and in order to cultivate 'zest for living', it is important to stress the indispensable aim of further advancing a way of thinking that respects individuality.

Amid 'room to grow', in schools, families and the community, children accumulate rich experiences, such as various living experiences, experiences of nature, social and volunteer experiences, as well as having exchanges with various people. Children use these sorts of experiences and exchanges with people as learning material, and through a process of trial and error, discover their interests in a process that must be referred to as the budding of individuality. Through this process they bring to life the knowledge they have gained from books, acquire 'zest for living' and have cultivated in them a rich sense of humanity.

(2) Translate 'Zest for Living' into well-known psychological terms
As the concept of 'Zest of Living' is very ambiguous, the author (Yumino) has translated the concept into well-known psychological terms. These are:

- Deeper understanding and multiple thinking ability (after Howard Gardner)
- Creativity
- Curiosity
- Presentation ability
- Self-efficacy
- Leadership and followership
- Abilities and attitudes in harmony with the environment
- Abilities and attitudes to cope with the 'information society'
- Skills and knowledge for international understanding.

For further information, see Yumino (2001a). This book includes the following topics; psychology of intelligence and creativity; academic achievement of Japanese children; zest for living and creative power; measuring and fostering zest for living; enlarging thinking and creative ability; developments in cognitive mapping; the development and evaluation of integrated study; and enlarging questioning abilities and curiosity using the internet.

Fostering creativity in schools

(1) Primary and secondary school level
All of Japan's schools have introduced the 'Period for Integrated Study', which mainly aims to foster 'zest for living'. In this period, students are given many kinds of experience. The National Institute for Educational Policy Research has differentiated the following 26 experiences:

- Experience of making things.
- Experience of breeding animals and cultivating plants.
- Observational experiences of animals and plants.
- Experience of social facilities (clubs, camping sites, etc)
- Experience of interactive education (international, visiting schools for the disabled, visiting schools of other regions, etc).
- Activities concerning human rights and the meanings of peace.
- Researching activities about local nature.
- Exploring activities for local regional history and traditional culture.

- Researching activities about local society.
- Activities concerning local unique business and industry.
- Exploring activities for local domestic living: e.g. dressing, eating, dwelling.
- Experiences that explore today's problems and how to solve them by trial and error.
- Creating some play and enjoying it in a real situation.
- Real experiences through volunteer and social welfare activities.
- Exchanging their own opinions among various people through a variety of topics.
- Activities that maintain the environment.
- Utilising many kinds of information devices & media.
- Astronomical and meteorological observation.
- Playing music and drama.
- Activities that maintain health, and physical education.
- Experiences from enrolling in activities in local society.
- Exploring and staying in a mountain or a field.
- Interactive activities with foreign people.
- Exploring foreign cultures.
- Actual job experiences that aim at realising one's own way of life.
- Experiences that grasp the meanings of life and death.

Some schools aim at fostering creativity through the above experiences. However, the number of such schools is very small.

(2) Senior-high school level
26 high schools in all of Japan were chosen as 'Super Science High School' in 2002. Students in the schools learn higher and progressive curricula that include fostering creativity in science and mathematics.

(3) Undergraduate & graduate level
There are many courses that aim at fostering creativity in the curriculum, in particular, engineering, information, business and education. Unfortunately, the programme that guarantees high-level creativity is very limited.

Yumino (2001b) has introduced a *creativity development programme* in the graduate course of teacher training. It includes many practical and theoretical issues; intelligence and creativity, period for integrated study, high information-oriented society, theories of creativity, methods of fostering creativity, such as NM (Nakayama Masakazu) Method, teaching lesson for fostering creativity, etc.

Comments on the Yumino creativity development programme

What kinds of knowledge, skills and values have students learned from a year-long lecture and seminar programme? Two students summarised their learning as follows:

Report from Student A

Learned from the lectures and seminars:
1) skills for raising children's interest, 2) making a classroom fascinating, 3) how to identify next step task in the reflection of learning, 4) the hours of orientation are very important, 5) for Integrated Study, it is important to prepare a cross-curricular type of learning that involves the main concepts of each subject, 6) fostering self efficacy is very important, 7) effective learning through the Internet, 8) creativity development techniques: brain-storming, NM Method, KJ Method, 9) for Integrated Study, it is profitable to initiate it from Local Area Study, 10) in the Participation Lesson, it is appropriate to create something as a group/class in brushing up individual ability/skills for the topic, 11) a portfolio is suitable for developing student's ability of reflection, 12) I totally grasped how to foster creative children.

Report from Student B

Concerning ways to develop creativity, the following points are important:
1) the wishes and hopes of children, 2) learning in real, not virtual, situations, 3) ways of learning that adapt to the rapidly changing society, 4) consider things from multiple viewpoints, 5) teach skills and knowledge for fostering children's creativity.

To achieve the above, it is essential to do the following teaching:
1) move from results-oriented teaching to process-oriented teaching, 2) move from a memory-oriented education to a thinking/creating-oriented education, 3) permit a free thinking style, 4) make a lesson involving children's everyday experiences, 5) do not scold the children's bad points, but praise good points, 6) evaluate children's performance properly, 7) do not teach knowledge completely, but leave room for acquiring, thinking and creating, 8) prepare tasks and learning materials suited to the developmental level of each child.

References

Yumino, K. (2001a) *Achievements in Integrated Study: How to Foster Creativity in the Classroom.* Tokyo: Meiji Tosyo Publishing Company.

Yumino, K. (2001b) Psychology of Creation. Unpublished lecture note.

Lynda Foster

Early influences on creativity in Great Britain

Upon my arrival in Great Britain from America over 25 years ago, I assumed that Great Britain would be a strong advocate of creativity in schools since it hosted the very first World Conference on Gifted Children which included creatively gifted children. I was very surprised when I visited schools here to find that there was very little emphasis on creativity in the classroom. Of the schools that I visited, I observed creativity in some schools by some teachers, but at that time each teacher or school set the curriculum and objectives, which may or may not have included the development of creativity. Each teacher was free to teach what he or she wanted without any evaluation of how the children were developing creatively.

When I asked teachers here all those many years ago if they did any testing for creativity, the answer was an unequivocal 'no'. The teachers explained to me that they did not believe in testing like the Americans and that something as personal as creativity should be left without measure. They were somewhat taken aback by the fact that I would even suggest testing for creativity. When I asked further how they would assess a child for creativity, they said just by observation. However, the teachers had their own ideas about what creativity was and thus, one would assume, each observation of creativity would have been different.

What I discovered in the UK was that in schools and in the wider community, creativity was thought to be something found only in the arts. Creativity, it was believed, could be found when children paint, draw, dance and the like, but it was not considered a factor in other 'more solid' subjects. Never would teachers consider creativity as part of maths or science or the teaching of history or language, for example. Creativity was considered an 'activity' that could be done after school and didn't necessarily have to be part of the curriculum.

Additionally, I found that the word 'creativity' had somewhat of a tarnished name in this country. It had transpired that in the 1960s, primary education in particular was dominated by self-expression, with no limits or real need for knowledge and structure. It was an 'anything goes' type of education and children were not to be evaluated too critically for what they had expressed or produced. This type of education became embedded in the minds of British society as what it means to be creative.

Needless to say, there was a backlash to this sort of education and 'creativity' was to blame. Children were not achieving according to traditional measures and, although they might have been happier and more at ease with themselves in the 60s, the government stepped in to say 'we want results' and not pretty pictures. Thus there was a return to a more traditional education with traditional measures of learning.

Of course, looking back we can instantly say that the 1960s education in Great Britain was not creativity but simply self-expression. We know that creativity does not occur in a vacuum but is based upon real knowledge. We know that the more knowledge one has, the more one has the basics with which to be creative. Our most creative authors, scientists, artists and musicians are those who attained a high level of knowledge in their chosen fields. They used what they knew to produce something new and pleasing for themselves and others.

Creativity in the UK therefore came to be associated with a lack of structure and, even in 2003, the average individual on the street still associates creativity with play, self-expression and solely with the arts. The UK has yet to make the leap from seeing creativity as a personal pleasure to seeing it as a vital part of learning, in any subject.

Where did this leave creative individuals in the years beyond the 60s? One would say they were left without any support or understanding of their needs. Education here became more and more knowledge and content-oriented to make up for the 'disastrous 60s'. Although the needs of creative children were somewhat met in the 60s, as time marched on, their needs were met less and less to the point that in 2003, the needs of creative children are still only met by chance if these children are lucky enough to have a teacher who spots their abilities.

Now, 25 years after my initial arrival in this country, the UK is one of the most tested countries in the world and, of course, the testing for the most part is for analytical, logical and deductive thinking. Children here are tested at ages 4, 7, 11, 14, 16, 17 and 18. Test results have become the single barometer to evaluate a child's achievement. The fact that the child has a unique and imaginative mind does not seem to matter. The days of the 60s are long past and it seems that parents are now demanding good test results so that their children can enter universities and attain good jobs. Creativity is low on the list of educational priorities, since how creative children are does not seem to matter. What seems to matter is how well they perform in tests. Parenthetically, how good a teacher or a school is seems equally to be measured by test performance.

In the many talks I've given in the UK over the years about creativity and what it entails, I have found a keen interest among parents, teachers and wider members of the community. Without fail, each of my talks has ended in a heated discussion of how schools are failing creative children and those who think differently. It seems that the tide is now changing and that the climate for creativity has finally taken hold here. In my talks I have found that people in the UK want more creativity in education. They now seem to see how narrow their testing society has become.

The Government has also responded to this groundswell of discontent in education. The 2003 Labour Party Conference announced that the past 30 years of education has not fulfilled our children. Labour is advocating a more active education where individual learning can take place. And the Government now sees that creativity must be included in education if we are to meet the needs of our present, ever-changing world where ideas are now important. The Government is saying that a knowledge-based education cannot now work.

As a Trustee of the Creativity Centre Educational Trust, a UK charity that promotes creativity in the home, school and community, I decided that it might be interesting to find out what creative individuals feel most influences their creativity and what helps or hinders it. If the UK is to promote creativity in schools, it is important that we know what factors most influence the development of creative thinking.

I thus constructed a questionnaire which I administered to 24 creative individuals aged from 18 to 60. These were people who were nominated as 'creative', using word of mouth, by at least 5 people in their professions and fields. There were 5 artists and sculptors, 2 drama teachers, 2 musicians, 3 nursery school teachers, 3 primary school teachers, 3 secondary school teachers, 2 university lecturers, 2 writers and 2 creative media specialists. Although the size of the sample involved is small and thus I cannot generalise to all creative individuals, I felt that by looking at individual responses to the questionnaire that we could at least attain a limited glimpse into how the creative individual views his developmental needs.

The four questions that I asked all respondents were:

1. What were the early influences on your creativity?
2. Was there anything in your schooling which helped your creativity?
3. Was there anything in your schooling which hindered your creativity?
4. What do you feel schools should do today to encourage creative thinking?

I wanted to keep the questionnaire simple so that respondents could write at length about that which they were most passionate. I was quite taken aback by the fervour provoked by question 4. I seemed to be unleashing a Pandora's Box by including this question. It seemed as if these individuals had been waiting a very long time for someone to ask this question.

Some of the *most common* responses to each question are given below. I was not able to list all the responses, since that would have taken up far too much space.

What were the early influences on your creativity?

- Parents encouraged our questioning and reasoning
- There were rich and varied experiences at home
- There were lots of books in the home
- Parents gave us time for solitary play
- We were taught to appreciate nature
- Parents were good story tellers and made up bedtime stories
- Parents at times were childlike and could engage at the child's level
- Parents enjoyed writing
- Parents liked to draw
- Parents had magazines available with rich pictures of art
- Parents took us to art galleries and we saw the works of great artists
- Parents encouraged us in creative play, puppetry, filmmaking and family concerts.

- There were musical instruments in the house
- Our emotions were valued by our parents and we were allowed plenty of expression of them.

Was there anything in your schooling which helped your creativity?

- Teachers who let children write stories and publish them in the class
- Teachers who had a class newspaper and allowed us to write fiction
- Being cast as a star in a play
- Being allowed to play the piano in school and accompany school assemblies
- Being exposed to good artists who came into the classroom
- Seeing my teacher emotionally moved when she read a story to us in class
- A music teacher who recognised my talent for the piano and encouraged me to pursue music further
- Teachers who encouraged us to look at things in different ways
- Teachers who were passionate about their subject
- Teachers who praised us for coming up with unusual ideas or questions.

Was there anything in your schooling which hindered your creativity?

- We had no school plays in secondary school
- I was made to feel that I couldn't draw or paint and art lessons were soul-destroying
- My physics teacher thought that science was not for girls
- We were not allowed to do creative writing
- The exam system straight-jacketed my secondary education
- We had no creative drama after the age of 15
- There was no art in class after the age of 11
- Boys were ridiculed by teachers and other students for doing art
- 'A' levels had to be chosen too early and I was pushed into the sciences by my teachers
- My teacher didn't notice my unusual thoughts or ideas.

What do you feel schools should do to encourage creative thinking?

- Passion, fantasy, intuition and feeling must all be acknowledged in schools
- Schools should be less syllabus bound and convergent
- Creative thinking should be used across the curriculum
- Schools should be more a community of future possibilities, than prisons
- There should be much less testing
- Encourage visiting artists and visits to art galleries and concerts
- Give more time in the day for experimentation and discovery
- Teachers should be judged on how creative they are and not by exam results
- Need a wider range of assessment for students and teachers
- Should be emphasis on lifelong learning rather than just for the exam
- Give children a role in assessment and decision making

- Students need time to have fun
- The key goal of education should be to enable people to be creative about every aspect of their life and work
- We should get back to the art of teaching
- Teachers should be allowed to use their own creativity without too much paperwork
- Give teachers goals and the freedom to reach them how they would like
- League tables should be thrown out
- Teachers need to be retooled and retrained in such things as respect for ideas, question asking and building good relationships with their pupils
- Teachers need to know how to handle creative responses
- We need to diagnose children for how creative they are
- There should be balanced learning experiences which incorporate the many different ways in which children learn
- Schools should unleash the human spirit of the teacher and the child
- The affective side of education should be addressed
- Teachers should be given the space to develop the love of their subject so that we have passionate teachers
- Testing should be done only at 11 and 18
- We should publish examples of the best creative practice in schools
- Students should not have to drop subjects too early.

What do these results tell us? First of all, it seems from the responses above that parents have a key role to play in the development of creative thinking. It seems that parents who are models of creative behaviour themselves by writing and making up their own stories, for example, encourage creativity in their children. Parents who give their children rich experiences both inside and outside the home also aid creative development. And most importantly, parents who encourage questioning and creative play within the home and who value emotional expression facilitate creative behaviour.

Within the schools, teachers do much to encourage creative thinking and development. It seems that teachers who set tasks that require creative thinking bring out creative behaviour in their students. By inviting others into the classroom who are engaged in creative professions, teachers demonstrate to the child in a practical way the benefits of creativity. Teachers who recognise creative talents and encourage creative responses to questions promote creativity which students can then carry though to their chosen professions.

We can see that teachers who deny creative expression are hindering creative development. Teachers who see no need for art or music or drama are depriving children of tools with which they can create. Inappropriate values and prejudices of teachers can block creativity and perhaps affect students for the rest of their lives.

In terms of what the questionnaire results say about the actions schools need to take to further creativity, it seems, as stated earlier, that creative individuals have many suggestions. To summarise, they feel that teachers should be passionate about their subjects, encourage questioning and experimentation, respect the student's ideas, individualise learning, and generally unleash the human spirit. Teachers themselves should be allowed the time and space to develop their own creativity and not be judged solely on the exam results of their students. Teachers should be allowed to get back to the art of teaching.

From the results of this questionnaire we can see that there is room for much improvement in the development of creativity in the UK, particularly within schools. In terms of the emphasis on exam results here, Dr. E. Paul Torrance tells us that if creative products are not received with appreciation and respect, creative talents do not develop. He states that:

> Teachers influence pupils though the kinds of tests they give, the way they react to the questions children ask and the ideas they produce, the grades they assign, the assignments they make, and even their wording in making an assignment. (Torrance, 1965, p.19)

We know that creative children ask questions which can cause teachers to lose track of their thinking. How would this affect the implementation of the National Curriculum, the body of knowledge requiring assessment? How would a teacher feel about a creative child who has a burning question that doesn't fit into the mould of the exam syllabus? Do UK teachers currently have the time to react positively to creative questions?

These and many other questions are what we now must be asking if the UK is to provide for the needs of creative students. We must look to creative individuals for guidance in meeting their self-defined needs. No one knows more than the creative individual how his or her needs can best be served.

Hopefully, by looking at the questionnaire I have given to creative individuals, we can at least attain a glimpse into how the creative mind and soul works, what they are looking for at home and in education, and the ways they see that others can help them. If we ignore their desire for a more suitable education, we may be ignoring a large well of talent in the UK.

As mentioned earlier, the UK Government has at last come to the realisation that for the past 30 years children have been educated in ways that deny their individual needs for learning. The 2003 Labour Manifesto argues that children can become more active in their learning and that each child can pursue independent learning with the aid of the teacher. Perhaps the role of the teacher will thus change from someone who is evaluated by the amount of knowledge he or she effectively imparts to someone who is judged by how well he or she inspires the students to learn. This is a time of great change in the UK educational system, and we can only hope that the concerns of the creative respondents in this survey will be addressed, so that creative children will flourish at last within UK schools.

Reference

Torrance, E. P (1965) *Rewarding Creative Behavior.* Englewood Cliffs NJ: Prentice-Hall.

Anna Craft

Creative thinking in the early years of education

This paper proposes a framework for exploring creative thinking in the early years of school. It explores creative thinking as characterised in two significant curriculum landmarks applicable to young children: Plowden from the 1960s and the Early Learning Goals from 2000. It proposes 'little c creativity' as a way of conceptualising creativity, arguing that it represents the start of a 'third wave' of understanding the meaning and potential of creativity in the early years of education.

Drawing on empirical observations from a number of nursery and early years classrooms in England it raises issues around the extent to which this idea may be culturally specific – and the extent to which it is possible to propose a 'universal' notion of little c creativity.

First, I try to step into the children's shoes, in two ways - a poem from Roger McGough and a tiny snapshot from a nursery classroom I worked in recently.

First day at School, by Roger McGough

A millionbillionwillion miles from home
Waiting for the bell to go. (To go where?)
Why are they all so big, other children?
So noisy? So much at home they
Must have been born in uniform
Lived all their lives in playgrounds
Spent the years inventing games
That don't let me in. Games
That are rough, that swallow you up.

And the railings,
All around, the railings.
Are they there to keep out wolves and monsters?
Things that carry off and eat children?
Things you don't take sweets from?
Perhaps they're there to stop us getting out.
Running away from the lessins. Lessin.
What does a lessin look like?
Sounds small and slimy.
They keep them in glassrooms.
Whole rooms made of glass. Imagine.

I wish I could remember my name.
Mummy said it would come in useful.
Like wellies. When there's puddles.
Yellowwellies. I wish she was here.

I think my name is sewn on somewhere.
Perhaps the teacher will read it for me.
Tea-cher. The one who makes the tea.

What can we learn from Roger McGough about the child's perspective on our provision?

Craig and the Lego

Just before lunch, Craig (aged 4) arrives at the carpeted area of the nursery classroom clutching a small Lego construction which he has been making painstakingly for the past twenty minutes in another part of the room. His teacher, frustrated at his late arrival and at his disregard for the rules that constructions are taken apart at the end of each session, scolds him, to which he responds 'I made that...'

What happens next for him? What will support his creativity? Why? What will be the implications for his teacher? And - you might ask - how is this creativity?

Introduction

There have been a number of points in recent English history in which creativity has been particularly recognised at policy level as significant in the education process. Perhaps the earliest policy example was the 1933 Hadow Report which recommended appropriate practical and cognitive provision for children from the nursery through to 7+, within the context of a child-focused rationale of the education of young children. It named imaginative activity and thinking as important (though tied it closely to reality rather than the realms of fancy) and also noted the significance of offering children contexts for self-expression.

The Hadow Report provided an important precursor to the Plowden Report, published in the 1960s and, together, they can be seen as representing the first 'wave' of policy recommendations and activity in practice in fostering creativity with early years children. This first wave, linked creativity to a particular, child-centred, discovery-based pedagogical approach and also to the arts. It represented a distinct position on what had preceded it. But it was such a 'free' approach to creativity which formed part of the critique of child-centred education practices by the Black Paper writers (Cox & Dyson, 1971) and which, arguably, laid the way for the introduction of a subject-content based national curriculum at the end of the 1980s. In addition, some thought that many schools were implementing the Plowden ideas incompetently (Alexander, 1995). Creativity, following the Plowden era, receded.

However, since the mid 1990s which could be seen as the start of the second period, there has been a growing recognition from policy makers and commentators that learner creativity is an extremely important aim for education. The economic imperative to foster creativity in business has helped raise the profile and credentials of creativity in education more generally.

During the recent review of the National Curriculum (Curriculum 2000) the Secretary of State for Education and Employment set up a number of advisory groups to provide input into the debate. One of these was the National Advisory Committee for Creative and Cultural Education (NACCCE) which submitted its final report in 1999. The report contained a wide range of recommendations, which called for further work and investigations into creativity and cultural education.

The first two waves of conceptualising creativity in the early years of education

The Plowden Report (CACE, 1967) and the Hadow recommendations that it incorporated, not only had a major general influence on the broad curriculum for this age range, it also crystallised thinking about creativity in education for the generation which followed it. It drew on a large body of so-called liberal thinking on the education of children.

The Plowden recommendations highlighted the importance of children learning by discovery and being permitted to take an active role in both the definition of their curriculum and the exploration of it. The trend towards active and individualised learning was endorsed, as was learning through first-hand experience of the natural social and constructed world beyond the classroom, although the roles of knowledge and skills were also acknowledged, as was the significance in education of what they described as 'learning by description' (para.553, p.202). A central role was given to play, which was seen as providing 'the roots of drama, expressive movement and art' (para. 525, p.193). Teachers were encouraged to enter the play world of the child, observing carefully what the children were learning and intervening to extend learning at appropriate times. Play was seen as a vehicle for fostering imagination as this quotation suggests: 'Their imagination seizes on particular facets of objects and leads them to invent as well as to create' (para.525, p.193). Play was also seen as providing a 'natural' stepping stone to more parts of the curriculum: for example, they claimed that 'Play can lead naturally to reading and writing' (Para. 536, p. 197).

Plowden made a significant contribution to the way in which creativity in early school education was understood. The report suggested that a child's creativity was:

- benign
- at the heart of all teaching and learning arrangements
- primarily associated with play.

It formed an early attempt to suggest how to stimulate creativity. It can also be seen as having provided an early foundation for the move in creativity research towards an emphasis on social systems rather than personality, cognition or psychodynamics.

The Plowden perspective on creativity is subject to all of the same criticisms made of the report in general. In other words:

- the fallacy of the necessity, posited in Plowden, of learning from concrete experience
- the ambiguity of the term 'discovery learning'
- the problem of defining a child's needs
- the view that the Piagetian and possibly Deweyesque notion underpinning Plowden, that the child's 'essential nature' unfolds by laws of growth merely by the child's exploration of a diverse physical environment is over-simplistic and misinformed
- the problematic nature of 'development'
- the naivete of the notion of a child's 'readiness to learn'
- the logical fallacy of the notion that what was natural (to the child) was also good
- the oversimplification of the notion of 'self-direction'
- disagreement with the notion that children could learn effectively without any structure or boundaries
- a fear of over-extension of individual autonomy.

I do not propose to re-visit these here as they have been explored to death in previous literatures. However, there are several problems arising from Plowden specifically associated with the fostering of creativity.

First, is *the problem of the role of knowledge*. Surely, if a child is to identify possibilities or exercise imagination in any context, this must be done with knowledge, for without it a child cannot logically go beyond what is 'given'. The difficulty with Plowden is that it implies that a child may be let loose to discover and learn without any prior knowledge.

Second, *there is some lack of context implied in the rationale for 'self-expression'*. Plowden appears to conceive of the child's growth and expression in a moral and ethical vacuum. I would argue that encouraging young children to have ideas and express them, should be set in a moral and ethical context within the classroom (Craft, 2000).

Third, Plowden suggests that play provides the foundation for a variety of other forms of knowledge and expression: 'In play are the roots of drama, expressive movement and art' (para.525). Whilst not wishing to take issue with this particular claim, I would argue that *it appears to connect play creativity within the arts only and not with creativity across the whole curriculum* (although Plowden does make much of the social foundations which both spawn play activities and to which children adjust through their play activities). The Plowden approach is not dissimilar to Herbert Read's thesis, that 'art should be the basis of education' (p.1). There is a further problem also which is that *play and creativity are not the same as one another*. Not all play is creative.

Plowden provided a landmark in envisioning a role for creativity in the curriculum. Creativity became associated with a range of other approaches which included discovery learning, child-centred pedagogy, an integrated curriculum, the embracing of self-referencing and the apparent move away from an emphasis on social norms for evaluative purposes. But because of the conceptual and practical problems with the progressive movement, it was later argued that the fostering of creativity was perceived as a rather loose notion

(NACCCE, 1999, p88), and was thus pushed to the back of policy makers' priorities in curriculum development.

Later in the 20th century, as the foundations of what was to become the National Curriculum were laid, the Plowden concept of creativity was left behind. No policy was put in its place initially, for the focus was on the formulation in 1989 of a curriculum with a high propositional knowledge content. Later, after the first revision of the National Curriculum in 1995, the attention of curriculum policy makers turned increasingly to thinking and other life skills involved in children's learning. And here we come to the second wave.

For this included some attention to the fostering of creativity, alongside a resurgence of interest in psychology and education research. The revival of research interest can be seen, Jeffrey & Craft argue (2001), as drawing in the role of social interaction in an unprecedented way.

In terms of curriculum policy, I want to look at three major initiatives. First, the inclusion of 'Creative Development' as one of the seven Early Learning Goals for early years children. Second, the commissioning of the National Advisory Committee on Creative and Cultural Education (NACCCE), which reported in 1999. The Committee gave advice on what would need to be done at a range of levels including policy making, to foster the development of pupil creativity within school education. Third, the Qualifications and Curriculum Authority (QCA) and Department for Education and Employment (DfEE) identified 'creative thinking skills' as a key skill in the National Curriculum (DfEE, QCA, 1999).

Looking at each of them in turn:

Creative Development: The codifying of this part of the early years curriculum for children up to the age of five, meshed closely with the existing norms and discourse about early education. 'Creative Development' encompasses art, craft and design and various forms of dramatic play and creative expression, all of which have traditionally formed a core part of early years provision. It emphasises the role of imagination and the importance of children developing a range of ways of expressing their ideas and communicating their feelings.

Although many welcomed the codifying of creativity in some form within the early learning curriculum, several problems may be detected with 'Creative Development'.

First, its formulation implies that creativity involves *specific parts of the curriculum and certain forms of learning, only*. Yet, I would argue that problem finding and solving, using imagination and posing 'what if?' questions could (and do) occur within a whole range of domains.

Second, *conceiving of creativity as something which may be 'developed' also opens it to the standard criticisms of developmentalism*. For it implies a ceiling or static end-state. There is an implication that, given the appropriate immediate learning environment, children will 'develop'. The presuppositions of a ceiling and of natural development are each problematic.

Thirdly, the implication is *that play and creativity are the same*. I would say they are not. Play may be, but is not necessarily, creative. For example, 'Snakes and Ladders', being dependent upon a mix of chance and a set structure, is not creative. But 'Hide and Seek' may well be, demanding the consideration of options and possibilities for hiding places and seeking strategies.

The NACCCE Report: The NACCCE Report linked the fostering of pupil creativity with the development of culture, in that original ideas and action are developed in a shifting cultural context. It suggested that the fostering of pupil creativity would contribute to the cultural development of society and that creativity rarely occurs without some form of interrogation of what has gone before or is occurring synchronously.

The Report distinguished between different definitions of creativity, proposing the 'democratic' definition as the one perhaps most appropriate to education, suggesting 'all people are capable of creative achievement in some area of activity, provided the conditions are right and they have acquired the relevant knowledge and skills.' (Para.25).

This notion, of 'democratic creativity', has some connection with Plowden, in that:

- pupils' self-expression is valued
- all people are seen as capable of creativity.

But the NACCCE 'democratic creativity' definition *contrasts* with the Plowden approach in a number of ways. First, it argues for the acquisition of knowledge and skills as the necessary foundation to creativity – reflecting the wider research context in the 'situating' of knowledge. Secondly, it has a great deal more to say on creativity than Plowden since that was its main focus.

Criticisms of NACCCE are few, the major one being that it gives an implicit message that creativity is arts-based.

The National Curriculum: By contrast, the National Curriculum Handbook for primary schools, proposes a *cross-curricular* role for creativity in the aims of the school curriculum, saying that 'the curriculum should enable pupils to think creatively.... It should give them the opportunity to become creative...' (1999, p11). Creativity is defined in the National Curriculum Handbook as a cross-curricular thinking skill. This reflects the notion proposed by some that creativity is not the preserve of the arts alone but that it arises in all domains of human endeavour.

Yet, identifying creativity as a skill could be seen as an over-simplification, for to operate creatively must necessarily presuppose an understanding of the domain and thus creativity cannot be seen as a knowledge-free, transferable skill. On the other hand, the National Curriculum, even in its revised form, is very knowledge-heavy and thus the curriculum framework itself does provide the knowledge base within which creativity is to operate. It is just left to teachers to make the connection.

These three major policy developments in the second wave reflect a wider burgeoning of interest in creativity beyond education at the start of the 21st century. This can be seen as reflecting social, technological and economic imperatives (Craft, 1997, 1998, 2000).

Although they have occurred almost simultaneously, a notable feature of them is their lack of coherence as a set of measures, in a number of ways:

- focus and detail (there are a variety of foci, including detailed discussion of creativity in the curriculum for different age stages in 'Creative Development', compared with a broad-brush description of creativity as a cross-curricular thinking skill but not mapped in at all, in the English National Curriculum, compared with a focus on creativity across learning, linked in with culture in the NACCCE Report);
- the way that creativity is defined (ranging from arts, play, aesthetic development and self-expression emphases in the Early Learning Goals, to broader, skill-based ones in the National Curriculum, as well as the NACCCE Report);
- the extent to which the guidance is statutory (the National Curriculum and the Early Learning Goals being statutory and the NACCCE Report not being).

This very incoherence suggests that the placing of creativity more centrally in the school curriculum has not yet occurred, despite a growing recognition of the need to ensure creativity is fostered in learners and teachers. Indeed, some say that the general direction being taken during the process of developing curricula for young children is that it has moved young children's learning firmly in the direction of formalised 'basic' skills and knowledge, and away from a 'child-focused' curriculum (Drummond, 1999; Schmidt, 1998; Pascal & Bertram, 1999).

It seems to me that we may now be experiencing the start of a third wave.

The third wave? Personal effectiveness as little c creativity

Uncertainty is a given in industrialised societies in today's world. Patterns of life which may have been more predictable in earlier times are now much less so. The very speed of change has itself introduced the need to exercise choice in a wide range of settings and at a spectrum of levels from the individual through to the collective. The growing culture of individualism, together with changes in technology and the marketplace, may be seen as demanding and offering an ever-growing role to the individual's own 'agency' in determining directions, routes and pathways through all sorts of aspects of life. Surviving and thriving in the 21st century seems to require a sort of 'personal effectiveness' in coping with unknown territory and in recognising and making choices.

I would like to call this 'creativity in everyday life', or *little c creativity* (to distinguish it from creativity in the arts, and/or the paradigm-shifting creativity of great figures in history). What then does personal effectiveness or little c creativity, involve? The first observation to make is that the terms 'little c creativity' and 'personal effectiveness' are distinct ideas. Little c creativity is the capacity to route-find, life-wide. Personal effectiveness is the capacity to take action which is in some way evaluated as 'effective' or successful. The term personal effectiveness implies the restriction of the activity to the 'personal' domain, for example, perhaps the social and emotional aspects of oneself.

I use the term 'little c creativity' to encompass personal effectiveness, a life-wide resourcefulness which is effective in successfully enabling the individual to chart a course of action by seeing opportunities as well as overcoming obstacles. This may occur in personal and social matters or in undertaking an activity in a curriculum area, such as mathematics or the humanities. Implied in 'little c creativity' is the notion that it is essentially a practical matter akin to Ryle's (1949) 'know-how' in that it is concerned with the skills involved in manoeuvring and operating with concepts, ideas and the physical and social world.

The kind of personal effectiveness being proposed here is in keeping with the liberal tradition and liberal ideas in general, in paying attention to the well-being of the individual. It focuses on the individual making something of his or her life, whilst being tied into the wider social, economic and ethical framework of society. It has something in common with the Romantic movement in the sense that it celebrates individuality and the potential for going beyond existing traditions.

Although it is a concept which emphasises the individual's freedom, little c creativity may also be developed in a context of constraint. Here I refer to Berlin's (1958) distinction between the notion of 'negative freedom' as being free through constraints, and 'positive freedom', i.e. being free to be one's own agent, being free to undertake a course of action, determined not by the collective but by the individual only. It seems to me that little c creativity could arise out of either form of freedom. A playgroup, for example, may at times provide for children to explore the play activities entirely independently, with a large degree of freedom. In such circumstances, a child may exercise personal effectiveness in the making of choices and in making something of friendships, and in exploring specific activities such as role-play and construction with bricks. By contrast, at other times the playgroup may constrain the children's choices so that they must choose between specified activities, for example, cutting and sticking, quiet time in the book corner, painting or a number activity. The constraining of choices does not necessarily mean that creativity may not be developed. This kind of creativity is not necessarily tied to a product-outcome, for it involves exercising imaginativeness.

The notion of little c creativity goes beyond 'doing it differently', 'finding alternatives' or 'producing novelty', for it involves having some grasp of the domain of application and thus of the appropriateness of the ideas. It involves the use of imagination, intelligence, self-creation and self-expression.

Little c creativity goes beyond the provision in both the Early Learning Goals and the National Curriculum 2000. Although it can be argued (Craft, 2000; Rowe & Humphries, 2001) that creativity can be encouraged in children aged 3 to 8 through these existing curricula, I want to suggest that this occurs in spite of, not because of, the statutory curriculum framework. Fostering young children's resourcefulness and encouraging them to consider and implement alternative possibilities in a range of contexts, including play, relationships, collective activity such as circle time and 'formal' curriculum areas such as early mathematics, requires the embracing of little c creativity.

It has something in common with the 'democratic' version of creativity proposed by the NACCCE Report (1999) which was: 'Imaginative activity fashioned so as to produce outcomes that are both original and of value'. But what is distinct about little c creativity is its emphasis on resourcefulness life-wide.

Overall my proposal is then, that there is a case for early education enabling children to develop confidence and skills in shaping themselves and their lives, both now as children and later as adults, that the existing Early Learning Goals and National Curriculum are insufficient on their own - and that fostering little c creativity involves harnessing children's inherent flexibility and resourcefulness.

To illustrate the kinds of activity that I would classify as little c creativity in early education, here are some short case studies from early years settings in the UK.

Case Study 1: Rowan and the computer game

Four year-old Rowan is playing on the computer, whilst his teacher works on the play mat nearby, helping some other boys do some drawing for their personal record books. Rowan completes the game which was on the screen, which is a teddy bear with 'clothes' that need to be placed over the correct part of his body. He looks around at his teacher and seeing him occupied, deftly finds the menu screen to select a new game. He seems to be concentrating hard on his task. After a few seconds he succeeds in bringing up a new game, this time involving sorting. His teacher notices what he is doing and comes over. 'Did you manage it all by yourself, Rowan?' he asks, appreciatively. Rowan nods and smiles. But this is a game he is unfamiliar with and he then seems puzzled about what to do next. His teacher asks, 'what do you think you might need to do for this game?'. Rowan is unsure and, meanwhile, another child from the carpeted area notices and calls out a suggestion. His teacher warmly acknowledges the suggestion, whilst at the same time encouraging Rowan to consider what the game might require. Rowan eventually decides on his own rules for the game, which involve putting all of the pieces into the 'rubbish bin'. Although this is not 'officially' the way the game works, Rowan sorts each of the fruits verbally, as he puts them into the bin (i.e. he does each fruit-type in groups). Rather than criticising this, his teacher praises his idea and his grouping and encourages him to continue to think about how this game works.

Case study 2: Possibilities and thinking thumbs

A small group of six-year-olds are working with a disparate selection of materials that their teacher has introduced to them. The materials include bread, glue, tissue paper, scissors, water and card. During the discussion before they start on their own individual projects, their teacher encourages them to explore the properties of each resource, showing that they are thinking by waggling their 'thinking thumbs'. She talks both gently but purposively with the children, trying to maintain a relationship with each as an individual. As the children come up with ideas of how the materials could be used, she uses language carefully to hint that each person will make up their own mind about how to use these materials. *'You* might be going to do that' she mentions several times in response to ideas.

Case Study 3: Manouella and the hoops

Manouella is leading a music and dance session with a group of children aged three and four, in a nursery school. She uses hoops during the session for a number of different imaginary things, including puddles, trays of cakes and handbags. Using music and song as the backdrop, the children jump into the 'puddles', hold the 'trays' and carry the 'bags'. They do all these things as children, as an old person, and so on, again listening to the mood of the music to help them determine how to move. Later in the morning, Manouella notices some of the same children are playing with their hoop play objects in exactly the same way, in the outdoor play area. Going over to them and bending down, she engages with their play, acknowledging their choice of imaginary object and again using her voice to encourage them to experiment further with direction (high pitch signifying 'up' and low pitch signifying 'down', etc), tempo and so on.

Case study 4

Two 3 year-olds were playing in the nursery sandpit with a long wooden plank, when it began to rain. As their teachers started to pack away the toys which belonged in the shed, one child ran indoors whilst the other began to drag the plank toward the shed, and after a few unsuccessful heaves at it, commissioned the observing researcher a few feet away, to take one end of it.

This particular call for 'ordinary' creativity is quite distinct from the first and second waves. Its distinguishing features are five-fold:

- its extension, beyond the curriculum subjects, to the width of ordinary life
- at the same time, conceptualising creativity as relevant across the curriculum
- the relationship suggested between little c creativity and the wider economic, social and technological context (Craft, 2000) (Here it contrasts with the 1960s approach to creativity, but is closer to the NACCCE and 2000 National Curriculum formulations)
- little c creativity is not necessarily tied to a particular pedagogy
- little c creativity is not value-free and is set in the context of humane morality.

But perhaps most importantly for today's discussion, in the context of early years education, I am proposing that it may have an importance which goes beyond ways in which creativity is currently conceived of in this phase of education.

Questions

I want to pose a few questions about the idea of little c creativity in the context of early years education, which are about its potential limits.

1. How culturally specific is this conceptualising of creativity? Creativity, whether 'high' or 'ordinary', is often presented as if it were a universally applicable concept. But it may, by contrast, be quite culturally specific, in its strong emphasis on individuality and the value it places on being able to think independently of social norms. For this may reflect peculiarly Western values, and a culture where the individual and the marketplace are held in high esteem. In a more repressive or conformist culture, creativity might be perceived to be less relevant and desirable. Clearly, cultural context may also affect a person's experiences of creativity and their ability to manifest it – although this may not be a totally predictable relationship. Thus, in a social context where choices and personal autonomy are severely restricted, the drive to find alternatives may be quite strong. On the other hand, it may be that avoidance of social or political sanctions and socialisation into submission, would, under such conditions, suffocate creativity.

It is also possible that creativity may be imbued with social class based assumptions such as resilience, self-reliance, persistence and control over one's environment – also future-orientation, and greater individualism (Craft, 2002, Kluckhohn and Strodtbeck, 1961).

On the other hand, it could be argued that both high and ordinary creativity reflect the globalisation of significant aspects of Western culture. And although there may be a strong element of 'cultural saturation' in the concept of creativity, it could also be said that the increasing global influence of Western culture, including its markets, means that the relevance of creativity as a universal concept may grow.

But, we still live in a world where there are distinct cultural identities both within and between nation-states, as well as different traditions and value-sets. The universalisation of creativity in the current world may be premature and inappropriate. Creativity, certainly in the sense of little c creativity, I would suggest, is limited by its cultural specificity.

2. Environmental limits The case for fostering creativity in education can be seen as a response to the conditions and pace of life and the global market economy. But, how desirable is the norm of innovation that the global economy demands? To what extent is it desirable to encourage and sustain the 'disposable' culture, where obsolescence is built in at the design stage of many consumer goods and where fashion dictates the need for constant change and updating? For there are clear environmental costs to giving high value to the market, as if it were a divine force. To what extent do we, in the marketplace at any rate, encourage innovation for it's own sake, without reference to genuine need? How desirable is it to encourage those values which present, via the market, 'wants' as if they were 'needs'? It could be said that a culture of 'make do and mend' might be something to be fostered, rather than looking to ways of changing what may be working perfectly well, whether that be a system, relationship, service or product.

3. *Ethical limits* How do we weigh up the use of creativity for destructive purposes? For creativity undoubtedly has a darker side. The human imagination is capable of immense destruction as well as of almost infinitely constructive possibilities. To what extent is it possible to generate systems which stimulate and celebrate creativity, within a profoundly humane framework, and to actively examine and encourage the critical examination of the values inherent in creative ideas and action? The role of educators is perhaps to encourage students to examine the possible wider effects of their own ideas and those of others, and to evaluate both choices and worth in the light of this. This inevitably means balancing conflicting perspectives and values which themselves may be irreconcilable.

4. *How do ordinary and high creativity connect?* There have been numerous attempts to distinguish between ordinary and high creativity. But what is their relationship to one another? Are they part of a continuum, as argued by Craft (2001a) and Worth (2000)? Weisberg's (1993) model of creativity has been proposed as one of a number which may unify ordinary and high creativity (Fowles, 2002). However, these assertions need more investigation, for our understanding of what factors may trigger an act of high creativity is still imperfect. This has implications for education. For example, it may be that by stimulating the creativity of all children, we produce more creative behaviour at all points in the continuum, including high creativity. This assumption seems to underpin both policy and also some commentary on creativity in education. But is the assumption sound? We are currently limited by our understanding of creativity itself.

Dilemmas for the educator

I have suggested, then, some fundamental difficulties with the concept. I have proposed that creativity cannot necessarily be seen as a universal concept, equally applicable and relevant to diverse contexts. So, what dilemmas of principle and practice are raised for the educator, by the argument that creativity is not a universal concept?

I want to propose three dilemmas of principle and several of practice. Dilemmas of principle, then:

- *If creativity is culturally specific, how appropriate is it to encourage it within education?* Stimulating creativity involves encouraging learners to adopt a way of life that not only presents itself as universal when it is not, but also the positive associations with creativity mask some possibly questionable values which are also associated with it. On the other hand, education in any cultural context will involve the teaching of some concepts as if they were universal; but like any other concept, creativity does not necessarily have to be taught in this way. Indeed, by its very nature, being about alternatives and possibilities, it offers inherent potential for evaluating the worth of any creative outcome, by considering the implications of any new idea, product, service, etc. Thus, although creativity is always situated within a cultural context, by interrogating this through evaluating the worth of any creative outcome, the assumption of cultural universalism may be challenged.

- *To what extent is the 'throw-away society' a given?* How appropriate is the implication that creativity is a good thing for the economy, for the society and therefore for education? Implicit in this is the idea that innovation is of itself a good thing. That the old, or the borrowed, the inherited and the unchanging are undesirable, whereas the new is, by contrast, of paramount value, by virtue of its newness. For creativity, in the sense of the process which leads to constant change and innovation in products, contributes to the economy, in that having a short shelf-life to any product means increased sales, and so on. How far is it appropriate for the fostering of creativity to occur without critical reflection on the environmental, social and other consequences in treating the 'market as God' in this way?
- *To what extent does the fostering of creativity feed or challenge the status quo?* Fostering creativity in the classroom could both feed the market as suggested. But fostering children's creativity could also lead to challenges to the status quo, and could lead to alternative modes of existence. How can classroom pedagogy reflect the schism between the assumption that creativity leads to increased wealth and the celebration of creativity as the 'other' or as the potential for the 'other'?

As to challenges of practice, I want to raise three of these, which probably speak for themselves:

- *The curriculum:* How can the curriculum be organised to stimulate creativity? A curriculum which is fixed, compulsory, which involves a great deal of propositional knowledge, and which takes up a great deal of learning time, may pose challenges to stimulating creativity - possibly more so than a curriculum which is more flexible. And how is *any* curriculum best organised - in discrete subject areas, or integrated?
- *Professional artistry within a centralised pedagogy.* The centralising not only of curriculum but also of pedagogy, in literacy and numeracy in any case, can be seen, as we know, as posing a challenge to professional artistry - and in this sense may be seen as restricting potential teacher creativity, at least in some parts of the curriculum and in some phases. So, how does a teacher balance professional creativity and judgement against the requirements to teach in certain ways?
- *The distinctions and potential tensions between teaching for creativity, creative teaching and creative learning.* The distinction between teaching for creativity and creative teaching was made by the NACCCE report (1999), which acknowledged that teaching for creativity (i.e. focusing on the child's creativity as an outcome) may or may not involve creative teaching

(which is essentially innovative professional practices). The notion of creative learning has been theorised as involving holism of pupil, learning and curriculum (Woods, 1995) and empowerment (Schiller, 1979) and is being further theorised at present (Craft, 2003, Jeffrey and Craft, 2003). There may be important practical distinctions between each of these in terms of pedagogy, which without care could be confused for one another.

Summing up

I hope what I have managed to start to do is to make a case for the significance of little c creativity in the curriculum of young children. Setting the second wave curriculum developments in historical context, I have suggested that they are insufficient on their own. I propose that within the creativity discourse in early years education, a third wave is emerging, and with it some important questions about its limits. And of course at the level of the classroom there are, as we might expect, some dilemmas of principle and pedagogy to grapple with.

To return to Craig and his Lego: what would have made his experience creative?

- hearing and acknowledging him: giving him time in a busy moment
- engaging with the knowledge that enabled him to construct the model
- enabling him to have the space to keep it - but with reference to the wider needs of the class
- celebrating the possibility thinking he brought to a rule-bound situation?

What would have been the consequences?

* overall needs of the class, and of the school - lunch was waiting
* other events like this?

To an extent, we are all like the children in Roger McGough's poem, in that we work with the constructions - the understandings - we have, and these are drawn from experience.

In the early years of education, the experiences of staff are of course wide and varied - possibly more so than anywhere else in the school. This paper has been designed to stimulate debate and discussion, to encourage reflection on the concept of little c creativity in the early years from participants' own experiences and contexts.

References

Alexander, R. (1995), *Versions of Primary Education,* London: Routledge.

Berlin, I. (1958), *Two Concepts of Liberty: An Inaugural Lecture*, Delivered before the University of Oxford, 31 October 1958, Oxford: The Clarendon Press.

Craft, A. (1997), 'Identity and Creativity: Educating for post-modernism?' *Teacher Development: An international journal of teachers' professional development*, Vol. 1, No. 1, 1997, pp 83 – 96 ISSN 1366-4530.

Craft, A. (1998), 'UK Educator Perspectives on Creativity', *Journal of Creative Behavior*, Vol 32 No4, fourth quarter, pp 244 – 257.

Craft, A. (1999), 'Creative development in the early years: implications of policy for practice', *The Curriculum Journal* Vol. 10 No. 1 Spring 1999 pp 135 - 150 .

Craft, A. (2000), *Creativity Across the Primary Curriculum*, London: Routledge.

Craft, A. (2003), A Language for Creativity? Paper given at *British Educational Research Association Conference*, Edinburgh University, September 2003, for Special Interest Group Creativity in Education.

Drummond, M.-J. (1999), Perceptions of Play in a Steiner Kindergarten, in Abbott, L., Moylett, H. (Eds) (1999), *Early Education Transformed*, London: Falmer Press.

Jeffrey, B. & Craft, A. (2001), The Universalization of Creativity, in Craft, A., Jeffrey, B. & Leibling, M. (Eds), (2001), *Creativity in Education*, London: Continuum.

Jeffrey, B. and Craft, A. (2003), Creative Learning and Possibility Thinking, Paper given at *British Educational Research Association Conference*, Edinburgh University, September 2003, for Special Interest Group Creativity in Education.

Qualifications and Curriculum Authority and Department for Education and Employment (2000*), Curriculum Guidance for the Foundation Stage*, London: DfEE/QCA.

Pascal, C. & Bertram, T. (1999), Accounting Early for Lifelong Learning, in Abbott, L., Moylett, H. (Eds) (1999), *Early Education Transformed*, London: Falmer Press.

Rowe, S. & Humphreys, S. (2001), Creating a Climate for Learning at Coombes Infant and Nursery School, in Craft, A., Jeffrey, B. & Leibling, M. (Eds), (2001), *Creativity in Education*, London: Continuum.

Qualifications and Curriculum Authority and Department for Education and Employment (1999*), The National Curriculum Handbook for primary teachers in England*, London: DfEE/QCA.

Ryle, G. (1949), *Concept of Mind*, London: Hutchinson.

Schiller, C. (1979), *Christian Schiller: in his own words*, London: Black.

Schmidt, S. (1998), *A Guide to Early Years Practice*, London: Routledge.

Woods, P. (1995), *Creative Teachers in Primary Schools*, Buckingham: Open University Press.

PLEASE DO NOT QUOTE FROM THIS PAPER WITHOUT AUTHOR'S PERMISSION

Rekha Sharma Sen
Neerja Sharma

Teachers' conception of creativity and its nurture in children: an Indian perspective

Introduction

Although creativity is a psychological construct, its meaning is based on a cultural definition of what it means to create something or to be creative. By adopting an ethnographic approach to the study of creativity theory, one can describe the creative process, products, individuals and environment in a cultural context, which makes it more meaningful than studying them in isolation (Hunsaker, 1992).

Research seems to indicate significant fundamental differences in the Western and Eastern conception of creativity and the process of creation. Creativity definitions may suffer from European and American-bound presuppositions and biases (Whitney, 1983; Mackinnon, 1987; Briggs, 1988). Research on the Eastern perspective of creativity indicates that the emphasis is not so much on producing something novel or original as being able to produce new and applicable responses to the daily challenges of living and, thereby, lead a creative life. According to the Eastern view, creativity involves a state of personal fulfillment, a connection to the primordial realm, the expression of an inner essence or ultimate reality, and spiritual and religious self-expression rather than an innovative solution to a problem (Chu, 1970; Mathur, 1982; Aron & Aron, 1982; Sherr, 1982; Kuo, 1996). Wonder and Blake (1992) argue that the Eastern view centres on artistic, poetic and everyday life domains of creative activity.

The Western view of the creative process, as one that is situated primarily in the individual person and results in a novel and socially useful tangible product/idea, seems to be fostered by individualistic cultures. The Indian society has been categorized as 'collectivist' in its orientation (Hofstede, 1980) and predominantly hierarchical (Sinha, 1980). Roland (1988), speaking of the collectivist orientation of the Indian society, refers to the 'familial self' of Indians. However, research also indicates that there is a kind of 'duality' of the Indian psyche, which makes people individualistic and collectivist at the same time (Bharati, 1985), with the bulk of the population lying somewhere between the two. An attempt to truly indigenize research in creativity has to begin with exploring how creativity is conceived, and the meaning that is ascribed to it, in India. This needs to be done with caution as the Indian society is multi-cultural. Thus, within and among various groups and communities in society, differences can exist in the way creativity is manifested and perceived.

While there has been extensive research on people's implicit theories of creativity in the West (Runco, 1984; Sternberg, 1985; Fryer & Collings, 1991;

Runco, Johnson & Baer, 1993; Runco, Nemiro & Walberg, 1998) and some studies have been carried out on Hong Kong and Chinese populations (Rudowicz & Hui, 1997; Rudowicz & Yue, 2001), in the Indian context it is difficult to find studies that investigate implicit theories of creativity. In a rare study, Kapur, Subramanyam & Shah (1997) explored Indian scientists' views of creativity, particularly with regard to Indian science. Eighty percent of the total sample (N=20) viewed creativity as involving something 'new'. Most of the scientists thought that family and educational institutions play a very significant role in fostering creativity, but also stated that in both contexts children's curiosity and explorations were largely stifled. It has been pointed out that it is the home and the school climate variables which make the crucial difference between creative and not so creative children (Mackinnon, 1962; Raina, 1975; Dehlavi & Torrance, 1979; Raina, Kumar & Raina, 1980). The belief systems and the 'psychology of the caretakers' provide powerful contextual meaning systems that influence child-rearing behaviours and expectations from children (Super & Harkness, 1986; 1997).

There has been a phenomenal growth in India's education sector since independence, in terms of quantity. However, analysts have also pointed out many ills in the system (Naik & Nurallah, 1974; Naik, 1975; Kamat, 1980). A major constraint is the curriculum load right from the primary classes which hinders the development of creative potential and offers few opportunities to explore and try things out (Hariharan, 1981; Mangla, 1981; Arora, Gupta & Madhulika, 1982; Mehra, 1982; Gore, 1985).

The 'Ideal Pupil' or 'Ideal Child' Checklist devised by Torrance and his colleagues (1975) has been used to determine the extent to which creativity-relevant traits are nurtured in various cultures. There have been a number of studies in the Indian context using the Ideal Pupil Checklist, with teachers as sample (Phatak's 1962-63 data reported in Torrance's study (1965); 1961 data reported in Torrance's analysis (1967; 1973); Raina (1970); Raina & Raina (1971); Raina (1982); 1977 data reported in Raina (1984); Raina (1985); Raina (1991) and these provide a cross-era comparison.

Except for the 1977 data reported in Raina (1984), when four of the traits nominated by the teachers were those most valued by Torrance's experts as relevant for creativity, in all the other studies cited above, only one or two traits associated with creative personality appeared in the teachers' ranking of top 10 traits. In fact, in Raina's (1991) study none of the traits most valued by experts appeared in the teachers' list of top 10 traits.

As regards the 10 traits least valued by the sample, the teachers in all eight Indian studies valued 'non conformity' least, whereas Torrance's experts least valued 'conformity'.

In the Indian studies there is consistently high correlation (0.83) among perception of Indian teachers across time. Coefficients of correlation between the Q-sort ratings of the teachers and those of Torrance's experts were largely low and not significant.

The stress on 'obedience', 'courteousness', 'affectionate', 'remembers well', 'does work on time', 'considerate of others' and 'altruistic' in most of the Indian studies has led researchers to postulate that the Indian teachers place more emphasis on the receptive nature of Man, as compared to the self-acting nature of Man (Raina, 1984). While teachers' opinions are reflecting the values nurtured in the larger social context, the consequences are grave from the viewpoint of creativity (Raina, 1991).

Creativity brings about cultural change, but is also facilitated by such changes. India has witnessed rapid changes at all levels in the past two decades, though change has not taken place at a uniform pace or in all regions. As Rao (1977) stated, the old exists with the new, 'what is' with 'what ought to be' and the traditional with the modern. However, the overall trend is in the direction of loosening controls – in the political, economic and social spheres. Given the complementary nature of the relationship that exists between change and creativity, the questions that arise are: Has the overall change in the Indian lifestyle had an impact on the education system? Have teachers' concepts of the ideal pupil changed? How do teachers construe creativity and creative teaching? Against this backdrop, the present study was undertaken with the following objectives:

- to determine if there has there been a change in teachers' conceptions of the 'ideal pupil' in the 40 years since the first Indian study in 1961
- to uncover teachers' implicit theories of creativity and to examine how they translate into creative teaching and learning.

Method

Sample
The sample comprised 29 teachers (7 male and 22 female), teaching grades nursery to XII, with teaching experience ranging from 5 to 30 years. The teachers were selected from four different schools - two high fee-paying private schools, catering for children from the middle and upper socioeconomic status groups; and two low fee-paying government schools, catering for children from the lower socioeconomic status group. They were identified from a universe of around 269 teachers in the four schools, based on predetermined criteria for selection, viz. a) level at which they were teaching; b) sex of the teacher; c) length of teaching experience; and d) willingness to give adequate time.

Measures
Data collection employed qualitative and quantitative methodologies. The following tools were used:

1. The 66-item *Ideal Pupil Checklist* (Torrance, 1975) to identify the characteristics teachers wanted to encourage and discourage in the child. The checklist was translated into Hindi and the accuracy of translation assessed using back translation.
2. In-depth semi-structured interview schedules for use with the teachers to understand how they construed creativity and creative teaching and learning, to identify the constraints they perceived in teaching creatively and to explore the extent of nurturance of children's creativity.

3. The interview schedule used in step two was converted into a questionnaire, containing open and close-ended questions, for the teachers to complete.

Procedure

The data was collected individually for each teacher during three meetings:

1. In the first meeting, the teacher completed the Ideal Pupil Checklist (IPC). Each teacher was asked to first rate the characteristics on a six-point scale ranging from +3 to −3 ('encourage very strongly' to 'discourage very strongly'). Additionally, she had to indicate, from the 66 characteristics of the IPC, the five most desirable that she would especially like to encourage and the five least desirable which she would want to strongly discourage.
2. In the second, an in-depth semi-structured interview was conducted, using the schedule described above. After the interview, the teacher was given the interview schedule in the form of a printed questionnaire.
3. In the third, a second interview with the teacher took place, based on the completed questionnaire. The total interview time per teacher ranged from 2½-3½ hours.

Analysis of data

1. 28 teachers responded to the IPC and there was one non-response. An index of desirability and undesirability was obtained with respect to each characteristic on the Ideal Pupil Checklist and they were rank-ordered. On the basis of this rank ordering, the 10 most and 10 least valued traits were identified and compared with similar data from the 8 Indian studies cited earlier; and with the ranking of the traits by Torrance's experts (1975).
2. The five characteristics to be especially encouraged and the five to be strongly discouraged that each teacher had additionally identified, were rank-ordered based on the frequency with which they were mentioned. Then, in each category, the traits which found a place in the first five ranks were identified as those which teachers wanted to especially encourage and strongly discourage.
3. The rank order coefficient of correlation was computed between the present study and Raina's study (1971) and the ranking by Torrance's experts (Torrance, 1975).
4. The teachers' responses to the interview and questionnaire were subjected to content analysis and themes were identified. Scale items were analysed in terms of the frequencies in each category.

Results and discussion

The results and discussion are presented in two sections: (i) teachers' conception of the ideal pupil, as indicated by the analysis of responses on the Ideal Pupil Checklist; (ii) teachers' conception of creativity, as obtained through interviews and the questionnaire.

Section 1: Teachers' conception of the ideal pupil

Table 1 presents the rank order of the 66 characteristics of the Ideal Pupil Checklist, from the most to the least valued.

SI No	Characteristics	Rank	SI No	Characteristics	Rank
1	Doing work on time	2	34	Never bored, always interested	34
2	Healthy	2	35	Obedient	35
3	Sincere	2	36	Spirited in disagreement	36
4	Courteous, polite	4.5	37	Asks questions about puzzling things	37
5	Competitive, trying to win	4.5	38	Becomes preoccupied with tasks	39
6	Self confident	6.5	39	Having a sense of beauty	39
7	Neat and orderly	6.5	40	Visionary, idealistic	39
8	Courageous in convictions	8.5	41	Preferring complex tasks	41
9	Desirous of excelling	8.5	42	Receptive to ideas of others	42
10	Affectionate, loving	10.5	43	Intuitive	43
11	Industrious, busy	10.5	44	Adventurous	44
12	Curious, searching	13	45	Willing to take risks	45
13	Independent in thinking	13	46	Feeling emotions strongly	46
14	Refined, free of coarseness	13	47	Truthful, even if it hurts	47
15	Physically strong	15.5	48	Guessing, hypothesizing	48
16	Socially well adjusted	15.5	49	Regressing occasionally	49
17	Remembering well	17.5	50	Emotionally sensitive	50
18	Versatile, well rounded	17.5	51	Quiet, not talkative	51
19	Altruistic	20.5	52	Willing to accept judgments of others	52
20	Determined, unflinching	20.5	53	Liking to work alone	53
21	Energetic,	20.5	54	Domineering, controlling	54
22	Persistent, persevering	20.5	55	Reserve	55
23	Popular, well liked	23	56	Conforming	56
24	Attempting difficult tasks	24	57	Unsophisticated	57
25	Considerate of others	25.5	58	Critical of others	58
26	Independent in judgment	25.5	59	Fault finding	59
27	Self-starting, initiating	27.5	60	Talkative	60
28	Self-sufficient	27.5	61	Negativistic	61.5
29	Having a sense of humour	30.5	62	Stubborn, obstinate	61.5
30	Striving for distant goals	30.5	63	Timid, shy, bashful	63
31	Thorough,	30.5	64	Haughty and self satisfied	64
32	Unwilling to accept things on mere say so	30.5	65	Disturbs procedures and organization of the group	65
33	Self assertive	33	66	Fearful, apprehensive	66

Table 1: Rank order of characteristics on the Ideal Pupil Checklist (N=28)

Table 2 compares the 10 traits most valued by the teachers in the present study, as obtained on the basis of rank ordering, with the traits ranked as important for creativity by Torrance's experts (Torrance, 1975). Four traits appear in both lists and are indicated in bold. In fact, the top three traits identified by the experts are present in the teachers' list. Besides these traits, 'self confidence' and 'determination' have also been associated with the creative individual (Torrance, 1963). These traits, too, find a place among the top 10 traits in the teachers' ranking. These findings are in contrast with the eight Indian studies cited earlier where, except in the 1977 study reported in Raina (1984), only one or two traits identified as most valued for creativity by Torrance's experts find a place in the teachers' list of 10 most valued traits.

SI No.	Teachers in 2002	Torrance's Experts
1	Doing work on time; healthy; sincere	**Courageous in convictions**
2	Courteous; competitive	**Curious**
3	*Self- confident*; neat and orderly	**Independent in thinking**
4	**Courageous in convictions**; desirous of excelling	Independent in judgment
5	Affectionate; industrious	Willing to take risks
6	**Curious; independent in thinking**; refined, free of coarseness	Intuitiveness
7	Physically strong; socially well-adjusted	Becomes pre-occupied with tasks
8	Remembering well; versatile	**Persistent**
9	Altruistic; energetic *determined;* **persistent**	Unwilling to accept things on mere say so
10	Popular, well liked	Visionary

Table 2: The most valued traits of the Ideal Pupil as perceived by teachers in the present study and traits ranked as most important for creativity by Torrance's experts (N=28).

With regard to the remaining six traits most valued for creativity by Torrance's experts, two ('independent in judgment' and 'unwilling to accept things on mere say so') appear in the first half of the teachers' ranking (ranked 25.5 & 30.5 respectively), and the remaining three in the third quarter (see Table 1).

On the other hand, some traits which are least valued for creativity by Torrance's experts (see Table 5) are among the traits most valued by teachers in the present study. These are 'courteous', 'neat & orderly', 'socially well adjusted' and 'doing work on time'. How does one reconcile the apparent contradictions – that the teachers seem to be valuing highly some of the experts' most valued and also least valued traits? Explanations can be posited at two levels.

(1) The first is that the teachers are truly aiming for an *ideal* child. This is evident if we regroup the 10 most valued characteristics identified by the teachers, as presented in Table 3. The traits in the first column refer to the health of the child and, as the teachers articulated, that is a prerequisite for any kind of effort on the child's part, including creative endeavours. The Indian cultural tradition with its 'other orientation' values highly the characteristics in the second column, and the teachers' ranking is mirroring these values. To continue through the education system from one class to the next, it is very important for the child to have the characteristics listed in the third column. The characteristics in the last column are creativity-relevant characteristics – and these seem to be as important to the teachers in the present study as the other characteristics. Further support for this analysis is provided when we look at the

data regarding the identification of five characteristics to be especially encouraged (see point 2 of Analysis). Of the eight characteristics which appear in the first five ranks, four are related to creativity (Table 4).

Traits valued for the health of the child	Traits valued in the Indian cultural tradition	Traits required for success in the education system	Creativity relevant traits
Healthy	Courteous	Neat and orderly	Courageous in convictions
Physically strong	Affectionate	Doing work on time	Curious
Energetic	Socially well adjusted	Remembers well	Independent in thinking
	Altruistic	Sincere	Persistence
	Popular	Industrious	Self confidence
		Desirous of excelling	Determined
		Competitive	

Table 3: Regrouping of traits most valued by teachers in the present study (N=28)

Characteristic	Worth special encouragement %
Self Confidence	39
Doing work on time	36
Healthy	32
Courageous in Convictions; Curious	21
Independent in thinking; Sincere; Courteous	18

Table 4: Characteristics from the Ideal Pupil Checklist located in the first five ranks, as those which must be especially encouraged, by teachers in the present study (N=28).

(2) The second explanation is that it is important to differentiate between those traits that may deter creative thinking (such as high premium on 'conformity', 'obedience' and 'accepting judgments of others') and traits which may not enhance creative thinking but whose presence does not deter creative thinking (such as 'courtesy', 'promptness in doing work', 'neatness and orderliness', 'affectionate'). It is possible that creative individuals may lack these traits (Torrance, 1963) but the converse is not necessarily true. It is significant that of the 10 traits most valued by the teachers in the present study, *none* is believed to counter creative thinking.

With respect to the 10 traits least valued by the sample, as identified on the basis of rank ordering, four are common to both the experts' and teachers' lists and are indicated in bold (Table 5). What is more significant is the comparison with the traits least valued by the teachers in the eight Indian studies mentioned earlier. We find that in the present study, *for the first time*, 'conforming' ranks among the least valued traits. This is in stark contrast with all the earlier Indian studies where 'non conformity' was ranked among the least valued traits. The teachers in the present study and Torrance's experts are in agreement here. Another related trait that deters creative thinking, 'willingness to accept judgments of others', is also rated quite low (ranked 52) by the teachers.

Another important difference between the present study and the previous eight Indian studies is that for the first time 'obedience' is not placed among the 10 most valued characteristics. In fact, it is ranked 35th in order of importance, which means that almost half of the traits are considered more important than 'obedience'.

Sl No	Teachers in 2002	Experts
1	**Fearful, apprehensive**	**Conformity**
2	Disturbs procedures and organisation of the group	Willing to accept judgments of authority
3	**Haughty and self satisfied**	**Fearfulness**
4	**Timid, shy, bashful**	**Timidity**
5	Stubborn; Negativistic	Obedience
6	Talkative	Courteous
7	Fault finding, objecting	Promptness in doing work
8	Critical of others	Socially well adjusted
9	Unsophisticated	**Haughty and self satisfied**
10	**Conforming**	Neatness and orderliness

Table 5: The least valued traits of the Ideal Pupil Checklist as perceived by teachers in the present study and Torrance's experts

Rank order coefficient of correlation was worked out between the present study and Raina's 1971 study. The value was .66, which is lower than the coefficient of correlation that has been found among the earlier Indian studies. The rank order coefficient of correlation between the experts' ranking and the ranking of teachers in the present study is .16. This is quite low and is similar to the values obtained in the earlier Indian studies.

The data as a whole regarding the ideal pupil supports the conclusion that, while the views of the present day teachers reflect continuity with those of teachers over the last 40 years (as indicated by moderate correlation between the present study and Raina's 1971 study), nevertheless their attitudes and views have undergone *some* change and have moved towards supporting creativity-relevant characteristics. Although the correlation between the experts' and teachers' rankings is low, traits considered important for creativity are amongst the teachers' most valued traits.

Section 2: Teachers' conceptions of creativity
While we may postulate on the basis of the analysis of the Ideal Pupil Checklist that creativity-relevant characteristics are perceived as desirable by the teachers, an associated question that arises is: How do the teachers themselves construe creativity and what do they view as creative teaching? In this section, the teachers' conception of creativity is presented as themes that emerged from in-depth content analysis of data.

Theme 1: Varied conceptions of creativity

Most teachers pointed out that they had not thought about creativity very consciously prior to the interview. In fact, almost all the teachers admitted that the interview became a process of thinking through and clarifying their ideas.

The teachers' responses to the opening question of the interview: 'What do you understand by the word 'creativity'?' were revealing. These were of two distinct types. For one set of teachers, there seemed to be clarity in their implicit ideas so that they responded naturally, spontaneously, immediately and unambiguously to the question, even though they had not previously articulated their thoughts. Of course, their implicit ideas varied and this will be discussed. For the other set of teachers, the implicit ideas did not seem clear; the question had to be rephrased several times and the teachers had to be helped to understand their own thinking. There were seven such teachers in the whole sample.

All the teachers regarded creativity as distinct from intelligence and academic achievement. However, there was a qualitative difference in their conception of creativity. For the purpose of analysis, the teachers' conception of creativity has been juxtaposed with the Western view of creativity which holds that the creative process results in the production of novel and useful products (Gilhooly, 1982; Gardner, 1989; Mumford, Reiter-Palmon & Redmond, 1994).

Based on content analysis of their responses, the teachers could be divided into three groups. The three teachers in the first group seemed to have no concept of 'creativity' or 'teaching creatively'. Despite the researcher rephrasing the question in several ways, these teachers could not respond to what was being asked.

Teachers in the second group viewed creativity in terms of 'doing something new or different', either in terms of ideas or work, and contrasted it with 'copying'. For these teachers, the originality of the idea/work, in some measure at least, was important. They maintained that if the person was implementing someone else's idea or work, it should be adapted or presented differently so as to reflect, to some extent, the new or original thinking of the person doing the adaptation. Such a conception of creativity is similar to the notion of creativity as dominant in Western scholarship. There were 18 teachers in this group.

The third group of teachers also had a clear conception of creativity but their conception was different from the second group's. To them creativity was the 'act of doing something', without it necessarily being new in some measure. Re-creating the work of another person or implementing another person's idea was regarded as being creative because 'she has done something... she has created something... she has done it after all'. They maintained: 'Wherever the idea is from, a book or another person, the point is that the person has implemented it and has shown a desire to try out something new'. Thus, the fact of doing something which the teacher has never done before and which she has now learnt to do, was of central importance.

These teachers with their 'reproductive' view of creativity stated: 'If the person does something new, then that is an advantage and is more creative than reproducing... but even if there is no element of 'newness' in what the person is doing, the person has still been creative'. The satisfaction derived from the act of creating by one's own hands, the teaching and learning of 'how to create' was emphasised more than whether the person executing the task was the one who had the original idea. In fact, 'newness' as a criterion for creative work was not reflected upon or mentioned by teachers in this group until the researcher posed it as a question. Some teachers emphasised that 'learning to do something' was an essential step towards producing something new in that domain. Thus, reproduction was regarded as a stepping-stone to newness and novelty. Seven teachers held such a view of creativity.

As evident from the findings, it can be said that in context of teachers, there is no one universal view of creativity. The conception of creativity among teachers ranges across a spectrum from re-creation and reproduction of the work/idea of another person to producing something new and original which reflects the person's own unique thinking. The emphasis in the Eastern view of creativity as 're-creating' has been reported in other studies as well. Hallman (1970) regards the reduced emphasis on originality as the greatest difference between Hindu and Western definitions of creativity. Kristeller (1983) states that in the Eastern view, creativity seems to involve the re-interpretation of traditional ideas – finding a new point of view – whereas in the Western approach, creativity involves a break with tradition.

Theme 2: Teaching creatively
Though teachers had not reflected upon creativity as such prior to the interview, most of them had been implementing, in varying degrees, what in their opinion were 'creative teaching strategies'. The teachers in both the second and third groups stated that teaching creatively was very important, as it helped to retain students' interest and led to better understanding of the concept. They contrasted 'teaching creatively' with what they called 'routine blackboard teaching', where the teacher uses the talk-and-chalk method of instruction. Both groups viewed creative teaching as 'activity-oriented teaching' but there were qualitative differences in what the two groups meant by this; and this was related to their conception of creativity itself.

For teachers in the third group (with the 'reproductive' view of creativity), activity-oriented teaching meant explaining concepts practically in the class using concrete objects and aids. Some examples of creative teaching included using a model; using maps; making diagrams on the board; using the price of wheat as printed in the newspapers over the years to calculate the price index; using the globe and the candle to explain day and night. In most of these examples, the teacher was the main protagonist in 'doing things practically' and the children were imbibing what the teacher was 'trying to make them understand'. The aids and activities mentioned by the teachers were all standard examples. Wherever children were involved in doing things, it was on the instruction of the teacher. The focus was on helping the children understand the concept as explained in the book. The teachers of this group, by and large, gave fewer examples of children's activities in class which they would consider creative. The examples they did provide included 'drawing neat and correct diagrams and the few questions asked by the children, which were usually to seek more clarification.

To summarise, the teachers in this group perceived themselves as teaching creatively because they were *doing* something practical in the class and the children *understood* the concept. It was not relevant to them whether what was being done by the teacher was the 'original' thinking of the teacher. Ownership of the idea and its implementation were seen as distinct and mutually exclusive activities, not necessarily to be performed by one person. A person performing either of the two activities was seen as being creative.

As stated earlier, the teachers in the second group (those with the 'originality' view of creativity) also perceived teaching creatively as activity-oriented teaching but what they described as examples of activities were new and original ideas, in some measure at least, borne out of their thinking. Also, the activities usually involved the child in actively exploring, doing something or thinking afresh. Some of their examples of creative teaching were: creating a new song or a story with children's active participation; extending the chapter on 'oil refinery' to include discussion on oil crisis, pollution and saving energy which led to poems, drawings and slogans created by the children, and finally a collage; conceptualising the atomic structure of complex compounds; dramatising a meeting of a company's board of members in an attempt to understand the working of organisations; relating a concept learnt in one context to another. Thus, teaching creatively was not a one-way transaction where the teacher did something and the children watched, but a mutual process where the 'teacher becomes a student again', as one teacher put it. The children themselves were encouraged to think of novel ideas. For these teachers, an element of *originality*, however small, in children's work defined that work as creative. The teachers in this group did not agree that explaining and clarifying concepts through the use of standard aids, examples and diagrams, was 'teaching creatively'.

Theme 3: Nurturance of creativity
All the teachers felt that creativity was nurtured during the preschool and primary years, and that the extent of its nurturance decreased as one progressed through the middle school and secondary school years. About 38% of the teachers said that they were 'never' or 'sometimes' able to teach creatively; 50% stated that they were 'often' able to teach creatively and 12% said that they were able to teach creatively 'all the time'. The last category comprised teachers teaching the nursery section and the art teacher.

The teachers indicated that children's academic performance was 'often' or 'very frequently' the topic of discussion, closely followed by discussions regarding children's intelligence. Children's creativity was discussed relatively less often. About 31% of the teachers said creativity was 'never' discussed; about 27% said children's creativity was 'sometimes' discussed and about 46% said this was 'often' or 'very frequently' discussed. However, some of the teachers in the latter group responded that children's creativity would become the focus of discussion only when cultural events or competitions were organised in the school.

Theme 4: Constraints in teaching creatively
Teachers articulated many constraints that they felt got in the way of their being able to teach creatively (Table 6).

Constraint	% of teachers finding this a constraint
Excessive non-teaching work load	69
Vastness of syllabus	62
Lack of awareness regarding how to teach creatively	62
Short teaching periods (insufficient lesson time)	58
Over large classes	54
Inadequate time to prepare for lessons	46
Excessive teaching load	42
Inadequate teaching resources	35
Constraints imposed due to school's philosophy	31
Unsuitable class accommodation	27
Inadequate non teaching resources	27
Constraints imposed due to attitude of the principal	23

Table 6: Constraints experienced by teachers in teaching creatively (N=26) *Source: 'Constraints' adopted from Fryer (1989) with permission*

While 62% of the sample felt that teachers may not know the 'how to' of creative teaching, the remaining felt that teachers *did know* how to teach creatively but lacked the motivation and interest to do so, because creative teaching was seen as requiring more time and effort on the part of the teacher. Only about one-fifth of the sample felt that putting creative teaching into practice did not require extra time and effort.

About half the sample stated unambiguously that the syllabus could not be completed if they implemented creative teaching/learning methodologies. The other half felt that the syllabus could be covered provided: lessons were well planned; all facilities were provided and teachers were not burdened with extra work load if they took extra classes; if the revision of the syllabus could be omitted; if only 30-40% of the classes were taught using creative teaching-learning methodologies.

One of the constraints attributed to the attitude of the principal was her approach towards the 'noise' created when the children were involved in exploring and doing something on their own. The teachers said that while noise and apparent disorganisation is bound to occur when children are given the freedom to be creative, this attracts censure from colleagues and the principal. It is also perceived that the class is having 'fun 'and is not 'seriously' studying. Thus, while teachers are expected to be creative in their teaching, the process involved in creative teaching and learning is sometimes looked upon with suspicion, leading to remarks such as: 'You can't control the class' or 'Time is being wasted'. Such experiences, if they happen regularly, de-motivate the teacher.

Theme 5: Motivational concerns and institutional priorities
All the teachers, from the low fee as well as the high fee-paying schools, agreed that creativity was nurtured more in the high fee-paying schools. The reasons for this, cited by the two groups of teachers, were however different. The teachers from high fee-paying schools cited the main cause as lack of motivation on the part of the teachers in the low fee-paying schools. However, the teachers from the low fee-paying schools cited the following reasons: poorer quality of students who enrol in the school, which is perceived as a limiting factor; the lack of adequate resources and equipment in the school due to economic constraints; less space; fewer teachers; lack of awareness and education among parents, so that what is done at school is not followed up at home; and economic constraints on the child's family. Thus, the factors responsible for creativity being accorded low priority in school were mostly seen as lying outside the teachers' control. A few teachers from the low fee-paying school, however, did articulate that a major reason for the low premium on creative teaching in their school was lack of motivation and interest on the part of the teachers and this stemmed largely from the fact that they had a secure job.

While the high fee-paying school teachers agreed that they were helped to implement creative teaching by the following factors: the better economic situation of their schools; better facilities for extra-curricular activities; more aware and economically better-off parents, who follow up at home what is done in school; they still saw themselves as considerably more motivated and interested.

Analysis indicates that the school's priorities as reflected in the actions of the principal and the management have a direct bearing on the extent to which teachers feel motivated to implement creative teaching. In one of the private high fee-paying schools, there was an explicit emphasis by the management and the principal on creativity and this directly translated into teaching practices. As some of the teachers said: 'There is so much pressure to be creative... the display board must be different each week'; 'I feel if that teacher can have a creative idea, why can't I?' In a way, there was a test-like situation for the teachers in these schools and while they stated that this caused pressure and tension, they also felt it spurred them to be creative.

However, the teachers from the high fee-paying schools also voiced the concern that the emphasis on creativity by the principal/management ought to be in the correct perspective. Sometimes, the emphasis on creativity causes the creative product to become more important than the process. This tends to defeat the purpose of the creative effort.

Conclusions and recommendations

The findings of the present study in terms of the 'reproductive' and the 'originality' views of creativity find a parallel in Rejskind's (1988) postulation of 'assimilative' and 'accommodative' creativity and Leary's (1964) conceptualisation of 'reproductive blocked', 'reproductive creator', and 'creative creator'. The teachers' conception of creativity influences their interpretation of 'teaching creatively'. Those with the 'originality 'view of creativity tend to be innovative themselves in their teaching/learning strategies. Those with the 'reproductive' view of creativity tend to teach in terms of what they have been taught, producing what has been produced before, occasionally manipulating these 'old' experiences into novel combinations.

The conception of creativity by the two groups of teachers is also, to some extent, a consequence of the type of school systems to which they belong. The group with the 'reproductive' view of creativity comprised seven teachers from the low fee-paying schools; the group with the 'originality' view of creativity comprised three teachers from the low fee-paying schools and 12 from high fee-paying schools. By and large, those with the 'originality' view of creativity had more exposure to a variety of concepts and ideas. The principal and the management of these schools explicitly demanded and supported innovation and this seemed to make the critical difference.

Much can be accomplished through a re-appraisal of inputs that go into teacher training so that the teachers perceive creativity as relevant to all subjects and all aspects of the curriculum and are equipped with the 'how to' of creative teaching. Seminars on this topic can be a means of providing in-service training to the teachers.

Analysis also indicates that a change is coming about in the teachers' conception of the ideal child and that creativity-relevant characteristics are becoming salient. However, it also needs to be recognised that teachers' attitudes and actions are influenced by aspects other than their personal preferences. Thus, while the teachers may be oriented to supporting creativity-relevant traits, the extent to which they succeed in their endeavours will be largely determined by the values of the education system. Presently, the system has a predominantly 'information' orientation, with a premium on marks, so that the cognitive processes that seem to bring rewards in terms of more marks are 'neatness', 'memory' and 'ability to reproduce'. A reappraisal of the educational system and its methodology of evaluation is needed (something frequently articulated by various committees and eminent educationalists in the country) so that children's creative expression is nurtured and taken into account in the evaluation of their performance in school.

References

Aron, E.N. & Aron, A. (1982) An introduction to Maharishi's theory of creativity: Its empirical base and description of the creative process. *Journal of Creative Behavior,* 16 (1), 29-49.

Arora, G. L., Gupta, B.P. & Madhulika (1982) *Comparison of the Curriculum Load at the Secondary Stage in Different States.* New Delhi: National Council of Educational Research and Training.

Bharati, A. (1985) The self in Hindu thought and action. In A.J. Marsella, G. Devos & F.L.K. Hsu (Eds.) *Culture and Self: Asian and Western Perspectives* (185-230). New York: Tavistock.

Briggs, J. (1988) *Fire in the Crucible: The Alchemy of Creative Genius.* New York: St. Martin's Press.

Chu, Y.K. (1970) Oriental views on creativity. In A. Angott & B. Shapiro (Eds.) *Psi Factors in Creativity* (35-50). New York: Parapsychology Foundation.

Dehlavi, N. & Torrance, E.P. (1979) Iranian mothers' perception of the ideal child. *Gifted and Talented Education,* 1, 107-11.

Fryer, M. (1989) Teachers' views on creativity. Unpublished PhD thesis, Leeds Metropolitan University, Leeds.

Fryer, M. & Collings, J.A. (1991) Teachers' views about creativity. *British Journal of Educational Psychology.* Vol. 61, 207-219.

Gardner, H. (1989) *To Open Minds.* New York: Basic.

Gilhooly, K.J. (1982) *Thinking: Directed, Undirected and Creative.* New York: Academic Press.

Gore, M. S. (1985) Creativity in higher education. *New Frontiers in Education,* 15, 98-105.

Hallman, R.J. (1970) Toward a Hindu theory of creativity. *Educational Theory,* 20 (4), 368-76.

Hariharan, A. (1981) A colossal national waste. *The Hindustan Times,* Feb.27.

Hofstede, G. (1980) *Culture's Consequences: International Differences in Work Related Values.* Beverly Hills, CA: Sage.

Hunsaker, S.L. (1992) Towards an ethnographic perspective on creativity research. *Journal of Creative Behavior,* 26 (4), 235-41.

Kamat, A.R. (1980) Educational policy in India. *Sociological Bulletin,* 29, 182-205.

Kapur, R.L. Subramanyam, S. & Shah, A. (1997) Creativity in Indian Science. *Psychology and Developing Societies,* Vol. 9, (2) 161-87.

Kristeller, P.O. (1983) Creativity' and 'tradition'. *Journal of the History of Ideas,* 44, 105-14.

Kuo, Y.Y. (1996) Taoistic psychology of creativity. *Journal of Creative Behavior,* 30 (3), 197-212.

Leary T. (1964) The effects of test score feedback on creative performance and of drugs on creative experience. In C.W. Taylor (Ed.) *Widening Horizons in Creativity* (94-96), New York: Wiley.

Mackinnon, D.W. (1962) The nature and nurture of creative talent. *American Psychologist,* 17, 489-95.

Mackinnon, D.W. (1987) Some critical issues for future research in creativity. In S.G. Isaksen (Ed.) *Frontiers of Creativity Research: Beyond the Basics* (120-30). Buffalo, NY: Bearly Limited.

Mangla. (1981) Are we educated. *The Hindustan Times* (weekly) October.

Mathur, S.G. (1982) Cross-cultural implications of creativity. *Indian Psychological Review,* 22 (1), 12-19.

Mehra, P. (1982) Education for sale. *Sunday Review,* Times of India, April 25.

Mumford, M.D., Reiter-Palmon, R. & Redmond, M.R. (1994) Problem construction & cognition: Applying problem representation in ill-defined domains. In M.A. Runco (Ed.) *Problem Finding, Problem Solving, and Creativity* (3-39). Norwood, N J: Ablex.

Naik, J.P. & Nurallah, S. (1974) *A Student History of Education in India (1800-1973)*. New Delhi: Macmillan.

Naik, J.P. (1975) *Policy and Performance in Indian Education*. New Delhi: Saiyidain Memorial Trust.

Raina, M.K. (1970) Prospective science teachers' perception of an ideal pupil. *Journal of Research in Science Teaching*, 7, 169-72.

Raina, M.K. (1975) Parental perception about the ideal child: A cross cultural study. *Journal of Marriage and the Family*, 37, 229-232.

Raina, M.K. (1984) *Social Cultural Change and Changes in Creative Functioning in Children*. New Delhi: National Council of Educational Research and Training.

Raina, M.K. (1999) Cross Cultural Differences. In M.A. Runco & S.R. Pritzker (Eds.) *Encyclopaedia of Creativity*, Volume 2. Academic Press.

Raina, M.K., Kumar, G. & Raina, V.K. (1980) A cross cultural study of parental perception of the ideal child. *Creative Child and Adult Quarterly*, 4, 234-41.

Raina, T.N. & Raina, M.K. (1971) Perception of teacher educators in India about the ideal pupil. *Journal of Educational Research*, 64 (7), 303-10.

Raina, V.K. (1982) The perception of Indian history teachers about the ideal pupil. *Teaching History*, 32, 6-7.

Raina, V.K. (1985) Perception of meritorious Indian teachers about the ideal pupil. *Gifted International*, 3 (1), 11-22.

Raina, U. (1991) *What is Honoured – Creativity or Conformity? Studies in the Area of Parental and Teacher Perceptions of the Ideal Child*. New Delhi, India: Indian Council of Social Science Research.

Rao, V. K. R.V. (1977) Some thoughts on social change in India. In M.N. Srinivas, S. Seshaiah & V.S. Parthasarthy (Eds.) *Dimensions of Social Change in India*. Bombay: Allied Publishers.

Rejskind, G. (1988) Personality correlates of divergent-thinking in gifted children. Presented at the meeting of the National Association for Gifted Children, Orlando, FL.

Roland, A. (1988) *In Search of Self in India and Japan: Towards a Cross Cultural Psychology*. Princeton, New Jersey: Princeton University Press.

Rudowicz, E. & Hui, A. (1997) The creative personality: Hong Kong perspective. *Journal of Social Behaviour and Personality*, 12 (1), 139-57.

Rudowicz, E. & Yue, X.D. (2001) Concepts of creativity: Similarities and differences among Mainland, Hong Kong and Taiwanese Chinese. *Journal of Creative Behavior*, 35, 2, 1-18.

Runco, M.A., Nemiro, J. & Walberg, H.J. (1998). Personal explicit theories of creativity. *Journal of Creative Behaviour*, 32 (1), 1-17.

Runco, M.A. (1984) Teachers' judgements of creativity and social validation of divergent thinking tests. *Perceptual and Motor Skills*, 59, 711-17.

Runco, M.A., Johnson, D.J. & Baer, P.K. (1993) Parents' and teachers' implicit theories of children's creativity. *Child Study Journal*, June.

Sherr, J. (1982) The universal structures and dynamics of creativity: Maharishi, Plato, Jung, and various creative geniuses on the creative process. *Journal of Creative Behavior,* 16 (3), 155-75.

Sinha, D. (1988) Basic Indian values and behaviour dispositions in the context of national development: An appraisal. In D. Sinha & H.S.R. Kao (Eds.) *Social Values and Development: Asian Perspectives* (37-55). New Delhi: Sage.

Sternberg, R.J. (1985) Implicit theories of intelligence, creativity and wisdom. *Journal of Personality and Social psychology,* Vol. 49 (3), 607-27.

Super, C. & Harkness, S. (1997) The cultural structuring of child development. In J.W. Berry, P.R. Dasen & T.S. Sarawathi (Eds.) *Handbook of Cross Cultural Psychology, Vol 2: Basic Processes and Human Development* (pp3-39). Allyn and Bacon.

Super, C. & Harkness, S. (1986) The developmental niche: A conceptualization at the interface of child and culture. *International J. of Behavioral Development,* 9, 545-70.

Torrance, E.P. (1963) The creative personality and the ideal pupil. *Teachers' College Record,* 65 (3), 220-26.

Torrance, E.P. (1963) What kind of person do you want your gifted child to become? *Gifted Child Quarterly,* 7 (3), 87-91.

Torrance, E.P. (1965) *Rewarding Creative Behavior.* Englewood Cliffs, NJ: Prentice-Hall.

Torrance, E.P. (1967) *Understanding the Fourth Grade Slump in Creative Thinking.* Athens, Georgia: University of Georgia.

Torrance, E.P. (1973) Cross cultural studies of creative development in seven selected cultures. *The Educational Trends,* 8, 28-38.

Torrance, E.P. (1975) *Preliminary Manual: Ideal Child Checklist.* Athens, GA: Georgia Studies of Creative Behavior, Dept. of Educational Psychology, University of Georgia.

Torrance, E.P. (1975) Assessing children, teachers and parents against the ideal child criterion. *Gifted Child Quarterly,* 19 (2), 130-39.

Whitney, L.D. (1983) Beyond decision-making: cultural ideology as heuristic paradigmatic models. *Presented at the American Anthropological Association, Chicago.* (ERIC Document Reproduction Service No. ED 245, 967).

Wonder, J. & Blake, J. (1992) Creativity East and West: intuition vs. logic. *Journal of Creative Behavior,* 26 (3), 172-85.

Acknowledgements

The authors express their deep gratitude to: The late E. P. Torrance, Prof. Emeritus, University of Georgia, Athens for advice on scoring the Ideal Pupil Checklist and for making readily available his book and related articles; Dr. M. Fryer, Director, The Creativity Centre, U.K., for her questionnaire 'Creativity Survey' and detailed comments on the interview schedule/questionnaire developed for the study; Prof. M. K. Raina, National Council of Educational Research & Training, for comments on the interview schedule and questionnaire and his insight into Indian researches. The timely responses and academic inputs from these experts are greatly appreciated.

Ma Xiaolei (Diana) and Wang Yan (Lily)

Using creative methods to teach English in China

Background

'Learning English is just like memorising mathematical formula and historical dates...' When we first distributed a questionnaire at the beginning of the term, asking, 'What do you think English study is like', a good number of our students from Senior One provided such answers. We felt shocked and sad. We couldn't help asking ourselves, 'What's wrong with English teaching in China?' which has been asked constantly by people from all walks of life for the past 10 years.

During the last two decades, various English teaching methods have been introduced to China and some of them became quite popular, such as the grammar-translation method, audio-lingual method and the most recent and prevalent one, communicative language teaching. Many methods have been created as well, according to the circumstances in China, like the 'Zhang Sizhong' English teaching method, Crazy English, and the 'Word, Sentence, Context' teaching method. We have explored this field quite vigorously; however, the students' learning results are far from satisfactory. In other words, there is a gap between what the students have grasped and what society requires.

One of the reasons for such undesirable results might be that we didn't master the essence of these imported ELT methods and used them in an inappropriate way. However, as Nunan (1991) points out, 'There is little evidence that methods are realised at the level of classroom action in the way intended by their creators'. Through the integration of the methods into real classroom practice, modifications are sure to occur.

Another important reason may be that Chinese English teachers have to face the reality of English teaching in China. Therefore, we must create our own methods. Actually, we are longing for appropriate and effective ELT methods to emerge; unfortunately, none of these are among those homemade methods mentioned above. For, most of them lack a solid theoretical foundation and mainly consist of the experiences of a successful English learner, or several learners, or at most, a particular group of learners.

However, language learning is such a complex process that we cannot ignore the theory of language and the theory of learning and claim that if a particular group of people can master English well in a certain way anyone else can accomplish it by simply following their steps. Another severe problem underlying these national products is that all of them serve mainly for the examination-oriented evaluation system. However, more important elements tend to be neglected, such as students' interests, their needs and different learning styles and so on. So high scores become the most common goal that teachers and students struggle for.

Hence, from the first day of our teaching practice we were determined to create our own teaching method in a typical Senior One classroom in China: 1) with a large class size (about 40-50 students); 2) with multi-level students (they are from different junior high schools and are at quite different levels in term of language proficiency); 3) with tremendous pressure from examinations (we observed their frustration when facing not only mid-term and final examinations, but the monthly tests).

Approach

Theory of language
Language is not only a set of rules and symbols to convey meaning, but serves important social functions in our daily lives.

There are seven functions of language (as cited in Brown, 1987, p.203):

1. The instrumental function refers to the particular power of language to handle things under certain circumstances. For example, 'No smoking, please,' and 'Don't move!'
2. The regulatory function of language allows people to maintain a regulatory relationship among one another, such as 'approval', 'disapproval', 'behavior control,' 'setting rules and laws,' etc. For instance, a doctor may tell his patient, 'Stay in bed for three days, have enough water and fruits, you'll be all right soon'.
3. The representational function means to 'represent' reality in one's own eyes in the ways of making statements or explanations, reporting facts, etc. For example, 'The earth is not the centre of the universe'.
4. The interactional function of language, referring to the maintenance of social contacts and certain relationships between human beings. 'Successful interactional communication requires knowledge of slang, jargon, jokes, folklore, cultural mores, politeness and formality expectations, and other keys to social exchange'.
5. The personal function allows people to express their feelings, emotions and opinions. Different people express themselves differently, so the particular use of language can reveal a person's individuality.
6. The heuristic function means people can use language to acquire knowledge and learn about the environment. The use of 'why' questions are a typical example of this function.
7. The imaginative function involves the creative capacity of language, such as writing novels and poems, or telling jokes and fairy tales. This function allows people to go beyond the reality and express whatever exists in their minds.

Although language is not just a set of grammatical rules, we cannot deny there is an underlying system within every language itself. This underlying system can be a great help in learning a language, especially in a foreign language context, where a naturalistic environment can hardly be established. In addition, when the language learners are above the age of 15 or so, they have this psychological need to question 'why must they be like that?' Thus, knowing and understanding some grammar helps them resolve their puzzles and facilitates their learning process (Ellis, 1994).

Moreover, some linguists have proposed recently that language may not only be a vehicle to convey meaning or a tool to achieve other goals, but it is so influential and so creative itself as to have a great impact on society: it can even shape people's conceptions and social constructions. This is as true of a foreign language as of one's native language (Widdowson, 1996).

Theory of learning

Since language is itself complex, language learning is a *highly* complicated process. Although a great deal of research has been conducted in the area of Second Language Acquisition, a lot of problematic issues still remain unresolved or are under investigation (Ellis, 1994).

Through our teaching experience and classroom research, we find that, in a foreign language context (especially in Chinese high schools), language learners can hardly master the target language (TL) through mechanical 'repetition' and 'reinforcement'. Language learning is a complex process which is highly sensitive to various external factors (e.g. attitudes to learning and other social factors), internal factors (e.g. transfer from one's natural language and other cognitive processes) and differences among learners. As in human behaviour generally, language learning cannot be the same as animals' 'stimuli-response' learning process; it is both 'cognitive' and 'affective' (Richards and Rodgers, 1986, p. 117).

Real language learning can only take place when learners show great interest in TL (or topics such as its people and culture), are highly motivated, employ appropriate and effective learning strategies, are exposed to various and intensified TL input, and obtain effective facilitation and instructions from the teacher inside and outside the classroom. In short, language learning is 'holistic'.

Design

Objectives

Since language learning is holistic, multi-level objectives must be designed in order to instruct and ensure effective learning.

The basic objective is certainly concerned with language proficiency: students must master English as a whole in terms of 'form', 'meaning' and 'use' (Celce-Murcia & Larsen-Freeman, 1999). This means that students should not only be familiar with a certain number of important grammar rules and structures, but also understand both the literal and deep meaning of the language to some extent. Furthermore, they should have the chance to observe how the forms and meanings they know are managed by native speakers in various means, and then try this themselves.

The fundamental objective is to help the students to arouse their own interests in language learning. Teachers should be able to find a number of ways of motivating their students. Every student is unique: they have distinct personalities, learning styles and learner needs, etc. As teachers, we are responsible for providing different kinds of tasks and activities, in which students may realise 'why I need to learn English' and 'what I can gain and enjoy through learning English'.

Accordingly, teachers must help them maintain their interests and assist them as independent learners. In Chinese high schools, students only have 4–5 English periods each week, which means students have only a maximum of 45 minutes every day (excluding the weekend) to spend on English classes. No matter how intensively they contact with the TL during the class, after class they may easily forget everything because they have few opportunities to practise it in such a foreign context. In addition, there are more than 40 students in every class; it is very hard for the teacher to pay attention to everyone during class. Therefore, the most effective and reasonable way is to train them to be independent learners, by providing or recommending to them diverse supplementary input and materials for self-study, and by introducing a range of learning strategies to students.

Recently, lifelong learning has been recognised as one of the crucial factors to ensure individual success and the social and economic progress of a nation. However, most of the high school students have been pushed very hard by the huge pressure of examinations. Many students work hard because they think English is very useful for getting a good job in the future. But how long can the effect of such external factors last? As Ellis (1994) points out, the 'fossilization' of L2 (foreign language) learning easily occurs when there is not enough input to refresh or opportunity to practise. If the teacher can show students the beauty of the TL, the philosophical meaning it conveys and the positive and profound influence it may have on one's life, they will learn it more eagerly as part of their lives.

The last but not least important objective concerns moral education. 'Words are the sounds from one's heart'. As English teachers, we should help the students to realise that by learning a foreign language: 1) we can understand more about English-speaking people, their lives, culture, tradition, literature and technology, etc.; 2) we can be more open-minded as we know more about the world; 3) we can cherish more the essence of our own culture while learning from other cultures; 4) furthermore, we will be able to think in different ways and make our lives more lively and colourful.

Syllabus
Basically, we follow the syllabus of the textbook Senior English for China, which is used on a nationwide scale.

Beyond that, we aim to help our students obtain high language abilities as well as high scores. Specifically, we need to improve their four basic skills, namely listening, speaking, reading and writing.

1. Speaking and listening are two areas of challenge for them. We offer them tapes and videos to listen and imitate which, together with the textbook, form a complete set. We show them whatever we have access to that is relevant to their textbook. We improve not only their pronunciation and intonation but also their awareness of the stress and rhythm of language. We also show them at least two English movies after class each term, to arouse their interest and give them a chance to know about foreign culture.

2. Our requirements for reading: a) students are able to read the passages in the textbook, b) each of them should find a set of self-study materials, such as Family Album U.S.A. or New Concept English, c) every student should be able to read some simplified English novels.

3. Requirements for writing: a) students are able to express themselves clearly and meaningfully in writing, b) they need to experiment a little bit on critical thinking in their writing assignment, c) they should produce some creative products, such as little poems, English songs, book reports and so on.

Types of learning/teaching activities
Language teaching and learning are integrative and holistic, so we agree with the communicative approach that acceptable teaching/learning activities are 'unlimited' (Richards and Rodgers, 1986, p76), provided they serve the following two general principles: 1) the activities make the students the central and active participants; and 2) the activities are designed to necessitate or at least facilitate communication.

Like the Natural Approach, we also emphasise the significance of the 'comprehensible input' during the class (*ibid*, p136). Nevertheless, we also advocate the variety and intensity of the English input for the following two reasons. First, in high schools, the students are not only numerous, but they are at different levels of language proficiency. Therefore, the input provided by the teacher must include different degrees of difficulty. That is, every student must be able to receive some comprehensible input in each class. Second, in a foreign language context, a naturalistic language environment can hardly exist in everyday life. If we can make good use of the 45-minute class, by presenting as much input as possible, classroom learning will not only be efficient but can serve as an effective guidance and impetus for self-study.

In each class, we prepare some facilitating activities which help to create a relaxing atmosphere, attract their attention, get rid of their tiredness and boredom, etc. During the process of teaching we find that these activities can not only ensure effective teaching and learning, but also help to establish a good rapport between teacher and students.

The learning activities in our class have two characteristics: First, most of the activities are fast-paced. We find this an effective way to get the students' attention and prevent them from being absent-minded. Second, the activities we designed for each class vary and cater for the needs and interests of different groups of students. Every student has his or her own personality and intelligence. Some are not good at logical thinking, but they may have 'musical intelligence' (Christian, 1998). All students have their own specialties; as teachers we should carefully design all sorts of activities to enhance their strong points. Hopefully, this can explore their potential and build up their confidence in English learning.

Learner roles
We believe that the learning experience can be enjoyable and consist of a series of self-achievements. Students are active participants in the activities, both during and after class. Only if they undergo the thorough experience of listening, speaking, reading and writing in a foreign language, can they really understand and grasp it.

Enthusiastic participation of the students derives from the sense of 'ownership' (Genesee & Upshur, 1998). It is very important for the teacher to help learners to recognise they are learning a foreign language for themselves instead of for their teachers and parents. The teachers should also respect their students as independent learners with distinct interests, personalities and learning styles. They should also trust the students: share the decision-making process with the students in some appropriate situations; or even tell their worries and difficulties to the students and ask them for advice. You will see how helpful they are and what constructive suggestions they will put forward. Students have great potential and what you need to do is just give them opportunities to display and exploit this.

We also train the students to be 'assistant teachers'. Sometimes, we give a challenging or interesting task for one or two students to deal with, such as to present a new grammar point, to make a brief introduction of a favourite singer, etc. Thus, they can have an opportunity to practise and get the feeling of being a 'teacher'.

Teacher roles
As teachers, we play several important roles in our English class:

Being facilitators. Students are the centre and focus of the learning process. The teacher should take the responsibility to create opportunities for them to practise, and enable them in every possible way to achieve their learning goals.

Being instructors. Besides imparting knowledge to the students, the teacher should also guide them in every aspect of learning, which includes cultivating good learning habits, selecting appropriate learning strategies, choosing self-study materials, etc.

Being friends. From the very beginning, we try to find every opportunity to be together with them and get to know them. We always put our feet in their shoes and thus we can understand them very well. We show our real care and concern to them and they would like to share their happiness as well as sadness with us. These may appear to have nothing to do with English teaching, but they do have a considerable influence on the teaching and learning process. Being friends, teachers and students can cooperate very well in class and the teaching/learning process can become enjoyable for both sides.

Other more specific roles are also very important for an English teacher: 1) The teacher should be able to motivate the students both on a daily basis, by designing good tasks (Wang, 1999); and in the long run by helping them set meaningful and achievable long-term goals; 2) Teachers are also responsible for creating an English language environment by collecting various authentic inputs and utilising them in a suitable way.

The role of the instructional materials

Instructional materials play an important role in: 1) arousing students' interests; 2) providing input; 3) creating a desirable language environment; and 4) developing some basic skills and abilities.

Text-based materials. We are required to use *Senior English for China* (People Education Press, 1995). The textbook is claimed to be based on the communicative approach, but can hardly justify itself. Therefore, we rely on it chiefly for basic structures and vocabulary that students are required to master. We also recommend them to learn New Concept English and Family Album U.S.A. after class, to improve their reading comprehension, enlarge their vocabulary and, most of all, cultivate their language sense.

Task-based materials. Handouts, newspapers, pictures, tapes, videotapes – are all useful materials you can utilise to design various tasks in the class. They have the advantage over text-based materials of being more flexible and up to date. As new material is added, old copies can be disposed of easily. Thus, they can serve as a good supplement for text-based materials.

Procedure

Since the purpose of our methods is to foster the students' holistic English ability in terms of listening, speaking, reading and writing, it is not feasible to address just one mode of learning in a single lesson. Characteristically, our class teaching is described as 'big capacity', 'fast paced' and offering 'rich variation' (according to the students' interests and motivation, the periods of class and the patterns of lessons), and there is a focus on the four English skills respectively. For example, the first lesson basically lays stress on the conversation practice. The following is a unit outline for our students in Senior One of a secondary school in Beijing.

1. As a warm-up exercise, at the beginning of class, a suitable tape-recorded English song based on the topic of the texts is played by the teacher. This can help the students' get involved in English circumstances and arouse their interests.
2. Questions and answers related to the students' personal experiences, but centred on the dialogue or the text theme, are usually raised by the teacher as one of the main components of the class.
3. Oral practice of the basic communicative expressions used in dialogue is mainly conducted in pairs or groups.

4. Vocabulary teaching relies on the English interpretation and illustration associated with the students' concerns and needs in their real lives. The students are encouraged to make their own sentences or compile a story according to the words and phrases exemplified by the teacher (learning new words in context).
5. Challenging and open-ended questions are often provided by the teacher to encourage the students to come up with multiple answers instead of 'one question to one answer' task which is boring and stressful for individuals.
6. Small group discussions, pair work, whole class debates and creative English games are frequently organised in class. The intellectual stimulation and personal attention lead to great interest and satisfaction.
7. English strategies are frequently offered to students to improve their effectiveness of language learning. It is very important to help students seek their own learning strategies according to their different abilities, potential, needs and motives.
8. The performance assessments are used to encourage the students to participate. They include presenting simplified novels, writing about their own experiences by sending emails, taking turns to be teachers' assistants, compiling a portfolio of their creative works etc. They are much more attractive than exclusively doing the traditional examination papers.

Application in China

In China, there is a common saying about language learning that goes: 'practice makes perfect'. However, only by practising with a strong desire rather than cramming, can such effort be effective. Suitable class management may create a warm and friendly atmosphere in the English classroom, where students feel at 'home', versus a language-producing 'factory'. Observing in our English class, you can appreciate this kind of human feeling, variety and enjoyment.

Ideally, as language teachers, our main responsibility should be to create a supportive and positive human language atmosphere in class in order to help learners not only to 'know what', but also 'know how'. Our view of learning is: 'Tell me and I forget; teach me and I remember; involve me and I learn' (cited in Richards & Rodgers, 1986, p. 20). 'Focusing on the learners' is an essential perspective for judging our language teaching, whether it can balance the mastery of linguistic principles and the need to activate and foster the capabilities of learners.

Relatively speaking, our teaching methods are popular among our students; and successful in achieving the goal 'high scores with high ability' (ranking the top in this final exam) by respecting, encouraging and stimulating the students' individual needs and potential, particularly, by devoting ourselves to English teaching. However, English teachers in China are struggling with specific and complicated teaching situations, in terms of class size, differentiation of students, tremendous pressure from the examinations and so forth. It is unreasonable if teachers just follow a single type of teaching method regardless of their actual situation. Furthermore, without systematic research, teaching simply remains static at an affective and empirical level. For higher level teaching, we must not only know what to teach, but also how to teach and why to teach.

English teachers in China should develop flexible and effective teaching methods which can truly encourage and inspire students of different abilities to reach the higher goals of learning. We should bear in mind to what extent we can help learners to study English efficiently by using all kinds of effective teaching methods; as a Chinese proverb says, there is: ' No typical method of effective teaching'.

Conclusion

If you are going to travel through a forest, you'd better bring a compass so as not to lose your direction. When you are in the forest, making marks step by step will help you remember the route clearly. Having a direction and knowing a route are very important in our lives as well as in education. If merely passing examinations is still the goal for teachers and students in China, this will lead to a wrong and dangerous direction, which puts both of them at risk of losing interest and enthusiasm in teaching and learning language and failing to achieve their potential in this route, just like losing yourself in a forest.

Therefore, understanding the conception of the goal of education is very crucial for us. Quality-oriented education should be the highest goal to achieve and this can be called a long-term goal. Passing an exam can be regarded as a target to reach step by step - a short-term goal. In other words, the aim for education should emphasise educating the student to be a whole person who will be ready to serve society in the future. And the aim of fostering students' learning capability is to help them readily absorb a variety of up-to-date information from all over the world, for their future success in their studies and careers.

Our aims show that the real achievement of teaching English goes far beyond gaining high scores in examinations. As a consequence, the real challenge for fostering the English capability of Chinese students is to balance the conflict between the long-term pursuit and the short-term need of learning a foreign language in China. In short, the question emerges: do we want our students to be creative learners or passive learners?

References

Brown, H. D. (1987) *Principles of Language Learning and Teaching*. Prentice Hall Regents.
Celce-Murcia, M. & Larsen-Freeman, D. (1999) *The Grammar Book – An ESL/EFL Teacher's Course*. Heinle & Heinle Publishing House.

Christian, M. A. (1998) Applying multiple intelligences theory in pre-service and in-service TEFL educational progress, in *English Teaching Forum*. Apr-Jun pp.2-11.

Ellis, R. (1994) *The Study of Second Language Acquisition*. Oxford University Press.

Genesee, F. and Upshur, J. A. (1998) *Classroom-based Evaluation in Second Language Education*. Cambridge Language Education.

Nunan, D. (1991) *Language Teaching Methodology*. Prentice Hall.

Richards, J. C. and Rodgers, T. S. (1986) *Approaches and Methods in Language Teaching*. Oxford University Press.

Wang, Q. (1999). *Language Learning Theory*. Foreign Language Department of BNU.

Widdowson, H.G. (1996) *Linguistics*. Oxford University Press.

Margaret Talboys

QCA's creativity project

In 2000, the review of the UK's national curriculum emphasised creativity as an important aim. The Secretary of State for Education and Skills asked the Qualifications and Curriculum Authority (QCA) to follow up this review by investigating how schools can promote pupils' creativity through the national curriculum.

What did we do?

We focused on key stages 1, 2 and 3.

In the first year of the project, we looked at how other countries were promoting creativity. We looked at their policies and curriculum requirements, and analysed a wide range of literature and research findings.

In the second year, we worked with 120 teachers in England to investigate how they could develop pupils' creativity through their existing schemes of work and lesson plans. We adopted the definition of creativity in 'All our Futures: Creativity, Culture and Education' (DfEE, 1999), a report from the National Advisory Committee on Creative and Cultural Education. We also drew on the previous year's research and discussions with experts as a basis for the work with schools. We asked the teachers to:

- identify the most effective ways to plan for, and foster, pupils' creativity
- collect examples of pupils' creative thinking and behaviour
- decide how the learning environment can best support the creative process.

The teachers looked through their plans for a term and chose lessons that they thought had potential for promoting pupils' creativity. They then adjusted their planning to maximise this potential, recording what happened and collecting evidence of pupils' creativity. They considered whether they had changed their teaching approach, the classroom or the learning environment and reflected on what happened.

We used the teachers' experiences to help us develop a set of information sheets and examples for teachers: 'Creativity: Find it, promote it'. We sent these materials to 1,000 teachers, headteachers, advisers, teacher educators and other people who work with schools, and asked them to complete a questionnaire telling us what they thought of them. We refined the materials in the light of their feedback and put the results on our website.

What did we learn?

Initially, the teachers involved in the project had very specific views on how to promote pupils' creativity. Some thought that creativity arose from unplanned or unstructured activities. Others thought that activities such as role-play, visits and debates were the key. Many art and design and music teachers assumed (wrongly) that because their subjects involve a creative process, pupils were thinking and behaving creatively all the time.

As the project progressed, the teachers began to realise that creating something is not the same thing as being creative. They saw that being creative has as much to do with the quality of thought taking place and the process or journey as with what is ultimately produced. They also discovered that creativity can happen in extended project work, discussion and short question-and-answer sessions.

Often, teachers identified a creative moment in a lesson, a moment when there appeared to be a breakthrough in thinking. This was almost always the result of much hard work on the part of individuals or groups of pupils. Teachers also realised that creativity did not happen in a vacuum. Pupils needed subject-specific knowledge and skills for their creativity to flourish.

By the end of the project, all of the teachers agreed that:

- opportunities for creativity arise in all types of activities
- by making only minor adjustments to their lesson plans, they could promote creativity
- to teach creatively, they needed to feel confident in their skills and subject knowledge
- sharing practice with teachers of other subjects and age groups was helpful
- pupils can't be expected to think and behave creatively in every single lesson
- thinking and behaving creatively is not appropriate in all lessons.

Many of the teachers involved in the project also believe that if creative thinking and behaviour are to become part of pupils' life in school, they must be expected and valued by the school as a whole.

References

DfEE (1999) *All Our Futures: Creativity, Culture and Education* (Report of the National Advisory Committee on Creative and Cultural Education). Sudbury: Department for Education and Employment.

Marilyn Fryer

The *Creativity & Cultural Diversity* international conference

Background and rationale

Our international conference on *Creativity & Cultural Diversity* was organised by The Creativity Centre in collaboration with The Creativity Centre Educational Trust. This five-day event was held in September 2002 at the University of Sussex. The impetus for this event came out of a recognition that, although creativity was increasingly becoming a 'hot topic' in the UK (and indeed in many other countries), this field of study hadn't moved forward very much in recent years. We were also very aware that the mainstream literature tended to reflect a mainly white, Western perspective. Valuable though this is, we knew it wasn't the whole story and we wanted to do something about that. We wanted the conference to be a catalyst for:

- widening access to the body of knowledge about creativity
- moving this whole field forward.

So we devised a programme of workshops and presentations to:

- reflect culturally diverse approaches to creativity
- allow new, young researchers a platform for presenting their findings
- enable creativity pioneers and keynote speakers working in different traditions to express their views, so as to provide access to a broad spectrum of landmark approaches to creativity.

Then we set about encouraging a wide range of delegates to take part and share their views. As far as we are aware, this was a unique event. To the best of our knowledge, creativity pioneers working in different traditions have never previously come together to present their views. That this occurred in the context of a variety of other workshops enriched this event and, judging from the feedback received from delegates, it was greatly appreciated. We were extremely fortunate that so many distinguished speakers and workshop leaders were willing to contribute to this conference.

Each day there were keynote presentations on creativity, as well as parallel workshops from which delegates could choose. These focused on creativity in one or more of the following areas: education, the arts, business, personal development, and the community. These sessions were complemented by a rich programme of multicultural entertainment. Theresa Gurner made a significant contribution to this and other aspects of the conference.

Conference themes

Four major themes were woven into the conference. They included:

- the contribution of diverse perspectives on creativity to our understanding of this complex field
- an awareness that cultural diversity is also highly complex
- the role of creativity in our lives, in organisations, and the environment
- the need to sustain minority viewpoints on creativity, in the face of globalisation and technological advances.

The keynote presentations

Alec Reed CBE

The conference was opened by Alec Reed, Founder and Chairman of Reed Executive plc, one of the largest recruitment solution providers in the UK. Alec Reed is a living example of creativity in action. Having started his company with just £75, he created a business of international repute with over 2600 staff, 280 branches and a turnover of £450m. Amongst his many achievements, Alec has set up the Reed Business School and founded The Academy of Enterprise, a non-profit initiative which promotes enterprising behaviour throughout the UK.

In his presentation, Alec agued that creativity was the most needed feature of any organisation and something which was becoming increasingly relevant. He made it clear that he regarded creative people as the lifeblood of organisations.

Kobus Neethling PhD

Kobus Neethling, President of the South African Creativity Foundation and founder and director of the Kobus Neethling Group, was the Conference Keynote Speaker. Kobus argued that, for the sake of the people of the world and their environment, the 21st Century needed a new kind of creativity, which he described as *strategic creativity*. He envisaged this as characterised by unselfishness, caring and compassion. He contrasted this with 20th Century creativity which he saw as mainly concerned with self gain; and characterised by wealth creation on the one hand but poverty, starvation and an impoverished environment on the other. Kobus said he saw 21st Century creativity as also involving wealth creation, but believed such wealth should be used to ensure a healthy planet and healthy people. He stressed that it was up to us to choose the kind of world in which we wanted to live. This, he thought, depended very much on how we chose to use our creativity.

M. K. Raina PhD

M. K. Raina presented a highly comprehensive and thought-provoking paper on creativity and cultural diversity (see his chapter). In this paper, M. K. argues for a *garland-making* perspective on creativity - one rich in diversity. It was particularly fitting that this paper was presented in the University's multi-faith chapel. There is a fuller description of Professor Raina's achievements on page 3.

Morris I Stein PhD, Sidney J Parnes PhD, Beatrice Parnes, and Vincent Nolan

A particular highlight of the conference was a panel session featuring creativity pioneers, Morris Stein, Sidney Parnes and Beatrice Parnes from the United States, and Vincent Nolan from the UK. They each spoke about their experiences and their pioneering work in the field of creativity and then took questions from the floor. This session was chaired by Professor Barry Fryer. Sidney and Beatrice Parnes also conducted conference workshops and Morris Stein took much trouble to spend time with delegates in discussions about creativity. These pioneers' contributions to the whole conference were highly valued by conference delegates, especially the new, young researchers.

A brief account of Vincent's achievements is given on page 3. Morris Stein is Professor Emeritus (Psychology) New York University and an internationally-acknowledged authority on creativity research. He has had a long and distinguished career, during which he has published 14 books as well as numerous papers. He has presented hundreds of lectures and talks all over the world, as well as acting as consultant to many large organisations. His many awards include: Fellow of the Center for Advanced Studies in the Behavioral Sciences, Stanford, 1954-55; Research Career Award, the National Institute of Mental Health, 1962-84; Sigma Chi, Best Teacher Award, New York University, 1990; Outstanding Lifetime Creative Achievement Award, the Creative Education Foundation, 1995, and the American Creativity Association Lifetime Creative Achievement Award, 2002. We are honoured to have him as the External Advisor to The Creativity Centre Educational Trust and as the Charity's sole Honorary Member, succeeding the late Dr E Paul Torrance in this post.

Dr Sidney Parnes is Professor Emeritus of Creative Studies and Founding Director of the Center for Studies in Creativity at the State University College at Buffalo. He attended his first Creative Problem Solving Institute (CPSI) in 1955 with Alex Osborn as his mentor. The following year he became Director of CPSI at the University of Buffalo. He worked with Alex Osborn during the period 1955-66 to develop the 'Osborn-Parnes' Creative Problem Solving Process. In 1967 he moved to the State University College at Buffalo, where he established the Interdisciplinary Center for Creative Studies, now the Center for Studies in Creativity. He also initiated the first Masters Degree programme in Creative Studies. From 1967-84 he served as President of the Creative Education Foundation, USA. He has presented and published throughout the world.

Beatrice Parnes is a highly talented and experienced facilitator of the Osborn Parnes CPS and Parnes' Visionizing programmes. She has a Masters degree in Special Education – a field in which she has worked for 35 years. At the Cantalician Center for Learning in Buffalo, New York, she taught children creative approaches to learning, using methods in her co-authored book, *Success Oriented Instruction*. SOI is based on more than 20 years' research by psychologists in a wide variety of aspects of intelligence.

Arthur Cropley PhD

Arthur Cropley talked about how he saw creativity as a social phenomenon (see his chapter). Like Paul Torrance, Arthur has done a great deal to champion creative education for all young people as well as conducting valuable research in this field. A brief description of his achievements is included on page 2.

Margaret Talboys

Margaret Talboys described a three year creative education project which she has directed at the Qualifications and Curriculum Authority (QCA). This project involved devising guidelines on creativity across the curriculum for all teachers of pupils from 5 -16 years in England. A fuller account of this project is included in her chapter, and a brief resume of Margaret's achievements is given on page 8.

Elizabeth Rasekoala D Univ.

Liz Rasekoala talked about the effect of being denied her African identity by British bureaucracy whilst growing up in Nigeria. One example she gave to illustrate this was the way in which her African name was not regarded as acceptable to the officials, so they gave her a Western name which had to be used on all official documents. Liz's presentation is included in her chapter and a brief account of her achievements on page 2.

Leon Secatero

Just before the conference began, we were delighted to hear that a distinguished group of Navajo and Cherokee Elders wanted to take part in this conference. So I set aside my own keynote presentation (giving only a brief presentation instead) to allow Leon Secatero, Canoncito Navajo Spiritual Elder, to speak about the urgent need for the peoples of this world to care for our planet. He and his fellow Elders expressed grave concern about the way in which current lifestyles are causing irreparable damage to the Earth and he stressed the importance of using creativity to take a new direction in the next 500 years. This period of time was significant since their sacred indigenous calendar created five hundred years ago was about to end, so it was time for the spiritual elders and leaders to create the next 500 year calendar.

Marilyn Fryer PhD

My brief keynote presentation focused on the need to enable minority and diverse viewpoints in the field of creativity to be heard, so that the mainstream body of knowledge could incorporate these and enable new research leads to emerge.

The workshops

Throughout the conference, there were parallel workshops on creativity in business, the arts, education, communication and individual development. The keynote speakers who also ran workshops included Kobus Neethling, Sidney and Beatrice Parnes, Arthur Cropley, Vincent Nolan and me. Some of the keynote presenters and workshop leaders have also contributed chapters to this book.

Creativity in business

The workshops that specifically focussed on creativity in the business environment were led by Dr Jon-Chao Hong, Dr Kanes Rajah, Tim Stockil, Andy Wilkins, Linda Caller, Graham Rawlinson and Claire Hewitt.

Dr Jon-Chao Hong's workshop topic is discussed in his chapter. Dr Kanes Rajah, Director of the Centre for Entrepreneurship at Greenwich University Business School, focussed on the use of Kirton's KAI measure and other studies designed to reveal individual creative styles and to discuss the implications for life and work.

Tim Stockil, Director of Creative Development, Arts & Business, drew on the work of Rob Goffee, Charles Handy and Jon Kao, as well as his own experience, to explore the personal and organisational attributes which foster creativity at work. Participants then took part in practical exercises and games to 'help unlock their innate creativity'.

Andy Wilkins, CPSB Group (UK), led a session on improving the climate for organisational creativity which he argues has a large, if not the largest, impact on an organisation's ability to innovate.

Linda Caller, Managing Director of Thought Agents Ltd, acknowledged the increasing demand from global brand owners for advertising that will run across borders. But how can advertising teams in one country understand what's important to consumers in another? How to resolve this was the focus of this workshop.

Graham Rawlinson, UK, introduced participants to TRIZ, a popular business innovation guide devised by Russian Genrikh Saulovich Altschuller, whilst Claire Hewitt, Partner, Synectics (UK), focussed on innovative teamwork in business and how to create the climate, develop innovative thinking and problem solving capabilities.

Creativity in education

Two of the education workshop leaders, Dr Lynda Foster and Anna Craft, have contributed chapters to this book which reflect their contributions to the conference. Amy Prentiss and Miriam Minkoff, USA, described some community schools projects in Buffalo, NY, in a really innovative way which included participation in Tai Chi, African and Samba music, movement, poetry and percussion.

Andrew Walker, UK, conducted a practical workshop exploring a number of different projects which use the creative arts in the development of young people and help reduce the number of school exclusions. Rekha Sharma Sen, India, ran a workshop based on her research with Indian teachers (see chapter). Dr Kenichi Yumino's education workshop is also the subject of his book chapter. Tony Claydon held a poster presentation on developing creativity in Higher Education. My own workshop explored creative teaching and learning, drawing on my own research, teaching experience and participants' contributions.

Individual creativity

Of course creativity in everyday life is just as valuable as in business. How to recognise and release this was the focus of Arthur Cropley's workshop.

Some of the thinking strategies we use when searching for creative solutions, whether in or out of the workplace, have been formalised into creativity development programmes. The opportunity to try out three such programmes was available to conference participants. These were:

- Synectics, developed by George Prince, following collaborative work with W. J. J. Gordon
- the Osborn Parnes Creative Problem Solving Process (CPS), developed by Sidney Parnes and Alex Osborn
- The NM Method, proposed by Masakazu Nakayama.

Sidney Parnes ran a workshop with Kobus Neethling on using the Osborn Parnes Creative Problem Solving Process (CPS) to help identify and implement creative solutions that work. Sidney and Beatrice Parnes also ran sessions in which participants could explore the role of visualisation as a tool in creative problem solving. They later ran a workshop which involved applying CPS to a series of challenges with a view to participants developing a personal plan of action for the future.

Maggie Dugan and Tim Dunne, an American couple now living in France, ran a workshop in which participants unfamiliar with CPS could get to grips with it. They also led a session on personal stakeholders and how these impact on the way in which we solve problems, make decisions and communicate with others.

Kenichi Yumino provided a workshop on the NM Method of creative thinking. And Vincent Nolan offered delegates a taste of Synectics, inviting them to bring their own challenges and *walk through* the steps of Synectics. Synectics particularly relies on the use of metaphor, so it was good that we were also able to include a workshop by Martha Leyton and Martin Shovel of CreativityWorks which specifically explored the role of metaphor in our lives (see their chapter).

Alice Lee from Malaysia, author of Creative Malaysians, discussed Dr Ng Aik Kwang's book *Why are Asians less creative than Westerners?* before sharing with delegates her research featuring highly creative Asian people (see chapter). Lillian Dabdoub of Mexico conducted a workshop on creativity from a Mexican perspective.

The Native American Elders ran sessions on learning from the old ways, whilst Joanna Kwasniewska from Poland gave a very good account of her research on the role of gender in creativity, which included a first rate poster presentation (see chapter).

The arts, culture and creativity

Every day it was possible to undertake a workshop which involved some physical activity. For example, Laurie Millar, Becca Tracey and Ben Tollefson, USA, conducted a yoga and soundscape session designed to strengthen the body and focus the mind. This team combined yoga with the healing properties of music. Olwen Wolfe from France and Sandra Minnee from Holland led a highly interactive, activity-based workshop which included exploring how the cultural context of Paris in the 1920s and 1930s nurtured a multi-cultural group of artists, including Picasso, Dali, Ernst, Breton, Magritte and Miro.

Amareza Buys, South Africa, presented a workshop on the visual and symbolic meanings of murals by children from ethnically-diverse backgrounds. This was complemented by a photographic display.

Corrine Shirman-Sarti led a workshop involving movement, breathing and voice, whilst Ed Wade Martins' workshop allowed participants to try out the music and movements of Capoeira – a dynamic Brazilian art form fusing martial arts, dance, acrobatics and game play with percussion and song.

Professional musician and dancer, Anthony Hyatt, USA, led a number of dance sessions including a practical workshop which drew on the work of Japanese dancers Eiko and Komo. Another of his workshops comprised a fun improvisational session in which participants could learn improvisational techniques to use in everyday life to enhance creativity. These sessions drew on Anthony's experience in the performing arts and incorporated elements of theatre, live music and dance. The principles underlying structures used were also discussed.

Juliet Russell, leader of the choir *Vocal Explosion*, offered a workshop which allowed participants to use simple, powerful melodies which built harmoniously into a celebration of sound. Lucky Moyo, Music for Change, led a participatory workshop which involved South African *a cappela* vocals, gum boot dancing and rhythms. The aims and work of Music for Change were also discussed.

Dr Manuela Romo, Spain, drew on her major research findings to examine the relationship between the way in which artistic creativity is perceived by Spanish artists and the general public, and how this impacts on artists. This included an account of the construction of a questionnaire for evaluating painters' identification with implicit theories of artistic creativity. She also discussed developments in Spain in the field of creativity.

Joanna Kwasniewska, Poland, had participants employ art materials in a practical exploration of the creative process.

Creativity and communication

Theresa Gurner and Luke Concannon, UK, led a series of practical activities aimed at unlocking creativity and improving communication. These activities drew on their work with young people with special needs and other groups. It involved the use of all the senses as well as music and the visual arts. Dido Fisher and Oliver MacDonald, UK, of *Red Zebra*, led a workshop which involved experiential learning to explore verbal and non-verbal communication through music, dance, drama and voice work.

Isabel Jacob and Collette Chambon from France helped participants explore the way in which our cultural backgrounds influence our values, how we represent reality, and how we interact with others. The aim was to facilitate better communication, leadership and inter-cultural team-building. They also led a silent, inter-cultural gaps game which comprised a non-threatening way of experiencing what it's like to be an outsider and how to deal with this. This game allows participants to explore the misunderstandings and inter-cultural gaps which may otherwise fuel conflict.

Saeeda Ahmed of Trescom, UK, helped participants explore how to involve and engage 'hard to reach groups' using examples from her work with such groups and a scenario activity. Saeeda also explored the role of creativity and innovation in the regeneration of cities.

The Navajo and Cherokee Elders introduced participants to a *talking circle*. In many native traditions, when Council is called, a talking stick is used as a way of honouring others' viewpoints.

Entertainment programme

The arts and entertainment programme complemented the conference's cultural diversity theme. Local choir, Vocal Explosion, performed interpretations of original songs by their leader, Juliet Russell. They were accompanied by members of Carnival Collective on percussion.

As part of the National Foundation for Youth Music's Song for Youth Initiative, nearly two hundred young people from 15 special schools in the South East performed Youth Music's *Drop in the Ocean*, as well as delivering an accomplished performance of other songs, music and dance, including wheel-chair dancing. This was greatly appreciated by the delegates. Ann West from Surrey County Arts, who organised the performance, commented, 'Singing is such a positive way for the children to communicate and the difference this has made to their confidence has been enormous'.

Paul Winter, teacher in charge of Ash Cottage, Downs View School - a school for pupils with learning difficulties - and teacher, Tim Dunkerley, introduced *Unified Rhythm* – a highly successful percussion band comprised of professional musicians and young people with learning difficulties from Downs View School, Ash Cottage and youth groups across Brighton. Paul and Tim discussed the benefit of creativity across the curriculum for special needs pupils. Then, led by Ollie MacDonald of Red Zebra, Unified Rhythm gave an accomplished outdoor performance. The day ended with a hugely enjoyable Irish ceilidh, led by Luke Colcannon and the *Quiet Men*.

An Arts & Diversity evening began with a viewing of art work by Catherine Lucktaylor and Pia von Kornow, followed by an Arts Walk through the sculptures of the South East Eco Arts Group, who make many of their totem-like structures from driftwood washed ashore at Brighton. Theresa Gurner then led delegates to an international buffet and theatre programme. Then the Mayor of Brighton & Hove, Councillor David Watkins, introduced Sita Ramamurthy, Director of the Arts Council of England's *Decibel Project*. Using a dramatic story-telling style, Sita described the Decibel Project, which aims to give people from ethnic minorities a greater voice in the arts.

Danny Horwood, Harmony in the Community, expertly compèred the rest of the evening, during which the Mayor joined the resident percussion band for a spot of drumming! Sound Spectrum performed sketches from 'Where are you *really* from?' which satirises attempts to classify British people into distinct ethnic groups and addresses potential inter-generational conflict. South Asian tac tac dancer Mayala, followed with a beautiful dance routine. The evening was rounded off with Sound Arc's rich tapestry of world music.

The closing ceremony

The last morning's workshops enabled conference participants to focus on next steps. This was followed by a closing ceremony introduced by Caroline Fryer, the main conference organiser and chief executive of CCET. Caroline thanked everyone for making the conference such a success. The Creativity Centre's goals to encourage broader cultural perspectives on creativity were re-affirmed. Then Caroline introduced some of the younger creativity researchers from around the world, who shared their often moving and really positive experiences of participating in the conference.

Appendix

The Creativity Centre Educational Trust

The Creativity Centre Educational Trust (CCET) is a registered charity which was founded by Dr Marilyn Fryer and Caroline Fryer in order to formalise the not-for-profits activities of their business, The Creativity Centre Ltd. The Creativity Centre Ltd is an independent company which provides research and consultancy services in creativity to organisations in the public and private sectors. The work of CCET follows the same principles but it caters for individual members of the public, the voluntary sector and young people. Projects run by CCET are funded by sponsorship and grants, with support from The Creativity Centre Ltd.

Board of Trustees

The work of CCET is overseen by its Board of Trustees. They are Sir Ernest Hall OBE DL (Chair), Sally Bassett, Coll Bell, Dr Lynda Foster, Becky Malby, John Mee, Dr Richard Perkin and Roger Standen. Morris I Stein PhD, Professor Emeritus (Psychology) New York University, is the Charity's External Advisor and Honorary Member.

Chief Executive

Caroline Fryer is Chief Executive of CCET. She has over ten years experience of creativity research, training, teaching and consultancy, which includes developing and coordinating creativity programmes for young people internationally. She also has a track record in media production, website design and management. Caroline has published internationally and was the main conference organiser for the Centre's 2002 international conference on *Creativity & Cultural Diversity*. As well as managing the Charity, she is project manager of *Science Alliance*.

Science Alliance

Science Alliance is a key project of CCET. The pilot phase, funded by NESTA, brought together four primary schools in Brighton & Hove to produce the *Science Alliance* website. Whole classes of Year 5 & 6 pupils used digital camcorders and still cameras to capture their school science projects for the site and worked together to design their own web pages.

This project is part of NESTA's ACRISAT initiative. Spearheaded by chemical engineer, Liz Rasekoala, ACRISAT seeks to advance the educational achievement and career aspirations of young people from African, African-Caribbean ethnic and other minority ethnic backgrounds, within science and technology. The aim is to nurture the ethos that the pursuit of such qualifications can be fun, empowering and achievable.

Through *Science Alliance* pupils can develop their creativity, learn media production skills, have increased confidence with new technology, as well as an appreciation of the contribution of ethnic minority scientists. Teachers receive additional support through information packs, teachers' workshops and useful links on the *Science Alliance* website. Phase Two of Science Alliance is about to begin. This will involve clusters of schools in various parts of the UK.

Contact details

The Creativity Centre Educational Trust
1 Whitehall Quay
Leeds LS1 4HR
UK
Tel: +44 (0) 113 390 6053
Fax: +44 (0) 113 390 6100
Email: ccet@creativitycentre.org.uk
Website: www.creativitycentre.org.uk
Science Alliance website: www.science-alliance.org.uk

Notes